The Caledonia Upgrade Guide for GroupWise 2014

Upgrading In-Place on Linux or Windows

By Danita Zanrè and Paul Lamontagne

Caledonia Network Press
2014

March 31, 2014

Version 1.0.0

The Caledonia Upgrade Guide for GroupWise 2014
Upgrading In-Place on Linux or Windows

By Danita Zanrè and Paul Lamontagne

ISBN 978-0-9745067-2-2

Published by:
Caledonia Network Press
20116 E. Aintree Court
Parker, CO 80138

http://www.caledonia.net

All rights reserved. No part of this book may be reproduced or transmitted in any form or by any means, electronic or mechanical, including photocopying, recording, or by any information storage and retrieval system, without written permission from the publisher.

Copyright ©2014 by Caledonia Network Press

Disclaimer

The authors and publisher have made every effort to make this book as complete and accurate as possible. The authors and Caledonia Network Press make no representations or warranties of any kind as to the accuracy of the contents of this book, and accept no liability whatsoever with respect to any loss or damages arising from the information contained in this book or from the use of any programs that may accompany it.

Trademarks

Novell, Inc. has intellectual property rights relating to the technology and software embodied that is described in this document. In particular, and without limitation, these intellectual property rights may include one or more of the U.S. patents listed on the Novell Legal Patents Web page (http://www.novell.com/company/legal/patents/) and one or more additional patents or pending patent applications in the U.S. and in other countries.

GroupWise and ZENWorks are registered trademarks of Novell, and copyrighted by Novell. Windows is copyrighted by Microsoft.

All other trademarks, service marks, and company names are properties of their respective owners.

Electronic Publication

This book is available in print and PDF versions. If this book is delivered to you as an electronic publication in PDF format, the book is formatted with the assumption that it will be printed duplexed. If you choose to print the document single-sided you will discover some blank pages that would have been pages facing a new chapter. You can discard these pages, as long as you keep in mind that the overall pagination of the document assumes these "place keeper" pages exist.

The ebook version is delivered to the purchaser electronically as a PDF file, and the purchaser is allowed to 1) make ONE printed copy and 2) possess ONE electronic copy at any given time. The electronic version of this book will not be placed on a network server, accessible by more than one person simultaneously. By following the requirements outlined above for electronic distribution of this book, the purchaser will, in effect have one copy of the book, which can be viewed by a single reader, as though the book were delivered in a bound copy.

You can find more about purchasing options for the print or ebook versions at

http://caledonia.net/store

Acknowledgements

Danita Zanrè:

A number of people have been very helpful in the course of writing this book.

Pam Robello at Novell is a constant that I could not do without! She always gives me support and help when I need it.

At Novell, the GroupWise Engineering team were the biggest help. Without them, we wouldn't have GroupWise 2014 at all! They endure a lot of my questions, and are always ready to give me straight answers and walk me through the difficult challenges. Morris Blackham, Dave Hansen, and Dan Christensen go above and beyond!.

My co-author Paul Lamontagne is tireless and a great sounding board. He tests my theories over and over to make sure I haven't lost my mind!

So many of my Knowledge Partner buddies helped out with reviewing, proof-reading and challenging! Aaron Burgemeister, Willem Meens, David Gersic, Geoffrey Carmen, Laura Buckley and Kevin Boyle. I could not have done all of this without you!

My daughters cheered me on, and my son stayed out of my hair. Most of all, my dear husband just put up with my work, work, work for the past few weeks.

Thanks to all who supported me through this!

Paul Lamontagne

No one truly works alone, there are always many people who help you along the way.

Pam Robello is without a doubt one of the best resources Novell has. Wish to thank her for all she does not only for Danita and me but for the entire GroupWise Community. A heartfelt Thank You Pam.

The Engineering Team, headed by Kevin Crutchfield, Jay Parker and Dirk Giles whose hard work and dedication, truly make GroupWise one of the best products on the market

To the Product Management Team, headed by Dean Lythgoe who continually strive to listen to and make customer requests a reality.

To the Project Manager, Tom Urquart, whose job it is to piece it all together and make sure a quality product is delivered. I think it is similar to herding cats.

To my Wife, Sandra, for all her patience and understanding, and realizing that I'll be done in 5 minutes really means another 2 hours.

Thanks to all who supported me through this.

About the Authors

Danita Zanrè (the "GroupWise Goddess") has been using "GroupWise" since 1989, when its precursor was known as WordPerfect Office 2.0. She has been involved closely with every version of the product since that time. Danita is widely regarded as one of the top experts in e-mail in general, and GroupWise specifically. She has written many books and articles, and has been a frequent speaker at BrainShare, GWAVACon, and other conferences throughout the world.

Paul Lamontagne @groupwiseguy has been using "GroupWise" since 1991, when it was still a WordPerfect product. Paul is regarded as one of the leading subject matter experts and trainers for all things GroupWise. Paul was the lead developer on Novell Authorized Training for GroupWise versions 8, 2012 and 2014. Paul has been a frequent speaker at Brainshare, ATTLive, GWAVACon, and The Open Horizon Summit EMEA.

Contents

Acknowledgements v

About the Authors vi

Foreword xvii

1   Introduction 1
     A Few Important Conventions 2
     How This Book is Organized 3

2   Preparing Your GroupWise System 5
     Server Requirements 5
     Administration Requirements 6
     WebAccess/Monitor Application/Calendar Publishing Host Requirements . .6
          SLES 11/OES11 6
          Windows Server 2008 R2/2012/2012R2 7
     GroupWise Client Requirements 7
          Windows 7
          Linux 7
          Mac 8
     Software Distribution Directory 8
     WebAccess Changes 8
     GWIA Considerations 9
     What about Document Management? 9
          Document Properties Maintenance .9
          No Application Integrations 10
     Enabling the HTTP Monitor for Your Agent 11

| Table of Contents

GroupWise High Availability Agent Considerations. 12
Verifying MTA Network Settings 12
Modifying Linux Network Settings 12
A Quick Health Check 13
Preparing Your LDAP System. 14
    Testing Your Current System 15
    Check the MTA Platform Settings 15
    Check or Create your LDAP Server 16
    Check or Configure eDirectory User Synchronization. 17
    Check Or Configure Your MTA Scheduled Event 21
The Upgrade Overview 22
    Small, Single Server System 22
    Small, Multiple Server System 23
    Complex GroupWise System on Multiple Servers 23

3 Installing the GroupWise Administration Service 25

Installing the GroupWise Administration Service on Linux 25
    Download the Installation Media 25
    Install the Administration Service 27
Installing the GroupWise Administration Service on Windows. 30
    Download the Installation Media 30
    Install the Administration Service 31
Re-enabling the GroupWise High Availability Agent on Linux 35
    Troubleshooting. 36
Accessing the GroupWise Installation Console. 36
Accessing the Installation Console for the First Time 38
Changing the Installation Console Access Method 39

4 Upgrading GroupWise Domains 43

How Does the Upgrade Work? 43
What About ConsoleOne? 44
Prepare The Domain Database 44
The Domain Upgrade Overview 45
    DC Files 45
    Startup Files 46
Performing the Domain Upgrade 46

Domain With or Without a GWIA (No Post Office) 48
Domain With Post Office (GWIA optional) 52
Verifying the Upgrade 55
Additional Post Office Steps 58
Where to from here? 58
    Single Server 58
    Multiple Servers. 58
    Primary Domain and Post Office on the Same Server 59
Troubleshooting Domain Upgrade Problems 59
Troubleshooting Post Office Upgrade Problems 59

5 Directory Integration and Synchronization 61

What is Directory Integration and Synchronization? 62
Directory Rights Requirements 63
    eDirectory 64
    Active Directory 64
What Is Directory Authentication? 64
Launching the New Administration Console 65
The Initial Directory Integration 66
    Associated Users 68
    Unassociated Users 69
    Non-Associated Users 70
The Directory Object 71
The LDAP Server Object 71
Verifying a Successful Directory Integration 73
    Verifying the Directory 73
    Verifying the LDAP Server 76
    Verifying User Associations 77
Correcting a Failed Directory Integration 81
    Verifying the Directory 82
    Verifying User Associations 86
    Verifying the LDAP Server 90
Integrating Active Directory into Your GroupWise System 92
    Associating GroupWise Users with Active Directory 95
        Associating Individual Users 95
        Associating Users En Masse 97

Creating the LDAP Server. 98
　Removing eDirectory Associations to become Stand-Alone 99
　External Entities 101
　Exporting Trusted Root Certificates 102
　　　iManager 102
　　　Windows 102
　Directory Plugins 102
　　　Installing the iManager Plugin 102
　　　Using the iManager Plugin 106
　　　MMC Plugin 109
　　　Using the MMC Plugin 112
　Cleaning up eDirectory 113

6 The GroupWise Administration Console 115

　The GroupWise Admin Service 115
　The GroupWise Administration Console 116
　　　Logging Into the Administration Console 117
　Accessing Objects from the Dashboard 118
　Global Search 119
　Context Specific Search 120
　Export 120
　Quick Lists 121
　System Settings 121
　　　Administrators 121
　　　Directory Associations 122
　　　Document Viewer Agents 122
　　　Email Address Lookup 122
　　　Legacy 122
　　　Link Configuration 122
　　　User Import 122
　Domain Settings 122
　　　Administrators 123
　　　Post Office Links 123
　　　Maintenance 123
　　　Client Options 123
　Message Transfer Agents 123

General	124
Post Office Settings	125
Administrators	125
Maintenance	125
Client Options	125
Replicate (Formerly Synchronize)	125
Post Office Agents	126
General	126
Agent Settings	127
Document Viewer Agents	127
Groups	128
Command Line Utilities	128
gwadminutil	129
Rebuilding a Secondary Domain Database	130
Validating or Rebuilding a Post Office Database	130
Checking Your Database Version	131
gwadmin-ipc	131
gwcheck.sh	132
Connecting to other Domain Administration Consoles	132
Reinstalling ConsoleOne Snapins on Linux	133

7 Upgrading GroupWise Post Offices . . . 135

How Does the Upgrade Work?	135
Enabling SOAP	137
Preparing the Post Office Database	137
Upgrading Your Post Office	137
Verifying the Upgrade	141
Configuring and Verifying a DVA for your Post Office	141
Troubleshooting	144

8 Upgrading GroupWise WebAccess . . . 145

Preparing For The Upgrade To GroupWise 2014 WebAccess	145
SLES 11/OES 11	146
Windows Server 2008/2008 R2/2010	146
Firewall Considerations	146
Shutting Down the WebAccess Agent	146

Table of Contents

      Linux 147
      Windows 147
   Upgrading WebAccess 148
      Linux WebAccess Installation 148
      Windows WebAccess Installation 152
   Loading the GroupWise WebAccess Application 155
      Linux 155
      Microsoft Windows Server 156
   Configuration Options 156
      Configuring Additional Post Office Agents 156
      Configuring Additional Document Viewer Agents 157
      Configuring HTTP Monitor for WebAccess 157
      Setting the GroupWise 2012 WebAccess as Your Default 158
      Security Timeouts 159
      Deleting Unneeded eDirectory Objects 159
   Troubleshooting 160

9   Upgrading GroupWise Monitor 161

   Preparing for the Upgrade 161
   GroupWise High Availability Agent Considerations 161
   Installing your Agent Software 162
      Linux 164
   Re-enabling the GroupWise High Availability Agent 166
      Troubleshooting GWHA 167
   Troubleshooting the GroupWise Monitor Agent 167
   Installing the Monitor Application Software 168
      Windows Monitor Application Installation 168
      Linux Monitor Application Installation 168
   Loading The GroupWise Monitor Application 170
      Linux 170
      Microsoft IIS – Web Server 171

10 Upgrading the GroupWise Calendar Publishing Host 173

   Preparing for the Upgrade 173
   Installing the Calendar Publishing Host Software 174
      Windows 174

| Linux 175
| Loading The GroupWise Calendar Publishing Host 176
| Linux 177
| Microsoft IIS — Web Server 177
| Checking the GroupWise Calendar Publishing Host 177
| Configuring Calendar Publishing Host Administration 178
| Enable the CalHost Administration Console 178
| Load the CalHost Administration Console 179
| Post Office Settings 179
| Logging Settings 180
| Authentication Settings 180
| Customize 181
| Updating your Changes 182
| Troubleshooting 182

11 Upgrading GroupWise Clients 185

   Choosing Your Windows Client Installation Method 185
   The Auto-Update Algorithm 185
   Auto-Update through Direct POA Access 186
   Auto-Update with POA Access Through a Web Server 191
     Preparing the Web Server 192
       Apache Specific Settings 193
       IIS Specific Settings 193
     Web Server Cleanup 194
     Test the Software Availability 194
     Enabling Auto-Update in GroupWise 194
     Upgrading the GroupWise Client with SETUPIP 199
       Configuring Your Web Server 199
       Apache Specific Settings 200
       IIS Specific Settings 201
     Web Server Cleanup 202
     Test the Software Availability 202
     Configure and Generate the setupip.exe Executable 202
       Troubleshooting SETUPIP 204
     Upgrading Users with ZENworks Configuration Management 204
       SETUP.INI 213

VERSION.INI 214
SETUP.CFG 214
Upgrading the Linux Cross-Platform Client 215
Upgrading the MAC Cross-Platform Client 215
Auditing the GroupWise Client Upgrade 215

Appendix 1: LDAP Attributes Map 217

Foreword

By Dean Lythgoe, Product Manager for Novell® GroupWise®

I have been connected with GroupWise in one way or another for almost 20 years. As an engineer, I have been involved in the design, coding, and feature development of areas like the Name Completion Control, Address Book, Proxy, Filters, and Disk Space Management. I have met and listened to many users suggest new capabilities, complain about usability, and dream about possibilities. As a Product Manager, I have seen how companies utilize collaboration to run their businesses and how simplicity and access have driven usability. I have seen GroupWise mature through those awkward teenage years to develop into this robust, modern collaboration set of functionalities that enable every organization to be agile, mobile, cost conscious, and responsible. I guess you could say this tweenie is all grown up!

Novell is very excited about Novell® GroupWise® 2014 and all of the interoperability and new capability it will provide our customers and partners. Novell® GroupWise® has always been a secure, reliable "home base" for workforce productivity. Now, Novell GroupWise 2014 enhances the email you love with all-new features and a sleek, dynamic user interface. With enhancements in all the places users work — as well as behind the scenes, where administrators live — GroupWise 2014 will help you get more done at every level of your organization.

We recognize that in order for customers to benefit from all of this effort, we need to make the upgrade process as familiar, stream-lined, and robust as possible. We encourage all of our customers to upgrade to Novell GroupWise 2014 at their earliest convenience. The Caledonia Upgrade Guide for GroupWise 2014 is researched, written, and provided by some of the most recognized and trusted voices in the GroupWise community. Every GroupWise system demands a knowledgeable professional to configure, update, optimize, and customize their collaboration ecosystem to benefit their organization. Danita and Paul are simply the best! Deep consultant experience, with an abundance of real-world expertise, make this technical resource invaluable for every GroupWise organization.

Make sure you get the most from your GroupWise investment by running GroupWise 2014 Today!

- Dean

March, 2014

1 Introduction

Danita and Paul here! Are you ready for a change? We sure hope so, because GroupWise 2014 is full of change and new functionality. Some of it will be intuitive, and some not so much. Hopefully by purchasing this book you will get through the newness of GroupWise 2014 without too much trouble.

As long-time GroupWise administrators, users and consultants, GroupWise 2014 brings with it many changes for us. We've both used GroupWise since before it was GroupWise! Danita started with WordPerfect 2.0 in 1989, and Paul started with WordPerfect Office 3.0 in 1991 and we've used every version since. Here's a little history that can help you appreciate just what is going on with GroupWise 2014.

Firstly, we do not wish to offend any long-time WordPerfect Office/GroupWise lovers, but we are not going to dwell too much on WordPerfect Office 2.x and 3.x. We will say that WordPerfect Office 3.x had great functionality, and was truly "enterprise worthy" in many respects. However, the seeds of the GroupWise that we know and love really started with WordPerfect Office 4.0 in 1993. This is when the FLAIM database became the engine (and some speculate FLAIM was one of the driving forces for Novell wanting to acquire WordPerfect Corporation), and the directory structure that we know and love actually came into being. If you've ever wondered why many directories in "GroupWise" are prefixed with wpcs, that is because it stood for "WordPerfect Connection Server", the original name of the Message Transfer Agent.

The "migration" from GroupWise 4.1 to GroupWise 5.0 was a really big deal. The 4.x versions of our beloved collaboration system were still rather simple in administration. A stand-alone administration tool, ad.exe, and a few command line utilities that did all of the work. When GroupWise 5.x came along, you were going to need NetWare 4.x and "NDS" (now eDirectory). We installed GroupWise at MANY sites in the beginning where we put a lone NetWare 4.x server with NDS on a desktop somewhere, and it often got turned off when no one needed to administer GroupWise! GroupWise 5.0 killed DOS, OS/2 and Unix agents (and we thought having to give up NetWare and the Mac/Linux clients with GroupWise 2012 was painful)! It dumped all character based clients for DOS and Unix. It was a major undertaking for most of the sites that had really just gotten started with their WPO/GroupWise systems. It was definitely not for the faint of heart. In fact, in the very first GroupWise Administrator's Guide that Danita co-wrote with Richard Beels and Scott Kunau for Sybex Network Press, she penned this:

> "How many of us have received an upgrade to a software package in the mail and just "gone for it"? Most of us are tempted to install software without advanced planning. The likelihood of a successful GroupWise 4.1-to-5.x migration in such a scenario is slim. Although many of the basic concepts behind GroupWise 5.x are familiar to GroupWise 4.x administrators, some major changes have occurred that impact the decision of how and when to move from GroupWise 4.x."

Looking back at the level of difficulty in a GroupWise 4.1 to 5.x migration, we can only smile. In many ways that was child's play compared to some of the changes that are included with GroupWise 2014. This is especially valid when you take into consideration that by the time of the initial GroupWise 5.0 release (1996) the familiarity with the basic structure was only 4 years in the making. We've had a relatively "consistent" GroupWise now for 17 years, and there is a certain comfort level among seasoned GroupWise administrators that could very well encourage folks to leap before they look.

Of course the biggest change that is introduced with GroupWise 2014 is the new web based Administration Console. Many folks will be inclined to compare it with the move from NWAdmin to ConsoleOne. Sorry! This is so much bigger than that. Think more in terms of how you felt when you originally moved from ConsoleOne to iManager for many Novell related tasks (albeit never for GroupWise, which managed to avoid iManager altogether - to mixed reviews). We'll warrant that no matter how much you thought you disliked ConsoleOne, you were lost and confused initially when you were faced with finding the new way to deal with once familiar tasks. However, for those of you who have fallen in love with iManager now, GroupWise 2014 has an iManager plugin, which we will discuss later in this guide.

We do want to assure you that the GroupWise team has done a really great job with the new Administrative Console. There was a great deal of thought and planning that went into designing this new administration tool, and it seems apparent that they also took into account some of the major complaints that revolved around the initial rollout of iManager and attempted to prevent the same frustration and confusion. That said, there is much that is simply "different" in the way the new administration model works, and you will really want to be prepared for real change when you make your move to GroupWise 2014.

We will discuss all of the changes that you need to know about GroupWise 2014 in the next chapter, *"Preparing Your GroupWise System"*. There are, however, two major changes that need to be addressed before you continue.

With GroupWise 2012, Novell discontinued NetWare as a server platform for GroupWise. This means that if you are still on NetWare, moving to GroupWise 2014 will not be a simple upgrade. Rather, we will need to do a migration/upgrade.

Novell does not support upgrading directly to GroupWise 2014 from any versions older than GroupWise 8. Thus if you have a GroupWise 7 or older system, you may need to do a two step upgrade for GroupWise 2014. That said, we have upgraded as far back as GroupWise 6.5 . We do not see any major problems upgrading from GroupWise 5.0 or later.

This guide has been written for a simple upgrade of GroupWise on Linux or Windows (i.e., no server migration is assumed, and all GroupWise components will continue to exist on the same servers they were on for GroupWise 2012 or prior). If you have your GroupWise system on NetWare, or need to migrate your system to new servers for any reason, you need our guide that has been designed for that purpose. If you have purchased this guide in error, and need the server migration guide, please contact info@caledonia.net and we will make sure you get the proper guide.

A Few Important Conventions

In writing this book, we've endeavored to be as consistent as possible with formatting and naming. Here are a few of the key things to keep in mind:

- URLs are shown in all lowercase.

- Filenames and locations are shown all in lowercase and in this format: **filename.ext**. Since this book must take into account Linux case sensitivity, we have opted to show all commands and file names in lowercase to help avoid confusion for administrators working with multiple OSs. If, however, a Linux process is in mixed case (like running **/usr/ConsoleOne/bin/ConsoleOne**), we will of course show the case requirements for the command.

- Information you must type, or commands you must execute will be formatted like this: **setup.exe**.
- We will refer to this version as GroupWise 2014 in this book, with the version number typically listed as merely 14.
- Since GroupWise Linux files always have the build number included in the file name (for example **novell-groupwise-server-14.0.0-115059.x86_64.rpm**), the names we show in this book might not have the same build number as your software. Substitute your build number in any commands we list in the guide.
- This guide is of course written for both Linux and Windows. We admittedly use Linux more for our own personal use. We will attempt to keep terminology straight. However, when we discuss the GroupWise "Server" directories on your server, these will be:
  - Linux: **/opt/novell/groupwise/**
  - Windows: **c:\Program Files\Novell\GroupWise Server**

  These GroupWise Server directories will be abbreviated throughout this guide as **<serverfiles>/** and as an example, **c:\Program Files\Novell\GroupWise Server\agents\data** will be simply listed as **<serverfiles>\agents\data**
- The installation files that you extracted from your download will be referred to as **<installationfiles>/** and as an example we might refer to the **install.sh** file being at **<installationfiles>/install.sh**

  We ask Windows administrators' forgiveness in advance if we occasionally just give the Linux paths to locations! Just substitute the Windows paths above when in doubt! Linux and Windows administrators alike should remember that Linux uses forward-slashes and Windows users back-slashes!

How This Book is Organized

The new upgrade procedures for GroupWise 2014 have necessitated a bit of a rework of our former upgrade guide organization. Rather than having separate chapters for upgrading the Primary Domain and Secondary Domains, all domain upgrades will be covered in a single chapter. You must simply remember that the FIRST domain to upgrade must be the primary. We will discuss upgrading a Post Office alone on its own server, and we will also combine a Post Office upgrade with a Domain on the same server in the Domain chapter. The GWIA chapter will be more of an overview of strategies for upgrading the GWIA, as it will be upgraded automatically with its Domain, and that is covered in the Domain chapter.

We are upgrading from GroupWise 8 and GroupWise 2012, and while we have tested GroupWise 6.5, Novell is not testing (and thus not officially supporting) any version prior to GroupWise 8 for a direct upgrade. Any time there is a version specific process to be dealt with, the version will be noted. We will upgrade our primary domain CNC, our CNC2 secondary domain, and our Caledonia post office in this guide. Additionally, we will upgrade our GroupWise Internet Agent, WebAccess, GroupWise Monitor, Calendar Publishing Host, and a couple of clients to usher you on your way.

Our figures may show GroupWise 2012 objects, GroupWise 8 objects, and in some cases perhaps even GroupWise 6.5 objects. We have tested upgrades with systems as old as GroupWise 6.5.

2 Preparing Your GroupWise System

For a new GroupWise administrator, the prospect of upgrading the GroupWise system can be a bit daunting. Of course, even those of us who have done hundreds of upgrades run into issues occasionally. There is an entirely new "wizard" for upgrading to GroupWise 2014, and while most of you know that we're not generally fans of wizards (except at Hogwarts) we will use the wizard in this book. Undoubtedly, it is the planning that is of utmost importance. In this chapter we will deal with the planning. It's important to know that even those of us who have literally done hundreds of GroupWise upgrades make a point to plan out even the simplest of upgrades, making sure to check off all of the necessary steps as we go. (Danita has even been known to carry around a copy of this book to customer sites to make sure nothing is forgotten). So, do not feel like you need to keep a lot of information to perform an upgrade in your head. Keep a copy of the upgrade guide close at hand, and refer to it often during your upgrade, and you'll be less likely to run into trouble.

Be certain to check the Errata Page for this book (http://www.caledonia.net/wiki/public/) prior to your upgrade to see if there are any important updates to the process that might not have been available when you downloaded the guide.

Server Requirements

We'll start with the technicalities! What do you need to be able to perform this upgrade? For the most part, your GroupWise 8.0 or higher server is likely to be adequate for your upgrade, but let's look at what Novell says you need (and what our recommendations are).

All Servers	64-bit/x86 processor
Any of the following, updated to the latest Support Pack*	
Linux	SUSE Linux Enterprise Server (SLES) 11, Novell Open Enterprise Server (OES) 11
Windows	Windows Server 2008 R2, Windows Server 2012, or Windows Server 2012 R2, all with the latest Service Pack
NetIQ eDirectory™ (optional)	8.8.7 or later, plus the latest Support Pack, with LDAP enabled
Microsoft Active Directory (optional)	

Memory and disk space requirements are not substantially different than prior GroupWise server requirements. There are a few agent components and options that can either be installed by default (for example the document viewer agent at the POA) or additionally (such as the

Calendar Publishing Host). Generally speaking, however, you will not need to upgrade your current Linux or Windows servers in order to upgrade your GroupWise systems so long as they meet the above requirements (although many sites take the opportunity to do so during the GroupWise upgrade).

You might have noticed a few interesting items in the table above. Let's talk about a few things to do with the servers:

- 64 bit OS is now required. Thus, regardless of the other hardware specs of your servers, if you are still running a 32 bit OS you will need to "migrate" your data from your current server to a 64 bit OS.

- For Linux, GroupWise 2014 is supported on SLES 11, which also means OES 11.

- NetWare is no longer an available option for GroupWise 2014 server OS. (This was discontinued with GroupWise 2012.)

Administration Requirements

ConsoleOne is not supported for GroupWise 2014 administration. As long as you have a mixed environment, you will need to keep ConsoleOne around for some administration of domains that are older than GroupWise 2014. Novell cautions against using ConsoleOne against a GroupWise 2014 domain. That said, you will need to keep ConsoleOne with GroupWise snapins around for managing Document Management Properties. We will discuss this later in the section entitled *"What about Document Management?"*

While there are many supported browsers for the Administration Console, in our opinion you will be happier if you simply use Firefox and do not try to force the issue with any other browser. That said, we've tested with Chrome and IE11. Safari on the Mac is a problem, because it seems to want a client certificate, even though one is not required, and in our testing no amount of offering a client certificate seems to be accepted.

There are some command line utilities that must be run for administration. On Linux it is best if these are run as root.

WebAccess/Monitor Application/Calendar Publishing Host Requirements

While GroupWise specific agents require a 64 bit processor, the Web based services such as WebAccess, Calendar Publisher and Monitor Application can be run on a 32 bit server – that assumes you still have any of those around!

For the Web Server running the WebAccess Application, Monitor Application, or the Calendar Publishing Host you will need one of the following:

SLES 11/OES11

Apache 2.2 plus:

- Tomcat 6.0 or later (this will be added by the GroupWise installation routine if required.)
- IBM Java 6 Runtime Environment (JRE)
- ModProxy Module

Have your Linux repository available when you begin your installation of these products. If any required files are missing during the installation, they will be installed as needed. However, if you do not have the repository available when you begin the installation, you will need to cancel the installation and make the repositories available before restarting the installation.

Windows Server 2008 R2/2012/2012R2

Microsoft Internet Information Server (IIS) 7 or later plus:

- Tomcat 6 or later
- IBM Java 6 Runtime Environment (JRE)
- Jakarta Connector 1.2 or later
- ISAPI Support

You must manually install IIS with ISAPI support prior to the GroupWise 2014 WebAccess installation. All other items above will be installed by the GroupWise installation routine if necessary.

GroupWise Client Requirements

For the GroupWise client, a few things have changed that are important.

Windows

Here are the specifics for the 2014 client:

- Windows XP SP 3 or better, on a 300 MHz or higher workstation with at least 128 MB of RAM
- Windows 7 on a 1 GHz or higher workstation with at least 1 GB of RAM
- Windows 8 or Windows 8.1 on a 1 GHz or higher workstation with at least 1 GB of RAM

Note: Windows 8 or later on a Microsoft Surface Pro tablet is not supported for use with the GroupWise client. Use GroupWise WebAccess instead.

- 200 MB of free disk space on each user's workstation is recommended to install the Windows client.

Linux

Novell has not updated the Linux client for GroupWise. You can use the GroupWise 8.0.2 HP3 Linux client. The only supported platform is SUSE Linux Enterprise Desktop 10. We have tested the client on various OpenSUSE versions, and even SLES 11, and it seems to perform

Mac

Again, Novell has not updated the GroupWise Mac client with GroupWise 2014. You can continue to use the GroupWise 8 Mac client. Interestingly, the Mac client seems to run on the most diverse versions of the operating system when compared to either Windows or Linux! You can run the GroupWise 8 Mac client on:

- Mac OS 10.4 through OS 10.9 Mavericks

If you are using the GroupWise Mobility Service, your Mac users might be interested in trying out TouchDown for Mac by Nitrodesk. Find out more here - http://nitrodesk.com/macplatform.html

Software Distribution Directory

The Software Distribution Directory is no more! GroupWise 2014 totally does away with the Software Distribution Directory. This means that those of you who never use it will be able to delete it from your systems with impunity! For those of you who actually used the SDD, you will still be able to perform auto-update. The procedure has simply changed. Also, you can use SetupIP or a desktop management program such as Novell ZENworks Configuration Management to roll out your clients.

WebAccess Changes

If you are upgrading a system older than GroupWise 2012, before you begin your upgrade, you need to understand some very fundamental changes to WebAccess. Prior to GroupWise 2012, WebAccess always consisted of two components: The WebAccess Agent, and the WebAccess Application. The WebAccess Agent (GWINTER) was a WebAccess component that acted as a GroupWise client which gathered information from the POA and supplied the information to the WebAccess Application (the web server component). GroupWise 2012 eliminated the WebAccess Agent altogether. The GroupWise 2012 and newer WebAccess Application communicates directly to the POA via the SOAP protocol.

Because of these changes, a GroupWise 2014 WebAccess installation cannot talk directly to older GroupWise Post Office Agents. Only a GroupWise 2014 POA "speaks" the proper SOAP language that the WebAccess Application will understand. This poses some challenges to sites with many post offices that will be upgraded over an extended period of time. If you will not be upgrading all of your post offices within a short time frame (perhaps a long weekend when you can indicate that WebAccess will be largely unavailable to users), you will need to either leave your WebAccess installation at your current GroupWise version, or you will need to provide for two separate web servers to serve as WebAccess applications for your current GroupWise version and for GroupWise 2014. There are settings for the GroupWise 2014 WebAccess Application that will allow it to serve as the default WebAccess entry point into your system, and then redirect older users to the appropriate web server hosting the GroupWise WebAccess Application for your current GroupWise version.

Like GroupWise 2012, the GroupWise 2014 WebAccess does not include the WebPublisher functionality. If you need WebPublisher, you must retain an older WebAccess installation for your existing GroupWise version to continue to provide the services of WebPublisher.

Of special note, the GroupWise WebAccess Agent had a section for controlling user access to WebAccess. Now that there is no WebAccess Agent, these settings are controlled by settings in the webacc.cfg file and the **gwac.xml** file. It is very important if you have access control settings in your GroupWise 8 or earlier WebAccess Agent that you export these prior to beginning your upgrade.

We will go over the details in Upgrading Your GroupWise WebAccess later in this guide.

GWIA Considerations

Upgrading your GroupWise Internet Agent is a fairly simple process. However, there are some challenges that are presented if you intend to have a "mixed" system (i.e., GroupWise 2012 AND older post offices) for any length of time. Here are the issues at hand:

- Your GWIA cannot be upgraded to GroupWise 2014 until the domain that owns it is upgraded to GroupWise 2014.
- When using the GWIA as a POP3 or IMAP4 "client", it is actually a client. You cannot access a GroupWise 2012 or earlier post office with the GWIA via IMAP4 or POP3, If it is attempted, you will see a "login failed: D058" in your GWIA log.
- On the other hand, if the GWIA is being used only for SMTP services, there are no issues with a mixed system.

So, as you can see, it's a good idea to get your post offices upgraded to GroupWise 2014 on a scheduled roll-out so that you are not surprised by any of the possible issues with mixed post offices. That said, many sites operate in a "mixed" system quite nicely for an extended period of time. You must simply make sure that your plans take the above caveats into account. If you need to have POP3 services for all users in your system, you might consider having two GWIAs - one for the GroupWise 2014 users, and one for your older post office users. If you are using IMAP4, you might consider opening up IMAP4 directly from the post office agent, rather than using the GWIA if you have a mixed system (versions 6.0 and later of GroupWise allow for IMAP4 at the post office agent).

What about Document Management?

Prior to GroupWise 2014 we would get asked about this at almost every upgrade, and our answer was always "Novell has not made any enhancements to GroupWise Document Management, but the functionality is generally the same". We cannot say that for GroupWise 2014. It is true that Document Management still works in GroupWise 2014. It is true that you can create new Libraries in the GroupWise Administration Console. It is true that you can manage all of the Rights and run Library Maintenance through the GroupWise Administration Console.

There are some definite changes that you need to be aware of though!.

Document Properties Maintenance

There is no facility in the Administration Console to edit the Document Properties for GroupWise Libraries. There is also no facility for this in ConsoleOne on Linux. In order to edit the properties, you must run **gwdpmb32.exe** on Windows. This is found in the **c:\novell\consoleone\1.2\bin** directory on a server or workstation where ConsoleOne with the GroupWise snapins is installed.

There is no requirement that you be logged into eDirectory to run this application. It DOES have dll dependencies provided by the Novell Client installation. Thus, you will need a PC or Windows server with the Novell Client loaded, with access to the Post Office directory in order to run this application.

If you are attempting to run this application on a 64 bit Windows server (and we'll bet you are!), you must add the **gwdpmb32.exe** application to your list of excluded programs in the Data Execution Prevention list. To do this, follow these steps:

1. Go to Control Panel | System | Advanced System Settings
2. Click on the Performance button.
3. Click the Data Execution Prevention tab.
4. If DEP is enabled, you must change the setting to "Turn on DEP except...."
5. Add c:\novell\consoleone\1.2\bin\gwdpmb32.exe to the list of exceptions.

To launch the application, run

    c:\novell\consoleone\1.2\bin\gwdpmb32.exe /po=<PathToPO>

so, for example,

    c:\novell\consoleone\1.2\bin\gwdpmb32.exe /po=d:\grpwise\pos\calpo

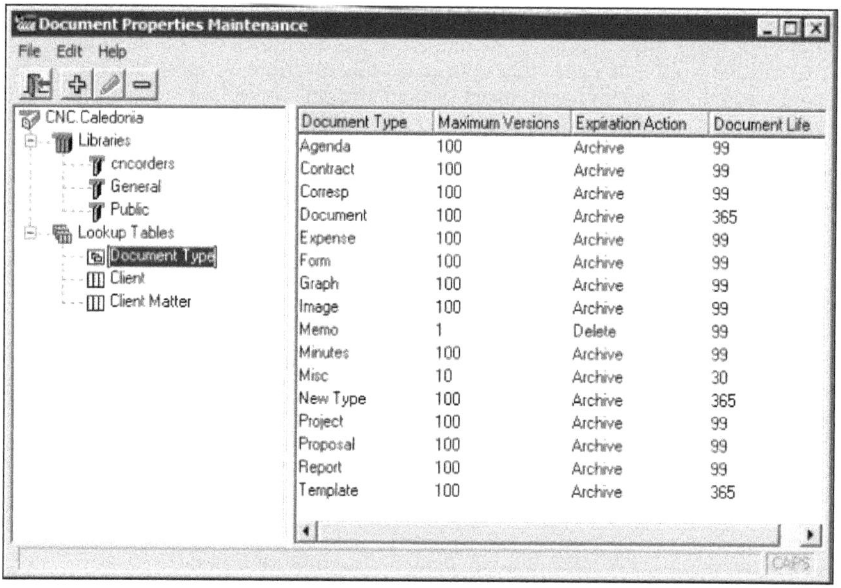

Figure 2-1: Running the Document Properties Maintenance Stand-Alone

No Application Integrations

The GroupWise 2014 client no longer provides any ODMA integrations for applications. Here are the ramifications of this:

- Users must create all new documents from the GroupWise client. There will no longer be the ability to save a document directly into the GroupWise client from once integrated applications like Word, WordPerfect, etc. (i.e., Save or Save As will no longer invoke a GroupWise save dialog).

- Documents must be opened from the GroupWise client. There will be no ability for a user to be in Word, for example, and choose File|Open and see a GroupWise dialog.

- Since ODMA integrations are no longer present, a user cannot rename a GroupWise document without breaking the link to the library. For example, if a user opens "Letter to Danita" into Word from GroupWise, makes changes and then saves the document as c:\temp\lettertopaul.docx, this document will no longer be in the GroupWise library. The GroupWise client monitors the document that was opened to the temp directory through the library, and when you close that file it is returned to the library. The file name is a very important part of this process.

If you rely heavily on GroupWise Document Management with Application Integrations, you may need to keep your current GroupWise client until users can be properly trained.

Enabling the HTTP Monitor for Your Agent

We have found that there are many GroupWise sites where the HTTP (Web) Monitor is not in use. Especially with GroupWise 8 and later, these HTTP Monitors have become more and more important. If you define a userid and password for the HTTP Monitors, you can perform all of the functions that you used to perform at the GUI Consoles for your agents, as well as new functions that were not available on the GUI Consoles. If you do not have your HTTP Monitor enabled, now is a good time to do so.

In ConsoleOne, click on the GroupWise System Globe, and perform the following steps:

1. In the dropdown list that typically shows "Users", change the setting to "Message Transfer Agents."
2. Find the MTA for your domain, right-click and choose Properties.
3. Now click on the triangle in the GroupWise tab and change to Network Address.
4. Make special note of the HTTP port that is defined for this agent. By default, the HTTP port for the MTA is 7180. For the POA, the default port is 7181. 9850 is the default for the GWIA.
5. If there is nothing in the HTTP port field, put 7180 (or another port of your choosing).
6. Now, on the GroupWise tab, change to the Agent Settings screen. Scroll down to the HTTP Monitor settings. If you have never enabled the HTTP monitors for your agents, you will need to decide on a good userid and password for the HTTP monitors. Please note that this is neither an eDirectory user nor a GroupWise user. This is an entirely made up user and password solely for the use of the HTTP monitors. If all administrators in your organization will have rights to use the HTTP monitors, then it is a good idea to have the same userid and password for all agents. If you need to limit rights to some agents to various groups, set up a userid and password for each group of agents that will be monitored. Enter the userid and password that you have decided on here in this screen.
7. Save your changes.

You should do this for all of your agents prior to beginning your upgrade so that you have access to them immediately after the upgrade if necessary. If you forget to do this, and they are needed during the upgrade, we will show you how to start the agents from the command line using the appropriate http monitor switches.

GroupWise High Availability Agent Considerations

If you are using the High Availability Agent, the settings will not come over after the upgrade. Thus, before you even install the GroupWise Administration Service, you must copy your High Availability settings so that you can re-enable the GWHA afterwards.

Edit the /etc/init.d/grpwise-ma script and find your MA_OPTIONS settings. For example, ours are:

MA_OPTIONS="--hauser gwha --hapassword gwhapassword --hapoll 120 --httpagentuser gwweb --httpagentpassword gwweb --httpmonuser gwmon --httpmonpassword gwmon"

Save this information in a text file for use in *"Re-enabling the GroupWise High Availability Agent"* on page 166.

Verifying MTA Network Settings

When we install the Administration Service in the following chapter, the MTA network settings for your domains will be very important.

In ConsoleOne, click on the GroupWise System Globe, and perform the following steps:

1. In the dropdown list that typically shows "Users", change the setting to "Message Transfer Agents."
2. Find the MTA for your domain, right-click and choose Properties.
3. Now click on the triangle in the GroupWise tab and change to Network Address.

The Admin Service will use the network address as defined on this page. If the network address is using an IP Address, then any time you are required to access the admin service during a system modification, you will need to use the IP Address. If the Network address is defined using a DNS name, then anytime you will be required to access the admin service you will need to use the DNS name. This will pertain to tasks such as adding or upgrading secondary domains or post offices that are not on the same server as the Primary domain, and installing the plugins for MMC or iManager.

Modifying Linux Network Settings

When configuring the network adaptor on SLES/OES, there is a setting in the Network Settings that reads "Assign Hostname to Loopback IP".

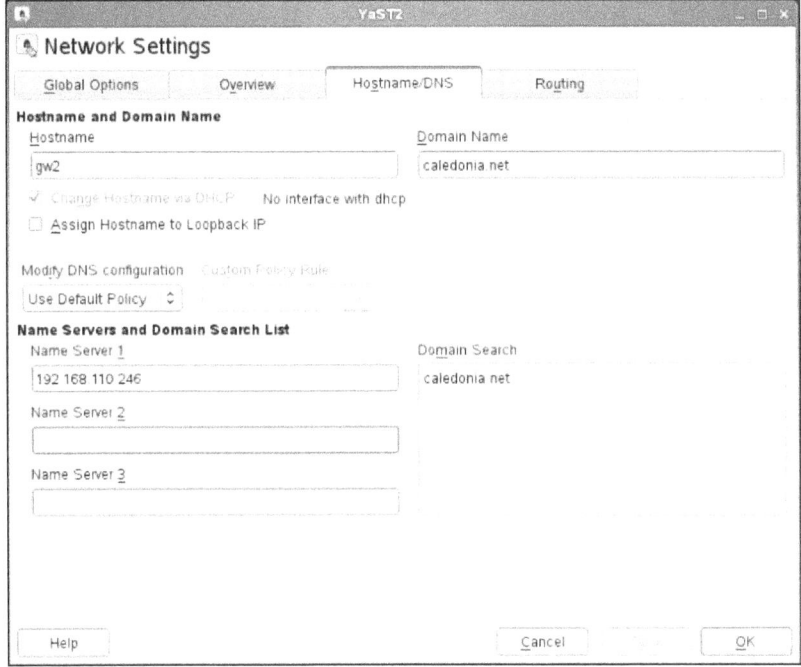

Figure 2-2: Linux Network Settings

On Linux (SLES and OES) do not configure the network Card with this setting enabled. If you do, the loopback address will become the IP Address that the Admin Service binds to *("Installing the GroupWise Administration Service"* on page 25), and this will prevent you from accessing the Admin Service from any process other than the Administration Console. This would affect iManager Plugin, MMC Plugin, the WebAccess Administration Console, etc.

A Quick Health Check

We hesitate to insist that major GroupWise maintenance be performed on your GroupWise system prior to the upgrade. You should ensure that your GroupWise system is in good working order, but because we feel that this should be done routinely anyway, and should not be left until the week of your upgrade! That said, there are a few things that you can do to make your GroupWise upgrade less stressful.

- Clean up your GroupWise system. Quite honestly, there is no real technical reason to get rid of old users, empty trash and implement cleanup options, but it's a perfect time to do so if you need to. Users are typically much more open to making cleanup changes when an upgrade is pending, simply because they accept that "changes" are coming and that might mean they need to help make the upgrade a smooth operation.

> There are licensing changes that will affect some sites regarding inactive accounts. If you have inactive accounts and wish to avoid paying for "inactive" GroupWise licenses, you may wish to archive the inactive accounts and delete them. It is not our intention to fully discuss GroupWise licensing policies, as we do not sell GroupWise product, and are certainly not the experts. Contact your GroupWise sales representative if you have any questions on licensing.

- Additionally, if you intend to integrate your existing eDirectory or Active Directory (yes, you read that right - GroupWise 2014 can integrate directly with Active Directory) with GroupWise, having a lean and clean directory will simplify some of the integration steps later. See the section below entitled *"Preparing Your LDAP System"* if you do intend to integrate and maintain the synchronization connection between your current eDirectory tree and GroupWise 2014.
- Run some basic GWCheck procedures. We know that you are running routine structure and contents checks on your post offices, but it's a good time to make sure that your routines are running properly, that there are no oddities in the logs, and that you are ready to upgrade!
- Verify that all links between MTAs and POAs are open and communicating properly.

Preparing Your LDAP System

GroupWise 2014 has new "directory" options, which we will discuss in detail in the Chapter entitled *"Directory Integration and Synchronization"* If you intend to continue to synchronize eDirectory with your GroupWise system, long-term, or just short-term while you transition to Active Directory, it is recommended that you verify that your GroupWise system is configured properly for LDAP synchronization. This is not the same thing as LDAP authentication (although LDAP authentication to eDirectory provides some of the pieces we need). LDAP synchronization is the mechanism that keeps the GroupWise address book synchronized with changes made in eDirectory (for example, changing a user's phone number, department or address, etc.). LDAP sync also permits the publishing of users' e-mail addresses back to the directory.

By default, MTA Directory Sync is not enabled with GroupWise 2012 and prior systems. eDirectory Sync at the MTA was only needed in the case of modifying eDirectory address book attributes outside of the GroupWise enabled ConsoleOne. So long as every administrator used ConsoleOne with GroupWise snapins, eDirectory changes such as phone numbers, street address, department and other eDirectory fields were automatically written to the **wpdomain.db** file and then spawned out to the other domains and post offices in the system. If, however, someone were to modify these directory fields in iManager, or use a third-party help desk tool that was not GroupWise aware, the MTA could synchronize the system during a daily scheduled event. Because MTA synchronization was disabled by default, and because it was only needed in specified instances, many systems are not enabled for eDirectory Synchronization.

If you have no need for further eDirectory synchronization (for example, you are moving to Active Directory, or you wish to dissociate your users from the eDirectory and run GroupWise as an entirely stand-alone system), then the following steps are not necessary for your installation. You can skip this section and continue on with *"The Upgrade Overview"* on page 22.

If your current system meets the following criteria, you may want to complete this section to ensure your LDAP Synchronization is properly set up and operational.

Note: While you can integrate your upgraded GroupWise system with your eDirectory LDAP server after the upgrade, it will require a few extra steps. It's better to get it done in your existing system.

- Your system will remain on eDirectory.
- You are running GroupWise 6.5 or later on Linux
- You are running GroupWise 8 or later on Windows

If your system is on NetWare, or does not meet the Windows criteria above, you will need to perform the post upgrade integration of eDirectory. Your NetWare MTA may even be properly set up to do eDirectory synchronization, but it does not use LDAP as the mechanism. Thus, a perfectly configured NetWare system will still need some re-configuration once you have migrated and upgraded to GroupWise 2014. So, if your GroupWise system is on NetWare, or a Windows version prior to GroupWise 8, you should skip this section and jump on down further in this chapter to *"The Upgrade Overview"*. After your upgrade, you can go to *"Correcting a Failed Directory Integration"* on page 81 to deal with eDirectory Integration.

Testing Your Current System

Since there are many steps involved with setting up eDirectory synchronization, before you dive in it's probably a good idea to see if your current system is already properly configured. eDirectory Synchronization is a Scheduled Event that is created for an MTA object. However, having the MTA Scheduled Event enabled is only one small step in the configuration. In fact, this event is enabled by default, so many sites just assume that eDirectory synchronization is always working. A very simple check would be to use iManager or a version of ConsoleOne without GroupWise snapins to edit the phone number field for a user today. Tomorrow go into the GroupWise Address Book in your client and see if the phone number has changed for the GroupWise Address Book. If it has, then eDirectory synchronization is activated and working. If it has not, then you can follow the steps below to configure and test eDirectory Sync. Now remember, if you have **NetWare** MTAs in your system, the above test may very well work, but it would still not necessarily be configured properly, unless you also have Linux/MTAs also performing the sync. Also, if you are using other tools like the IDM driver for GroupWise, you could see your changes sync to GroupWise and assume that GroupWise's own eDirectory synchronization is making the changes. If you have any doubts about the configuration, then the next steps should be completed.

Check the MTA Platform Settings

1. In ConsoleOne, click on the Primary Domain in the GroupWise View. The reason we specify the Primary Domain is that since you must upgrade the Primary Domain first, it's just less confusing to configure this MTA prior to your initial domain upgrade.
2. Change the item dropdown to Message Transfer Agents.
3. Choose your MTA and edit the properties.
4. Verify that your Platform is correct. We find that many times systems have been moved from NetWare to Linux or Windows, but the Platform for the agents was not modified. Having the wrong platform designation here can cause the synchronization setup to fail.

16 | Preparing Your GroupWise System

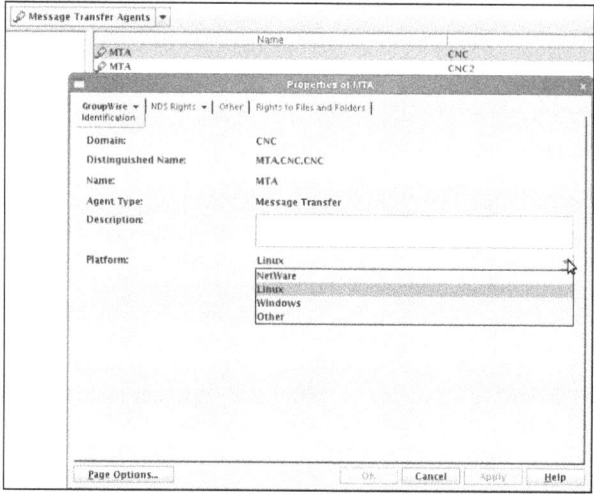

Figure 2-3: The MTA Properties

5. Save the change.

Check or Create your LDAP Server

Once your MTA platform has been verified, we can continue.

1. In ConsoleOne, go to **Tools|GroupWise System Operations|LDAP Servers**. If you have never used LDAP Authentication for your users, or if you have never set up eDirectory Synchronization for a Linux or Windows MTA, this window might be empty. If LDAP servers exist in this section, and you are using LDAP authentication for your users, then we can generally assume that the LDAP servers are properly configured, and you can move on. If not, perform the steps below to define your eDirectory LDAP servers.

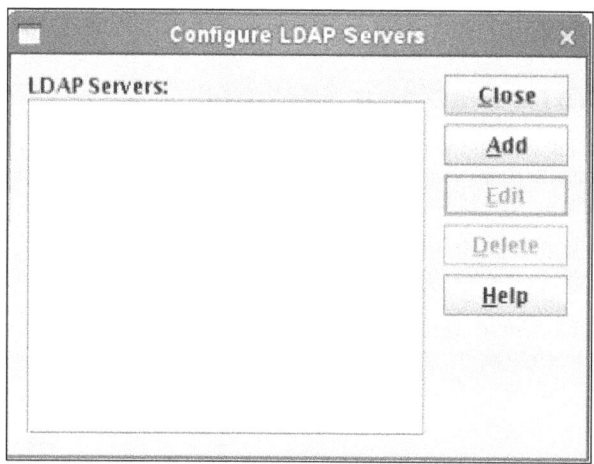

Figure 2-4: Empty LDAP Servers list

2. To add a new server, click Add.
3. Give your LDAP Server a name
4. If your server requires SSL for LDAP, check the SSL box and point to the server certificate key file for the LDAP server.
5. Enter the IP address for your LDAP server.
6. Most people will set their servers to Bind for the authentication method. This allows password restrictions to be honored for the logins.
7. Click OK

If you have a single tree for your GroupWise system, you will need only configure your primary domain MTA for eDirectory synchronization. If you have multiple trees represented in your GroupWise system, you will need to configure a separate MTA (and LDAP server) for each tree. Make sure you have LDAP servers for each eDirectory tree before you move on.

Check or Configure eDirectory User Synchronization

When you have finished the LDAP server configuration, go to **Tools|GroupWise System Operations|eDirectory User Synchronization**. You may see multiple MTAs listed here, but as mentioned, you only need to configure one MTA per LDAP tree in order to complete the tasks at hand. In our situation, our MTAs show disabled. Even if your MTAs show enabled, it is a good idea to check the settings.

Figure 2-5: The eDirectory User Synchronization Configuration

1. Click on the MTA you wish to configure/verify and choose Configure Agents.
2. A list of your agents will appear. If you have never configured eDirectory synchronization it is likely that all of your agents will show "No" in the eDirectory Access. Regardless of the settings here (i.e., Enabled/Disabled or eDirectory access available/unavailable), choose your Primary Domain MTA and click Set Up eDirectory Access.

18 | Preparing Your GroupWise System

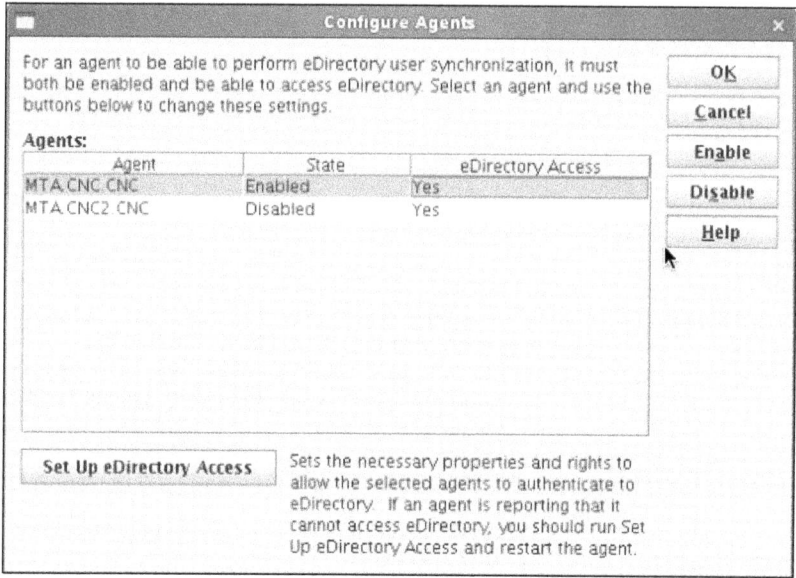

Figure 2-6: Configure Agents

3. You should see the figure in Figure 2-7 below. If you sec the figure in Figure 2-8 below, your MTA is still identified as NetWare, and you will need to go back to the steps in *"Check the MTA Platform Settings"* above to modify the Platform and turn to this section. If your MTA really IS running on NetWare, then these steps are not useful to you. You should stop now and configure your eDirectory synchronization after the upgrade has been performed.

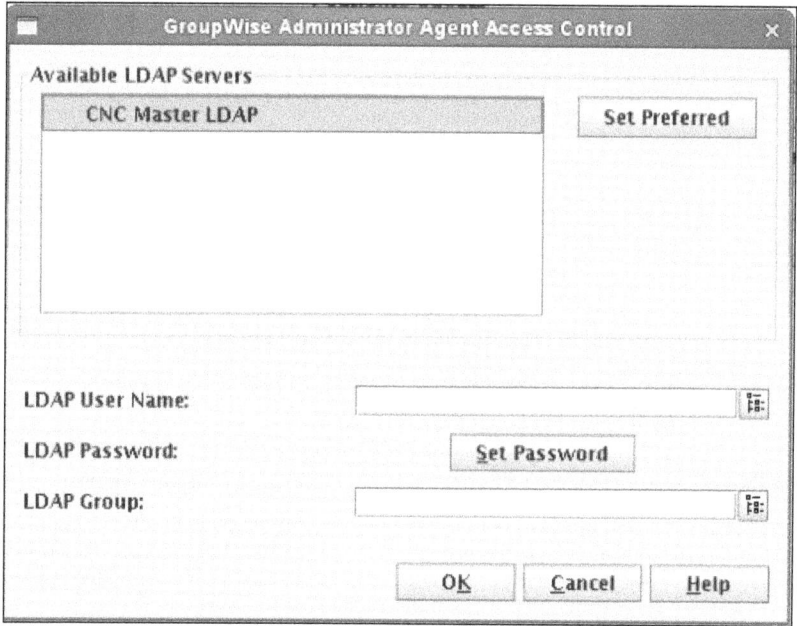

Figure 2-7: Agent Access Control

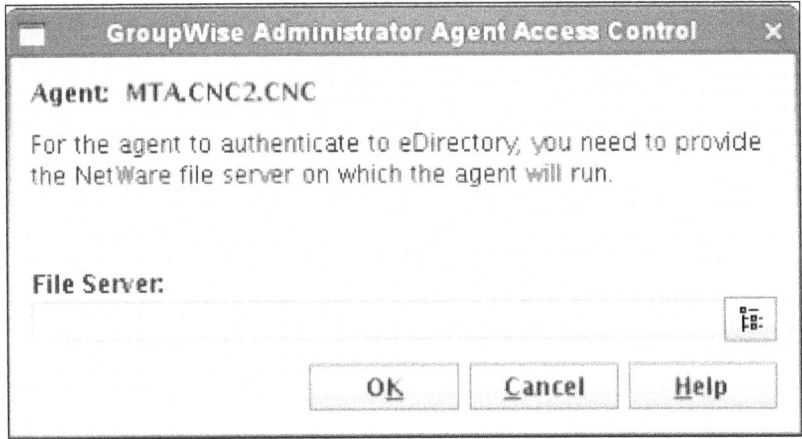

Figure 2-8: NetWare Agent Access Control

4. Choose the LDAP server you wish to use for Synchronization and click Set Preferred.
5. Browse for an LDAP user for a user who has browse rights to the user objects in your system, as well as create rights to user properties in order to publish email addresses back to the directory. We have listed the specific attributes affected in *"Directory Rights Requirements"* on page 63.
6. Browse to and select the LDAP Group for your eDirectory server.
7. Click "Set Password" and enter the password for the LDAP user you chose.

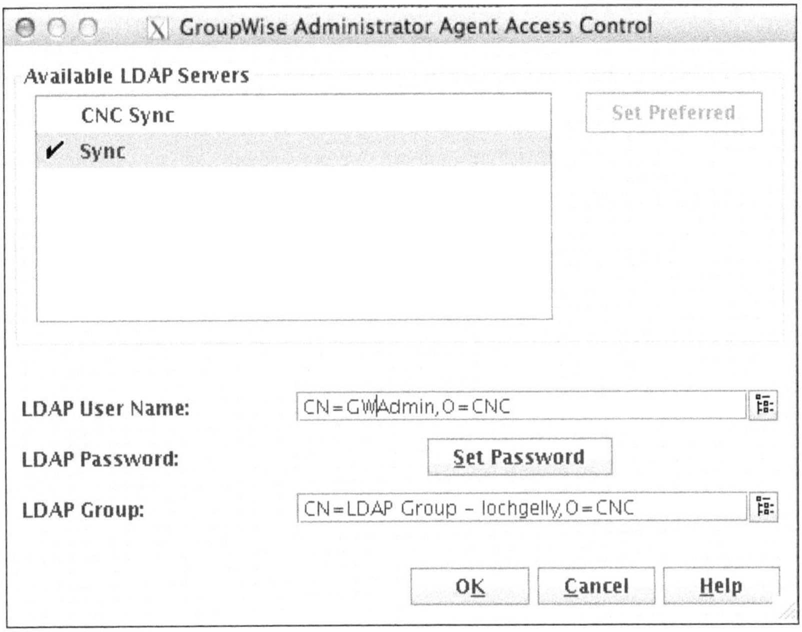

Figure 2-9: 9. LDAP Server Setup

Preparing Your GroupWise System

8. Make certain that you click "Set Preferred" here. If there is not a check box next to your LDAP server, even if there is only one listed, your sync will fail.
9. Click Okay to return the MTA list. The eDirectory Access field for this agent should say Yes.
10. If the State is Disabled, click the Enable button.

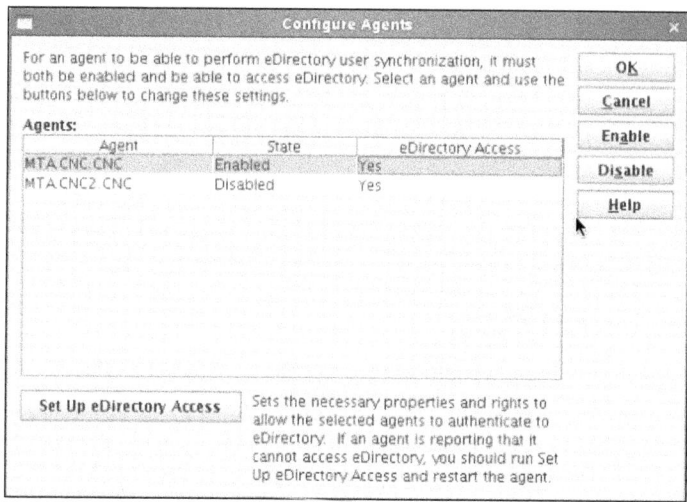

Figure 2-10: Enable your agent

11. You will be returned to the eDirectory User Synchronization Configuration screen. You may very well still see a status of Disabled.
12. Click Change Assignment
13. Click on your primary MTA that you have enabled above and click OK.
14. Now at your final screen your MTA should show enabled.

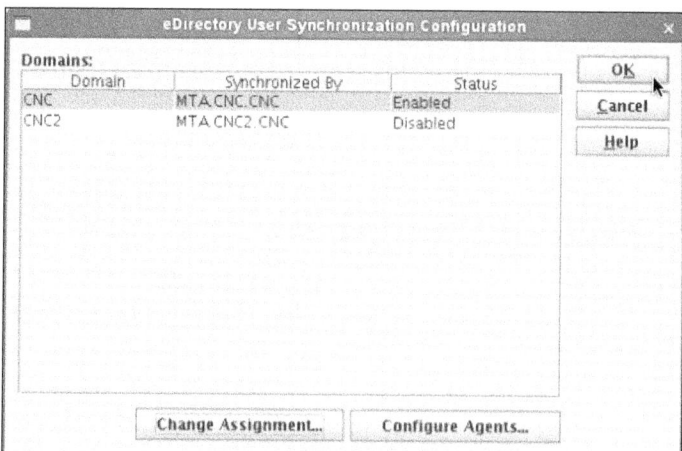

Figure 2-11: MTA is enabled

Check Or Configure Your MTA Scheduled Event

Finally we must check that a Scheduled Event is enabled for eDirectory Synchronization.

1. In ConsoleOne, click on the Primary Domain in the GroupWise View.
2. Change the item dropdown to Message Transfer Agents.
3. Choose your MTA and edit the properties.
4. On the GroupWise Tab, click on the triangle to the right, and select Scheduled Events. There will be an entry for Default eDirectory (or NDS) User Synchronization Event.
5. Click Edit to see the details.

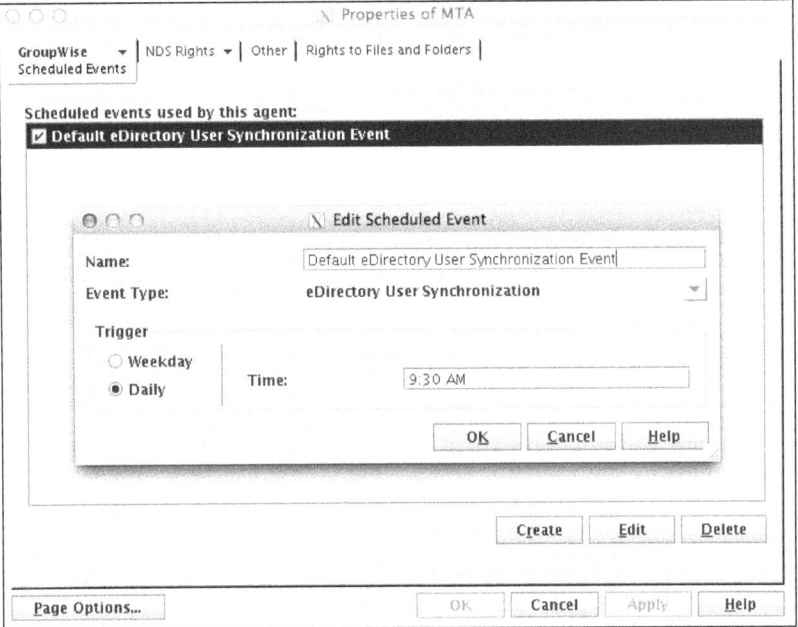

Figure 2-12: The Default eDirectory User Synchronization Event

The default for this event is 1:00 a.m. local time. In order to test this now, rather than waiting until tomorrow, you can change the time. We recommend that you make this at least 30 minutes in the future, to allow for other back-end synchronization processes to have occurred before you proceed. Ours has been changed to 9:30 a.m.

6. Click Okay, and make certain that the event is enabled (checked).
7. If you look at your MTA log, you will see a restart command, and then you should see an entry like this:

09:19:04 F4C5 Scheduled Event Settings:

09:19:04 F4C5   Today's eDirectory User Sync Event Times:

09:19:04 F4C5   09:30:21

If you do not see the restart command, it is helpful to manually restart the MTA.

8. Use iManager or ConsoleOne without any GroupWise snapins to change something that needs to synchronize to GroupWise. For example, a phone number.

At the appointed time (9:30 a.m. in our case), your MTA verbose log should show something similar to the following:

```
09:30:21 F3C7 Start eDirectory user synchronization.
09:30:21 F3C7 Connecting to LDAP server Sync at address 192.168.110.210
09:30:21 F3C7 Checking Beta
09:30:22 F3C7 Checking Caledonia
09:30:22 F3C7 Sync Users for Domain: Caledonia
09:30:22 F3C7 Checking post office: Highlands.GW-Cal.CNC.CNC
09:30:22 F3C7 Checking Caledonia.Highlands.Nessie
09:30:22 F3C7    Update NGW: GroupWise ID:Diane.CNC
  .
  .
09:30:23 F3C7 Checking Caledonia.Highlands.Dominique
09:30:23 F3D7    Update Telephone Number:555-555-7368
09:30:23 F3D7 Checking Caledonia.Highlands.Joe
  .
  .
09:30:24 F3C7 eDirectory user synchronization finished.
```

Now, when we later perform our upgrade, your eDirectory synchronization should be properly configured automatically.

The Upgrade Overview

Before we jump right in and begin our upgrade, we'll take a few moments to go over the process of what we will be doing. How you perform your upgrade will be dictated in part by the size, location and complexity of your system. Here are a few possible scenarios:

Small, Single Server System

First of all, we always recommend that you have at least two GroupWise domains for redundancy. So, if your single server system only has one domain, during your upgrade, you might consider creating a new domain for your GWIA on a separate server to satisfy this recommendation. If you truly can only dedicate one server to your GroupWise system, you can run two MTAs on the same server to allow for a second domain. This, of course, does not give you the same type of redundancy, but can provide a backup of your domain in case of database corruption that cannot be otherwise restored.

In any event, if your GroupWise system is contained all on a single server, you will need to plan to perform your entire upgrade (except for the clients) in a single sitting. It is vital that all components of the GroupWise system that reside on the same server be upgraded at the same time. Thus, if you have a small system, you would go through the steps of:

"Installing the GroupWise Administration Service"

"Upgrading GroupWise Domains" for the Primary Domain along with the GWIA.

"Directory Integration and Synchronization" to verify that your Directory Integration has succeeded and correct any errors.

"The GroupWise Administration Console" to familiarize yourself with the Administration Console

"Upgrading GroupWise Post Offices"

"Upgrading GroupWise WebAccess"

"Upgrading GroupWise Monitor"

"Upgrading the GroupWise Calendar Publishing Host"

"Upgrading GroupWise Clients"

Of course, you may not have all of those components in your system, but this is the order we recommend they be installed.

Small, Multiple Server System

If your GroupWise system is fairly small (perhaps even a single post office with primary domain and gateways on another server), you have some options. The key is that all components on the same server must be upgraded at the same time. Your first step of course will be to deal with upgrading your GroupWise Primary Domain. If the Post Office is on the same server as your primary domain, then you will need to upgrade it at the same time. So long as you upgrade all items on each server together, you should not run into any problems.

Complex GroupWise System on Multiple Servers

If you have a very complex GroupWise system, you need to consider a few things that will crop up with the inevitability of not being able to upgrade all of your post offices at the same time. Here are the most important "gotchas" of a gradual upgrade:

- GroupWise 2014 clients cannot access older post offices. Thus, you cannot begin your client rollout before you actually perform the post office upgrade. This also means that GroupWise 2014 clients cannot proxy to an older GroupWise post office. If you have users on your GroupWise 2014 post offices that need to proxy to an older GroupWise post office, that particular GroupWise 2014 user will need to continue to use the older GroupWise client.
- If you use your GWIA for POP3/IMAP4 access, you will not be able to upgrade your GWIA to GroupWise 2014 until all of your post offices that service such users have been upgraded. In other words, a GroupWise 2014 GWIA running as a POP3 or IMAP4 server is a GroupWise "client" and cannot access older GroupWise post offices. We will discuss this in more detail in Upgrading Your GroupWise Internet Agent. You may need to provide for an older GroupWise GWIA for your users on older post offices if you wish to upgrade your GWIA before you upgrade all of your post offices. If you are accessing through IMAP4, you might consider allowing your GroupWise Post Office Agents to serve as IMAP4 servers for your GroupWise 6 and newer users, thus allowing

you to upgrade the GWIA to GroupWise 2014 right away. There are actually very few good reasons to keep POP3 around (one of them being external processes that cannot use IMAP4). If you can convert all of your external access to IMAP4, moving the IMAP access to your POAs would definitely solve your migration issues.

- Web Access is also a "client", and as such a GroupWise 2014 WebAccess Application cannot access an older GroupWise post office. If you can provide for only one WebAccess Application server, you will need to wait until all post offices are upgraded to GroupWise 2014 before you upgrade your WebAccess. If you can provide two WebAccess Application servers, you can create a new WebAccess for GroupWise 2014, and even use it as your "default" WebAccess location. If a user for an older GroupWise version connects to the GroupWise 2014 WebAccess, the user is redirected to the older WebAccess version. We will discuss this in more detail when we get to Upgrading Your GroupWise WebAccess later in the book.

So, it's time to get started. We would recommend that you read this entire book before you begin your upgrade. We will discuss issues throughout the book that can influence your upgrade plan, and it's best to look at all of the options before beginning.

Before we actually get down to the business of upgrading we need to discuss the new GroupWise Administration Service. The next chapter will be dedicated to that!

3 Installing the GroupWise Administration Service

The GroupWise Administration Service (sometimes referred to during installation as the GroupWise Server) is a new process that runs on each GroupWise server that houses agents. Installing the Administration Server is the first thing you will do on any server as you work through your upgrade. This cannot be done in advance for an in-place upgrade as it replaces the agent binaries. Since you are doing an in-place upgrade, you will complete this process immediately prior to performing your upgrade. Once you begin installing the Administration Service, files will be changed on your server that will require you continue your upgrade immediately after installing the Administration Service

As we move through this upgrade guide, you will learn more about the functionality and purpose of the GroupWise Administrative Service.

The Administrative Service is installed at the same time as the GroupWise agents, and must exist on any server where GroupWise 2014 agents are running. You should start to think of the Administrative Service as a core component of your system.

The initial step in upgrading your GroupWise system is to install the GroupWise Administrative Service, so that it can be prepared to manage the newly upgraded GroupWise system.

In the following section we will show how to install the Administration Server on both Linux and Windows. We highly recommend that your server OS is fully patched before you install the GroupWise Administration Service.

Installing the GroupWise Administration Service on Linux

Download the Installation Media

The first thing you need to do is access the GroupWise 2014 installation media. This will typically be a downloaded compressed file from either http://download.novell.com, or from your Novell Customer Center portal.

Copy this compressed file to a location on your GroupWise server and extract it. To extract the GroupWise tar file, you would use the following command:

tar xfvz nameofgwfile.tar.gz

then cd into the name of the resultant directory. The directory is generally named **gw14.0.0-build_full_linux_multi.tar.gz**

This is the perfect time to point out that even though the files are typically named "multi", there is no longer an English only version. Let's look at the directory structure as it now exists.

26 | Installing the GroupWise Administration Service

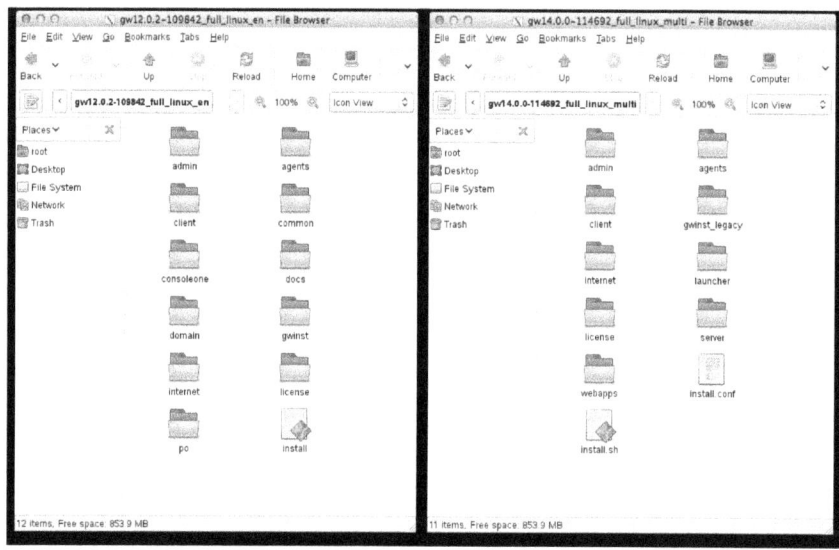

Figure 3-1: Old and new directory structures

As you can see here, there are a few directories missing from what you are accustomed to seeing. Indeed the directory layout is quite different. Gone are the **domain** and **po** directories that held the .dc files. WebAccess has been moved under **Webapps**. Monitor has been relegated to the "**gwinst_legacy**" directory! Now, in theory, it doesn't really matter that the entire folder structure has changed, because you will just be installing everything with the script (renamed from just "**install**" to "**install.sh**"). In practice, we wish sometimes that we could just go grab the dbcopy rpm and install it manually, rather than having to go through some other hoops.

If you have been a "do it manually" type in the past, Novell has made it much more difficult for you. There is no gwcheck rpm to install manually. There is no dbcopy rpm to install manually. Everything is included in the "server" installation. For all but the most hands-on types (and the rare instances where something just "goes wrong"), using the wizards and installation scripts will work out just fine! That said, if you just really want to see what is "there" without performing an installation, you could do the following by changing to the server installation directory):

    cd <installationfiles>/server/linux/x86_64

then run

    rpm2cpio novell-groupwise-server.64bit.rpm | cpio -idmv ./pathtodir/*

Note the **.** before **/pathtodir/** is important.

You can even do the following to extract all files matching a pattern

    rpm2cpio novell-groupwise-server.64bit.rpm | cpio -idmv .*pattern*

so you could use

    rpm2cpio novell-groupwise-server.64bit.rpm | cpio -idmv .*dc

This would allow you to extract the **.dc** files to your current directory, should they somehow become corrupted or lost from your installation.

During the installation, all agents controlled through the gwha.conf file will be shut down.

Also, the installation procedure will attempt to refresh all software repositories and perform a check for certain required dependencies and updated files. We have found that if your server has no Internet connection, the installation can fail. While we do not run into this issue often, if for some reason you have no access to nu.novell.com from your server during the installation, you can turn off the repositories.

1. Load YaST
2. Choose **Software|Software Repositories**
3. Click on each of the Repositories that show "enabled" and disable them.

Install the Administration Service

So, let's install the Administration Service. Before we do, please note that if this is on a production GroupWise server, the installation will actually shut down all of your agents! So, if you're not actually ready to upgrade your agent files, do not run this routine. After the installation, the new GroupWise 2014 agents will be loaded, but your databases will not have yet be upgraded. Thus you will be running GroupWise 2014 agents against your GroupWise 2012 databases.

In reality, even though all of this happens, the only thing that could break would be GWIA access as a POP3/IMAP4 server to your users. The 2014 GWIA is a "client", and cannot access older Post Offices to fulfill POP3/IMAP4 requests. All other functionality would continue, even if your older domain and post office were using GroupWise 2014 agents. That said, you should not install the new GroupWise 2014 server until you are ready to upgrade.

1. If you are in a GUI file browser like Nautilus or Konqueror, just click on **install.sh** and choose Run in Terminal (this is a text based installation, and will only run from the terminal). If you are at a terminal window, type **./install.sh** in the directory where the script resides. Here's the installation screen!

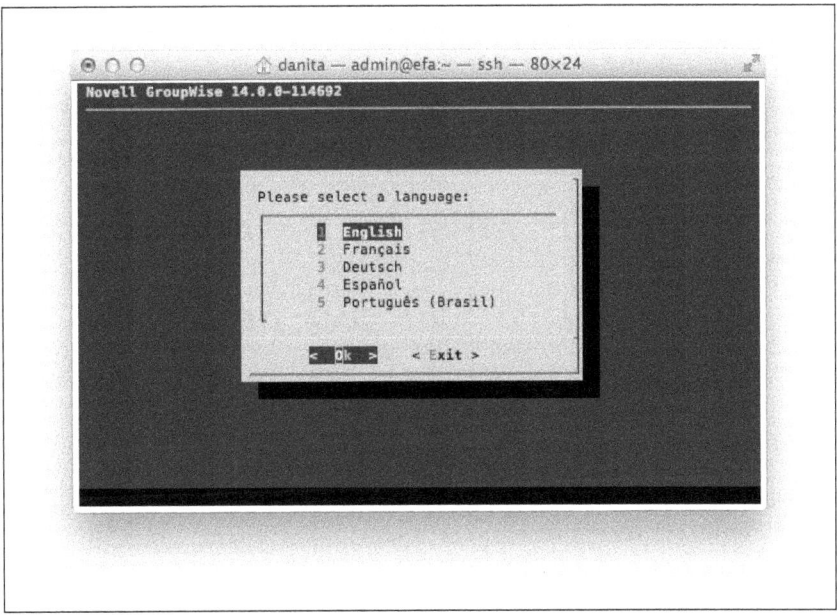

Figure 3-2: The Installation Window

28 | Installing the GroupWise Administration Service

Notice that this is no longer a GUI installation. Everything is text based. In many builds of this installation routine, we have noticed that the arrow keys do not work, and you must use the tab key. If you have issues with arrowing around, use the tab and shift-tab.

2. You have 5 languages to choose from here. Choose your language, and we'll move on.

3. At the next screen you will have two choices: Documentation and Installation. Documentation will attempt to open a web browser and take you to the Novell docs. Remember that the installation can be done in a totally text based environment, thus if you have no GUI/browser available to you, only the Readme be able to view if you choose to look at the documentation.

4. The next screen will present you with the EULA. When you agree to the EULA you are moved to the following screen:

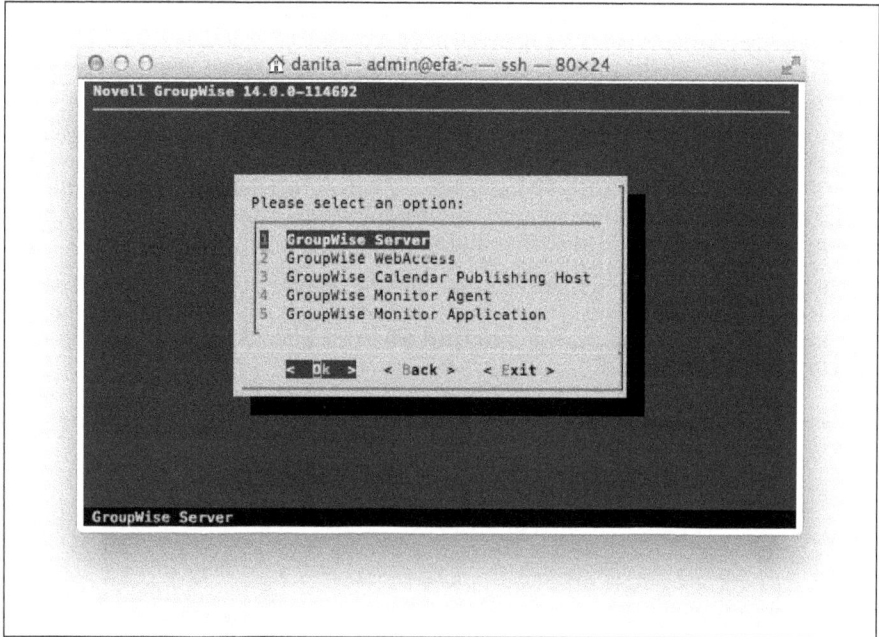

Figure 3-3: The Main Installation Screen

5. Here we can choose to install the GroupWise Server (i.e., all of the components necessary to run a GroupWise system), GroupWise WebAccess, GroupWise Calendar Publishing Host, GroupWise Monitor Agent or GroupWise Monitor Application. We'll choose GroupWise Server.

The GroupWise server is responsible for installing the GroupWise Administration Service, as well as installing the software for the Domains (MTA), Post Offices (POA), GroupWise Document Viewer Agent (GWDVA) and Internet Agent (GWIA). Additionally, the Server installation installs dbcopy and gwcheck on the server as well.

6. Next you have the option of Install or Configure

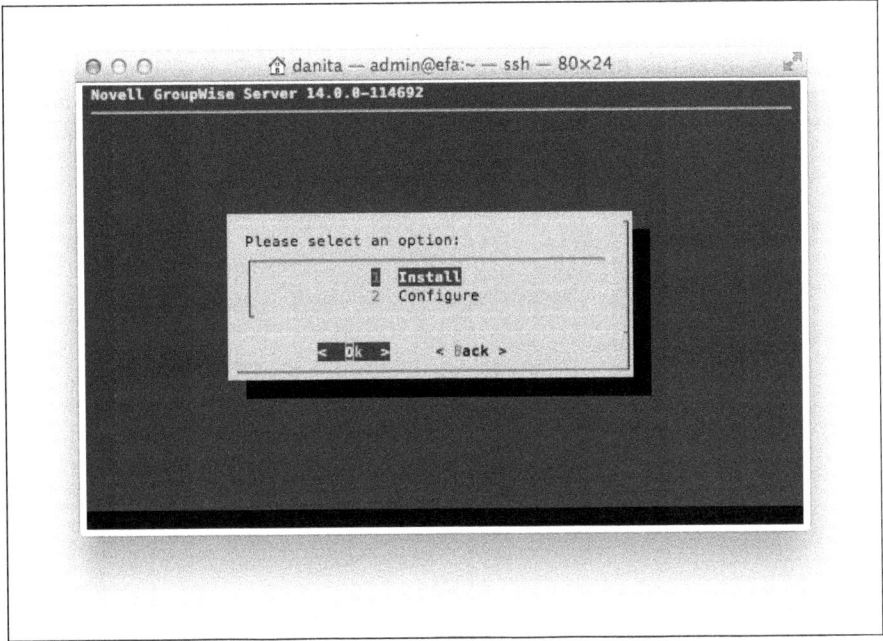

Figure 3-4: Installation Screen

We'll of course choose Install. This will install the actual files. We will later go to configure.

The installation routine will immediately shut down all of the agents that are configured on this server, as listed in the **gwha.conf** file. It will then remove any unsupported files on this server. This includes the GroupWise 8 client for Linux (if it is installed on this server), as well as the ConsoleOne Snapins for GroupWise. While it is Novell's contention that you will never need the ConsoleOne Snapins again on this server, we will show you in *"Reinstalling ConsoleOne Snapins on Linux"* on page 133 how to bring them back if you find yourself in a situation where you absolutely need them!

7. After the agents are shut down, the installation will attempt to refresh nu.novell.com to look for any new versions of OpenMotif.

8. GroupWise will then start installing OpenMotif and all of the required GroupWise files. During this process, the installation also creates a GroupWise Certificate Authority, and creates a certificate for the GroupWise Administration Service.

9. Once the installation has completed, you will be prompted with "press any key to return . . .". This will take you back to the Install/Configure menu.

After installing the Administrative Service, if you were to run an **rcgrpwise status**, you would see something like this:

windermere:~ # rcgrpwise status

Checking status [gwadminservice]   **running**

Back at Figure 3-4 we can now choose Configure.

In prior versions of GroupWise, selecting "Configure" would launch a routine to configure your GroupWise agent startup files, and create the **gwha.conf** for your system. With this new installation process, the "Configure" option in the menu will launch the admin service, and present you with URLs to access for administration.

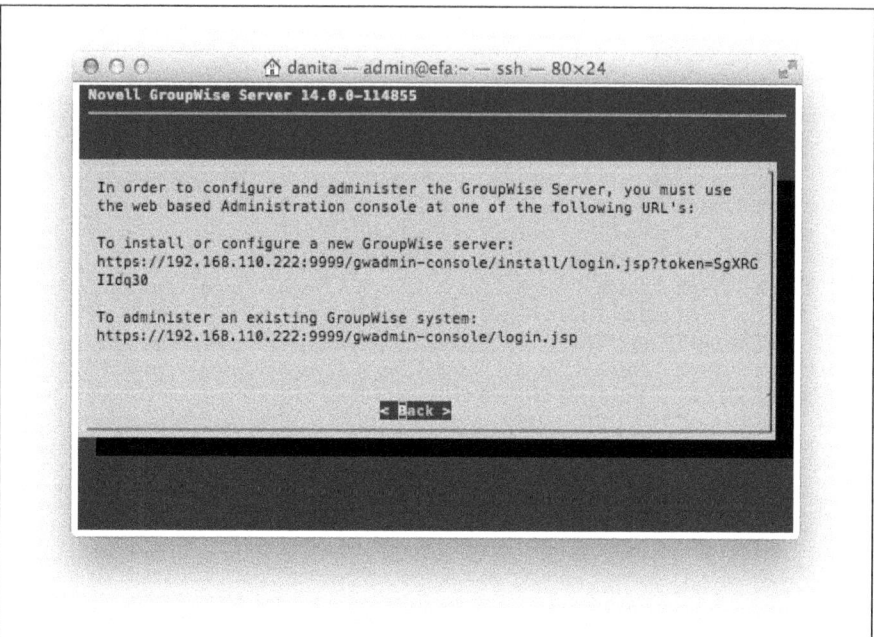

Figure 3-5: The Configuration screen

You can copy the text on this screen for the URL in order to paste it into your browser. If you are installing in X, and have a browser available to you on the server, these URLs are actually clickable. It's absolutely possible though, that you have simply ssh'd into the server to run the installation (since it needs no GUI), and will need to copy the URLs to your browser.

To access the Installation Console on Linux, continue with the section entitled *"Accessing the GroupWise Installation Console"*

Installing the GroupWise Administration Service on Windows

Download the Installation Media

The first thing you need to do is access the GroupWise 2014 installation media. This will typically be a downloaded compressed file from either http://download.novell.com, or from your Novell Customer Center portal.

Extract this file to a location on your GroupWise server. This is a zip file, and you can simply right-click on the file and choose "Extract All" to unzip the entire package to a directory of your choice. The files will then all be extracted into a folder named "groupwise". Thus, if you were to choose c:\installs as the destination folder for the extraction, you would then have c:\installs\groupwise for your files.

This is the perfect time to point out that even though the files are typically named "multi", there is no longer an English-only version. Let's look at the directory structure as it now exists.

GroupWise 2012 & Earlier		GroupWise 2014
admin	AGENTS	admin
CLIENT	COMMON	client
ConsoleOne	DOCS	common
DOMAIN	gwinst	freebusy
INTERNET	LICENSE	launcher
PO	_setup.dll	license
autorun	data1	mmcplugin
data1.hdr	data2	runtimes
ISSetup.dll	layout.bin	server
setup	setup	webapps
setup	setup.inx	setup
setup.isn		

Figure 3-6: Old and new directory structures

As you can see here, there are a few directories missing from what you are accustomed to seeing. Indeed the directory layout is quite different. Gone are the domain and po directories that held the .dc files. WebAccess has been moved under "**Webapps**". Monitor has been relegated to the "**gwinst_legacy**" directory! Now, in theory, it doesn't really matter that the entire folder structure has changed, because you will just be installing everything with **setup.exe**. In practice, we wish sometimes that we could just go grab the dbcopy rpm and install it manually, rather than having to go through some other hoops.

If you need access to the files prior to installation, you can extract all of the files to a temporary location to do so run:

setup.exe /extract path

so you could use

setup.exe /extract c:\gwtemp

During the installation, the GroupWise agents remain running, but a reboot is required to complete the installation.

Install the Administration Service

So, let's install the Administration Service. Before we do, please note that if this is on a production GroupWise server, the installation will install the new agent software, RENAME your GroupWise services, and on reboot load everything back up! This will load GroupWise 2014

32 | Installing the GroupWise Administration Service

agents, but your databases will not have yet be upgraded. Thus you will be running GroupWise 2014 agents against your GroupWise 2012 databases.

In reality, even though all of this happens, the only thing that could break would be GWIA access as a POP3/IMAP4 server to your users. The 2014 GWIA is a "client", and cannot access older Post Offices to fulfill POP3/IMAP4 requests. All other functionality would continue, even if your older domain and post office were using GroupWise 2014 agents. That said, you should not install the new GroupWise 2014 server until you are ready to upgrade.

Our Windows server is running a GroupWise domain, post office and GWIA. Notice the services that are running:

Figure 3-7: GroupWise Agents

Prior to GroupWise 2014, when you installed agents on a Windows server, the services would be named after the startup files. So the services can be spread out all through the list. In the case above, we have a calpo POA, CNC MTA and a GWIA - without any easy way to find them in the list if you are not sure of the startup files names. This will change during this installation, and we will revisit this later in this setup.

Note: Since the GroupWise Agent Services have no description defined, one way to find them in the list is to sort the services by description. This makes them at least float to the top!

1. From Windows Explorer, double-click on **setup.exe** in your installation directory. Here's the installation screen!

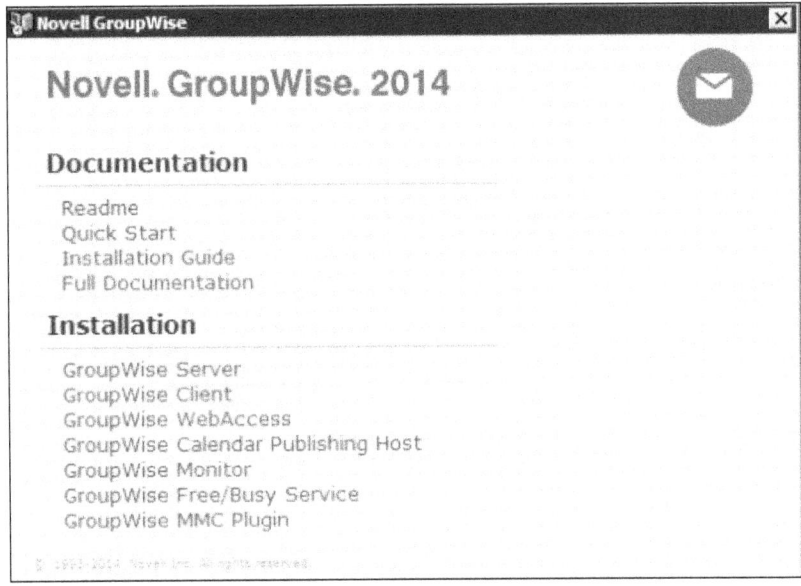

Figure 3-8: The Installation Window

2. Here we can choose to install the GroupWise Server (i.e., all of the components necessary to run a GroupWise system), the GroupWise Client, GroupWise WebAccess, GroupWise Calendar Publishing Host, GroupWise Monitor, the GroupWise Free/Busy Service or the GroupWise MMC Plugins. We'll choose GroupWise Server. Other components will be discussed in future chapters.

   The GroupWise server is responsible for installing the GroupWise Administration Service, as well as installing the software for the Domains (MTA), Post Offices (POA), GroupWise Document Viewer Agent (GWDVA) and Internet Agent (GWIA). Additionally, the Server installation installs dbcopy and gwcheck on the server as well.

   During this time you will see a few popups for the installation of some required redistributables such as vcruntime and c++ . It can take several minutes before the GroupWise installation continues.

3. You have 5 languages to choose from here. Choose your language, and we'll move on.

4. At the "Welcome" window, click next,

5. The next screen will present you with the EULA. When you agree to the EULA you are moved to the following screen:

34 | Installing the GroupWise Administration Service

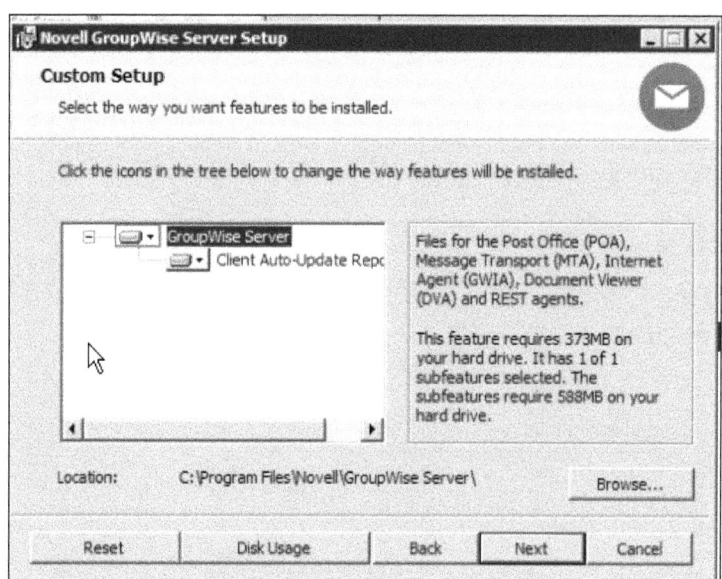

Figure 3-9: The Custom Setup Screen

6. Our only real option here is to decide whether to install the Client Auto-Update Repository, and to choose the location for our executable files. Space is cheap. We generally recommend that you keep the default and install all files.

   You will be brought to a confirmation window, allowing you to cancel or go back before you begin the installation. Click Install to proceed.

   Files will be copied, and you will be at the completion window.

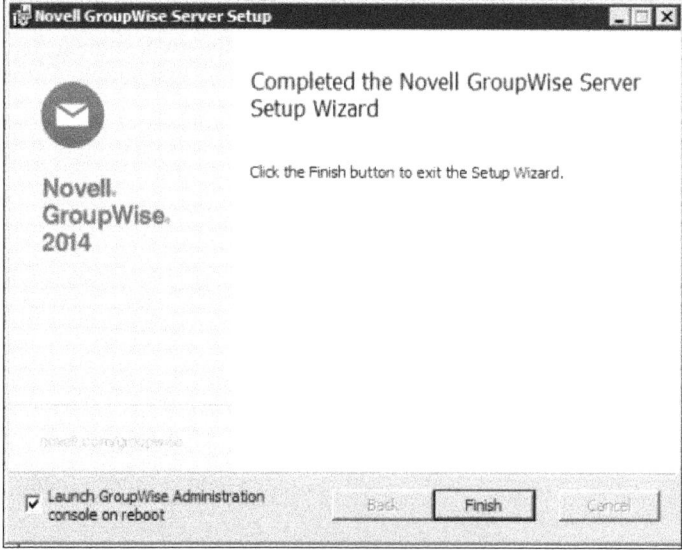

Figure 3-10: Completion Screen

7. You will be prompted to restart your server when the installation is completed. If you keep the box checked for Launching the Administration service after the reboot, you will be brought directly to the Installation Console. The particular "token" that allows you to access the Installation Console (which we'll discuss later in this chapter) will expire after 5 minutes. So you might as well uncheck the box and load up the Installation Console manually when you are ready.

By the way, it can take a good while for the Administration Service to load after the reboot. You'll see a command window with "Waiting for the Administration Service to start . . . ." and then eventually your browser will load.

After installing the Administration Service and rebooting your server, go and take a look at your services again (click the **Start button|Administration Tools|Services**. You will notice that all of your GroupWise services have been renamed, and are now sorted together under "GroupWise".

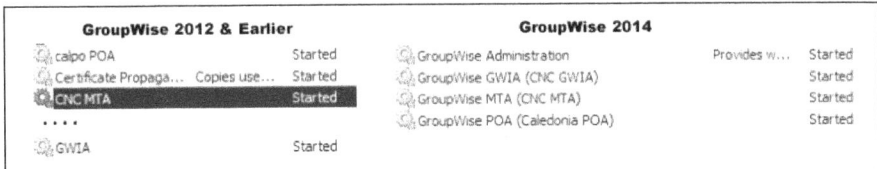

We also have a new service called "GroupWise Administration. This new service, as well as the GroupWise 2014 agents are now running.

Now WHAT, you say? I've updated my agents, and my GroupWise 2012 (or earlier!) domain and post office are being accessed by 2014 agents? Won't that hurt my system? For the short-term, the answer is no. If you DO have a GWIA on this server, and if users are utilizing IMAP4 or POP3, they will be unable to access their mailboxes (you've essentially installed a GroupWise 2014 client with the GWIA, and the newer client cannot access older POs). The SMTP service for the GWIA, and the MTA and POA will work just fine. In the figure below, notice that in our case we have a GroupWise 2014 agent running, but our domain database is still version 8.

Figure 3-11: GroupWise 2014 MTA with a Domain database that has not yet been upgraded.

Re-enabling the GroupWise High Availability Agent on Linux

During the Administration Service installation, all GroupWise related executable files are also upgraded. This includes the GroupWise High Availability Agent on Linux. The original GWHA settings are not preserved. Thus you will be required to do a bit of reconfiguring. During our preparations in *"GroupWise High Availability Agent Considerations"* on page 12, we had you copy your MA_OPTIONS line and place it in a text file for user in our reconfiguration.

Installing the GroupWise Administration Service

After the Administration Service has been installed, check your GroupWise Monitor agent to verify it loaded (i.e. go to http://yourserver:8200). If the agent is loaded, and operational, go back to your Linux server and type:

rcgrpwise-ma stop

Now, go edit **/etc/sysconfig/grpwise-ma.** Look for the line that starts GROUPWISE_MA_OPTIONS. Replace the switches there with those that were in your MA_OPTIONS you saved earlier. Our line would look like this:

GROUPWISE_MA_OPTIONS="--hauser gwha --hapassword gwhapassword --hapoll 120 --httpagentuser gwweb --httpagentpassword gwweb --httpmonuser gwmon --httpmonpassword gwmon"

Note that the option has changed from **MA_OPTIONS** to **GROUPWISE_MA_OPTIONS**.

Now start the Monitor Agent again:

rcgrpwise-ma stop

Test the High Availability Agent by shutting down one of your agents. For example, we might shut down the MTA on our system:

rcgrpwise stop CNC

What the status of the agent (either through the monitor or by running **rcgrpwise status**) to verify that the agent restarts.

Troubleshooting

The gwha service should still be configured. You can verify this by going to /etc/sysconfig and looking at the gwha file. Unless this file has a line that reads

disabled = yes

then the service is still enabled. If the above line has appeared, remove it.

If the Monitor Agent will not load, double check the hauser and hapassword switches. If you type them by hand, remember that it is hapassword, not hapass as Danita tends to type (over and over!).

Accessing the GroupWise Installation Console

The installation routine will also create two icons on your server desktop – one for GroupWise Installation and one for the GroupWise Admin Console.

Figure 3-12: GroupWise Administration Icons

These shortcut icons work the same on both Windows and Linux.

Let's take a moment to look at these URLs.

When the Administration Service is first installed, it is configured to run on port 9710. While you can change this later if you like, it is not our recommendation that you do. Some sites change the default ports as a type of security. Firstly, there are almost NO instances of a GroupWise agent being compromised. Secondly, if you change these ports around, it causes a great deal of confusion when GroupWise consultants try to help you (yes, we are thinking of ourselves here). Now, if you absolutely must change these, then we'll show you how later, but consider why you might want to do this, and only change the defaults if absolutely necessary. The two URLs that are called by these icons are:

https://yourserver:9710/gwadmin-console/login.jsp

and

https://yourserver:9710/gwadmin-console/install/login.jsp

These two URLs show that the Administration Service is running on port 9710, and that you need to go to either **/gwadmin-console/install** or **/gwadmin-console** to login. We'll have plenty of time to look at the Administration Console. Let's talk about the installation option in some detail.

Our image in Figure 3-5 on page 30 above shows a token at the end of the installation URL, after the "login.jsp" portion of the URL. This is visible on the Linux installation. On the Windows installation, a command is passed on reboot that runs **gwadmin-ipc** to request a token and pass the token to the web browser to launch the Installation Console.

So just what is this token? The token is a way for the installation procedure in the Administration Console to authenticate you so that not just anyone can hit the installation URL and start to make system changes. This token is only good for about 5 minutes. Thus, if you walk away from this screen and then attempt to access the Installation Console, you will be given a new token to use for verification. We'll show you how this works when we get to *"Accessing the Installation Console for the First Time"* below.

When you click on the URL to launch it in Firefox on your Linux server, or copy the URL to your own workstation browser, you will first be notified that the SSL certificate is untrusted. This, of course, is because the installation created a self-signed certificate in the steps above for your GroupWise system to use for the Administration Console and any agent that does not already have a certificate installed. So you will be warned that you are accessing an "untrusted" site, but can happily accept the certificate. If for some reason you get a time-out trying to access the Administrative Console right after installing the system, try again in a few seconds. You might simply be too fast for the Administration Service to have loaded in the background.

Accessing the Installation Console for the First Time

If for some reason you wait longer than 5 minutes to use this token, it will be invalid, and if you access the Installation Console, you will see the screen shown in the figure below:

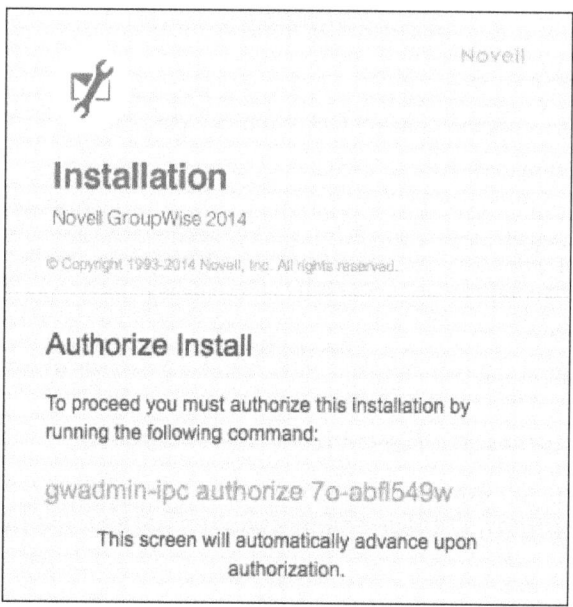

Figure 3-13: Authorize Installation

Notice that the command we're told to run above is "**gwadmin-ipc authorize 7o-abfl549w**" - this shows a program "**gwadmin-ipc**" a switch "authorize" and the token. You can copy this string and execute it on your Linux or Windows server.

In Windows, Novell has added the **<serverfiles>\admin** to the Path in System Variables. On Linux, Novell has included an **/etc/profiles.d/gwadmin.sh** file to add the Path on Linux as well.

We will discuss the programs in the **/opt/novell/groupwise/admin** (**c:\Program Files\Novell\GroupWise Server\admin** on Windows) directory in more detail later.

Let's look at the Installation Console now.

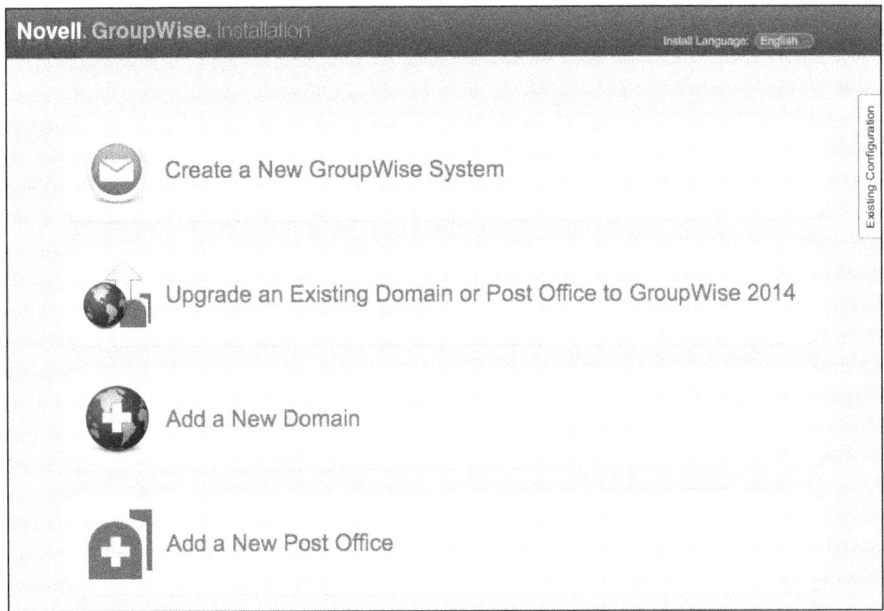

Figure 3-14: The Installation Console

Here you can Install a new system, Upgrade an existing system, or add some components.

Changing the Installation Console Access Method

If you have a simple system, dealing with the token to install or upgrade your system doesn't seem like a big deal. If you have a large system, it can become a bit annoying. So, let's look at how you can bypass the token.

First, let's look in the

/opt/novell/groupwise/admin

or

c:\Program Files\Novell\GroupWise Server\admin

directory on your server. Here you will find a file called **install.cfg**. By default, the contents of the file will look something like this:

#Tue Feb 04 21:12:28 MST 2014
    mode=token

We can change this with the **gwadminutil.sh** script or the **gwadminutil.cmd** file. There are three modes you can use for the Installation configuration:

- token
- user
- disabled.

Token is the default, and you have seen how it works. Now let's look at the other two modes.

Change to **/opt/novell/groupwise/admin** or **c:\Program Files\Novell\GroupWise Server\admin**. You can look to see all of the functions of **gwadminutil.sh** by running it with no switches (on Windows, just type **gwadminutil.cmd** instead). For example:

windermere:/opt/novell/groupwise/admin # ./gwadminutil.sh

GroupWise Admin Command Line Utility (14.0.0.114855)

Usage: gwadminutil <command>

Commands:

validate	**setadmin**
recover	**upgrade**
reclaim	**ca**
reindex	**certinst**
rebuild	**dbinfo**
sync	**installcfg**
convert	**services**
release	**config**
merge	

We will look at all of these switches later in this guide. For now, we are interested in **installcfg**. So let's run **gwadminutil.sh** (or **gwadminutil.cmd**) again with the **installcfg** switch to see the help screen for it.

windermere:/opt/novell/groupwise/admin # ./gwadminutil.sh installcfg

usage: gwadminutil installcfg [-u <username>] [-p [<password>]] -m <mode>

example: gwadminutil installcfg

Configure the admin service installation authentication

-m,--mode <mode>   **Installation mode (token|user|disabled)**

-p,--password <password>   **Install password (if mode is 'user')**

-u,--username <username>   **Install username (if mode is 'user')**

If we run

./gwadminutil installcfg -m disabled

this would prevent any access to the Installation Console. Of course someone with proper access to this directory can change the mode, but this prevents someone from accidentally stumbling upon the URL and trying to muck around.

Let's set the configuration to user:

./gwadminutil installcfg -m user -user gwinstall -p mypass

The resultant config file would look like this:

windermere:/opt/novell/groupwise/admin # cat install.cfg

#Tue Feb 04 21:25:29 MST 2014

user=gwinstall

hash=6b2e94d8c3c0f6c055eaa40daf8d0bb23f57305a

mode=user

You cannot simply edit this file and modify the parameters for user mode, since the **gwadminutil** performs a password hash and writes the hash value to the file rather than a password in clear text. You CAN however, copy this file to other servers. So if you will have many servers to upgrade over the course of your project, copying the file to each server will avoid having to deal with tokens as you move through your upgrade process. The user that you designate here is very much like the http monitor users – it is neither a GroupWise nor an LDAP user, and should be unique for the situation, and the password known to only those who need access.

The ability to copy a file with the hash means that your first level of security is to limit the people who have access to the **/opt/novell/groupwise/admin** or **c:\Program Files\Novell\ GroupWise Server\admin** folder on any particular server. What could someone do with this information? Create a new GroupWise system, upgrade components before you are ready, and install new domains or post offices. However, protecting file level access to your server is your best defense here.

Now that we've installed the Administration Service, you can upgrade the objects on this server.

4 Upgrading GroupWise Domains

This chapter will cover upgrading GroupWise Domains of all kinds. Primary Domains, Secondary Domains, Domains with GWIAs, Domains with Post Offices. If there is a domain involved, this chapter will address it.

If you have multiple servers to upgrade, after this domain chapter, we will deal with issues regarding Directory Services, and then give you an overview of the new Administration Console before we jump into upgrading the rest of your system.

Most of the images in this chapter will be for the Linux installation. If there are notable differences for Windows, we will point those out.

Now that we've looked at the overview of the upgrade process, the first step of the actual work is to upgrade your primary domain to GroupWise 2014. If your GroupWise system is a simple one server system, or even a multi-server system managed by a single administrator, this is a pretty easy task. Your primary domain gets upgraded, and you are on your way! However, if you happen to be in a larger system where the administration is distributed across multiple departments, locations, or even continents, this becomes more complicated. The primary domain MUST upgrade first. In most larger organizations, the primary domain will be a domain that is created solely for the purpose of administration and routing. It will not own any post offices or gateways, and will reside on a separate server. This is done often in larger organizations, and if this is the case, hopefully the owner of that domain will be willing to upgrade it quickly. However, if the administrator owning the primary is not as eager as you to upgrade, then you have a few choices.

- Wait for your primary domain to upgrade
- Request that a domain in your control be promoted to primary temporarily until the location that owns the current primary domain decides to upgrade.

While in some organizations this is often seen as a political matter, the primary domain's main purpose is to provide uniqueness of names throughout the system and replicate all changes in the system to other domains. It is generally not a problem to promote another secondary domain to primary if required in order to begin your upgrade.

How Does the Upgrade Work?

At the domain level, a GroupWise upgrade is really just a database conversion from one version to another. The former GroupWise domain database (version 5.0 through 2014 works the same), is RECOVERED by the administrative thread and CONVERTED to the new version. For a primary domain, this requires a few simple components and prerequisites:

- The Message Transfer Agent software must be at GroupWise version 2014
- The dc (dictionary files) in the domain directory must be at version 2014
- The Primary Domain must be upgraded before any Secondary Domain can upgrade.

- Secondary Domains must have received the notification from the Primary Domain (through administrative messages passed by the MTAs) that the Primary is at version 2014, and they Secondaries are permitted to upgrade.

The actual process is as follows: The Admin Service first makes a full copy of the **wpdomain.db** file in the same directory as the domain, and names it **recover.ddb**. Then the Admin Service also creates a file called **creating.ddb** in the domain directory. At the point that the **creating.ddb** file is fully created, the Admin Service puts an internal record lock on the primary domain's **wpdomain.db** file, carves the file out from the header down, and places the information from the **creating.ddb** file into the **wpdomain.db** file.

Prior to GroupWise 2014, this really was all there was to it. There are a few new twists with GroupWise 2014, involving creating an Administration Console user and assigning Administration Server ports.

This update then triggers a message to be sent to any post offices that might be owned by the domain. If you are upgrading the Primary Domain, the message is also sent to any Secondary Domains that are in the system. This message updates the post offices and secondary domain databases with the information that the primary domain is now a GroupWise 2014 domain. Unless this message is properly delivered (MTAs are down, POAs are down, etc.), the other domains and post offices will not upgrade, even though they may be running the GroupWise 2014 software for their agents. We'll discuss this more as we walk through this upgrade.

What About ConsoleOne?

As we've discussed previously, GroupWise 2014 does not use ConsoleOne for administration, and it is not recommended that you use ConsoleOne with your 2014 domains. Until your upgrade is complete, you will need to keep ConsoleOne around to do some administration of your older version domains and post offices. Since most administrative tasks in a GroupWise system are "store and forward" processes, the 2014 Administration Console can deal with tasks such as creating users, changing passwords, kicking off a GWCheck, etc. for all of the domains and post offices in the system, regardless of version. There will be times when you need access to ConsoleOne for older domains and post offices (rebuilding databases, and the like), so you will need to keep ConsoleOne with GroupWise snapins around on a workstation or two until the upgrade is complete. If you utilize GroupWise Document Management, you will want to revisit the discussion in *"What about Document Management?"* on page 9.

Prepare The Domain Database

We cannot overstate the importance of validating your databases prior to an upgrade. The only times we've seen GroupWise upgrades go very badly were when there was corruption in the domain or post office databases prior to upgrading. Due to the complications introduced with the new administration model, and the requirement that databases with versions prior to 2014 be rebuilt at the command line, some administrators will want to skip this step. Do so at your own peril.

From here on out, we will assume that you understand that the Primary Domain must be upgraded first, and references to domains in this chapter will generally be relevant for Primary or Secondary Domains. If there is something specific to a Primary Domain, we'll let you know! In fact, in the case of preparing the Primary Domain for upgrade, you will use ConsoleOne. Once the Primary Domain has been upgraded, you will need to use new GroupWise 2014 Command Line Utilities to do any database rebuilds that may be required. Thus, if you are upgrading a domain and post office on the same server, we recommend you do the validate on both the domain and post office at the same time from ConsoleOne for simplicity's sake.

When you are ready to continue your upgrade, we will first check the domain to make sure that it is ready to upgrade. In ConsoleOne, select the domain object and choose **Tools|GroupWise Utilities|System Maintenance|Validate Database**. If your database shows as valid, you can proceed. If for some reason the database does NOT validate, you should rebuild it. In order to rebuild the database you must first shut down the MTA and any gateways that attach to the domain database. Just be to safe, make a copy of the **wpdomain.db** file in case something unexpected were to happen during the rebuild (power outage, server room flood, etc.). If this is the Primary Domain, once the agents are shut down, return to ConsoleOne and choose **Tools|GroupWise Utilities|System Maintenance**, and this time choose **Rebuild Database.**

If you are checking a Secondary Domain, you can use ConsoleOne to check the validity of the Secondary Domain. If for some reason however, the domain database fails validation, you will need to rebuild the domain database from the new GroupWise 2014 Primary Domain server! Please see the section entitled *"Command Line Utilities"* on page 128 in the Chapter on *"The GroupWise Administration Console"* if a rebuild of a Secondary Domain is warranted.

The Domain Upgrade Overview

From this point forward, everything you've ever known about upgrading GroupWise has changed!!! The installation routine is different. The upgrade wizard is different. The administration is different. Onward and Upward!

Depending on your setup, you may be simply upgrading your domain during this sitting, or you may be doing more than that. If any other GroupWise components exist on the same server as your domain, you need to upgrade them now too. Let's look at the possible scenarios.

- Simple single server – you need to do everything. You will upgrade the Domain (which upgrades the GWIA) and Post Office, and then move to upgrading your WebAccess, etc.
- MTA & POA on same server – the procedure will upgrade both the domain and the post office, and you're done with this server.
- MTA on its own server – perform the steps to upgrade the domain and verify.
- MTA & GWIA. By default, upgrading the Domain upgrades the GWIA.

Before we go to the administration console, we'll go over a few structural changes here:

DC Files

In the past, the dictionary (.dc) files were found in the **/domain** and **/po** directories of your installation file location. We often had to copy those files directly to the domain directory in order for an upgrade to commence. In theory this should never be required again. These files are now installed along with the GroupWise Server files, and reside in **/opt/novell/groupwise/admin/data** directory (**c:\Program Files\Novell\GroupWise Server\admin\data** on Windows). Since the GroupWise Administration Service knows where these files are now (before they literally could have been anywhere), the upgrade procedure copies the files to the domain directory automatically, and avoids the problem of having the incorrect .dc files in the directory during the upgrade attempt.

Startup Files

Also, in the past, startup files for all agents on Linux were maintained by default in the **/opt/novell/groupwise/agents/share** directory. On Windows they were maintained in the agent executable directories. If GroupWise was in a cluster, these were typically maintained in the domain or post office directory. When you install a new domain or post office with GroupWise 2014, the startup file will be saved in the domain or post office directory. If you are upgrading on Linux and the startup file is in **/opt/novell/groupwise/agents/share**, it will remain in that directory after the upgrade. On Windows the startup files will all be located in the domain or post office or gwia directories. That said, we have seen instances on Linux where the file was recreated in the domain or post office directory, and you would see two of them on the server. This can happen if the installation routine gets confused and believes there is no file in the share directory, or the paths in the original startup file are believed to be incorrect.

The downside to this is that on Linux starting agents by hand can be a bit more cumbersome. Since it was assumed that startup files were in the share directory, you could start the agents from the **/opt/novell/groupwise/agents/bin** directory with a simple command like:

./gwmta @domain.mta

If the startup file is not in the share directory, you will need to specify the location thusly:

./gwmta @/grpwise/domains/cnc/cnc.mta

You can move these files back to the **/opt/novell/groupwise/agents/share** directory if that is your preference, but you will also need to edit the paths in the **gwha.conf** file if you choose to do this.

Alternatively, you could also create a symlink for the file. For example, if our file was **/grpwise/domains/cnc/cnc.mta**, we could change to **/opt/novell/groupwise/agents/bin** and create a symlink as follows:

ln -s /grpwise/domains/cnc/cnc.mta cnc.mta

Then we would no longer need to type the full path to the startup file.

So, let's get down to it.

In our last chapter, we installed the GroupWise Administration Server. This installed all agent software required for the GroupWise Agents (MTA, POA, GWIA).

Now that your agent software has been updated, we need to move on to the actual process of upgrading the domain to GroupWise 2014.

Performing the Domain Upgrade

At this point, you have installed the software required to take your domain to GroupWise 2014, but your domain has not actually upgraded. This will not happen until you access the Installation Console and choose to upgrade your system. Let's discuss how this has changed from the methods we used in GroupWise 2012 and earlier.

For prior versions of GroupWise, the key to an upgrade was providing the primary domain with new dictionary (.dc) files, and loading the new agents up to perform the upgrade. It really was as simple as that. Barring any complications, those two steps performed a successful upgrade every time. While these two steps are also necessary with GroupWise 2014, there are some additional steps required, and the locations of files have moved around a bit.

Back in the *"Installing the GroupWise Administration Service"* section, we loaded up the Installation Console after installing the Administration Service. Now we need to look at the upgrade steps for our system.

Hopefully you set your Installation configuration to use "user" mode as we described in *"Changing the Installation Console Access Method"*. Otherwise you will need to follow the "token" instructions above in that section to access the Installation Console (assuming it's been more than 5 minutes since you completed the installation of the files and received your first token).

1. Go to **https://yourserver:9710/gwadmin-console/install**

    We have set our installation mode to "user", so we can login with our "gwinstall" user we defined above.

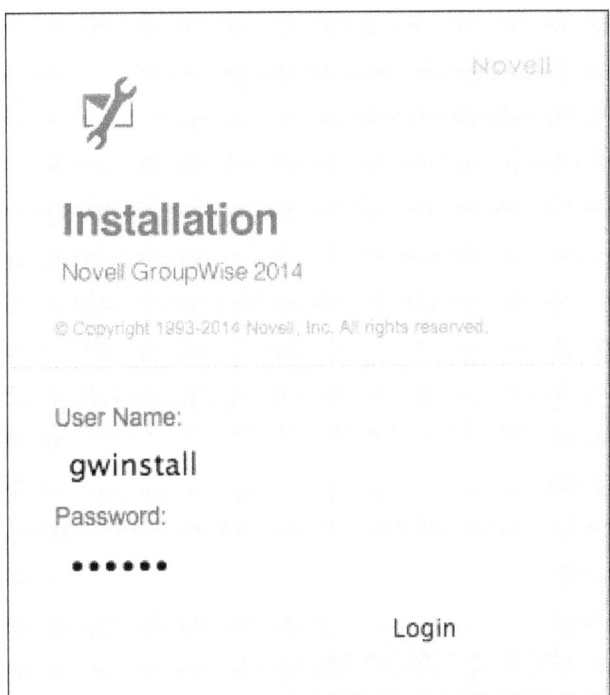

Figure 4-1: The Installation Login Screen

2. We now see the Installation options screen

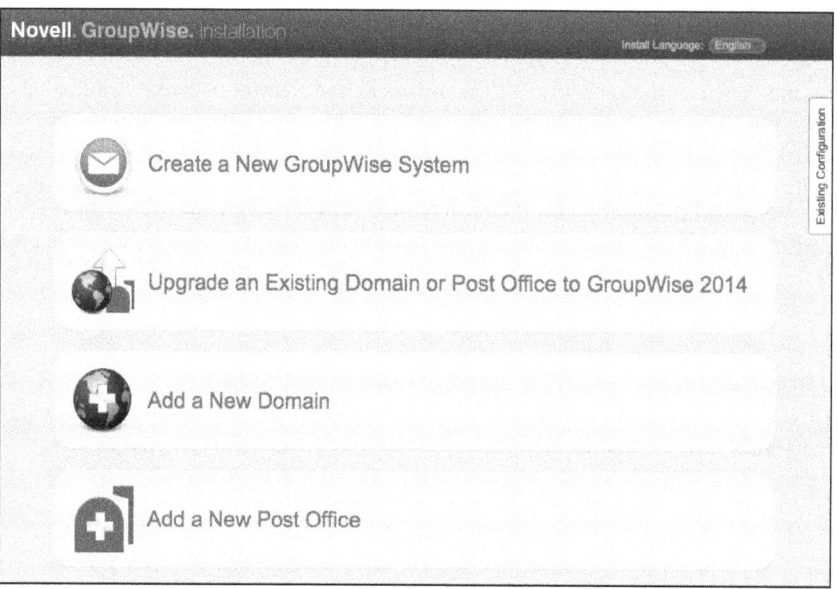

Figure 4-2: Installation Options

3. Click on "Upgrade an Existing Domain or Post Office to GroupWise 2014". We will show two examples in this chapter as follows:

   • Domain (Primary or Secondary) with or without a GWIA but no Post Office
   • Domain (Primary or Secondary) with GWIA and/or Post Office

Domain With or Without a GWIA (No Post Office)

In this section, we have a Domain, but no Post Office. Since all agents on the same server must be upgraded together, a domain that owns a GWIA will have the GWIA upgraded transparently during the upgrade procedure. There are some considerations for upgrading GWIAs. You will not be prompted for anything regarding the GWIA during the upgrade. If changes need to be made (for example, changing the IP address if this is a move/migration), you can make those after the upgrade. Please remember that the GWIA acts as a client. Thus, if you are using IMAP4 or POP3 to access your Post Offices, you cannot upgrade the GWIA until after all of the affected Post Offices have also been upgraded.

1. In our figure below, when we click on the "Upgrade" option, we see our domain called CNC. This is the only GroupWise agent configured in the **gwha.conf** or defined as a service on this server.

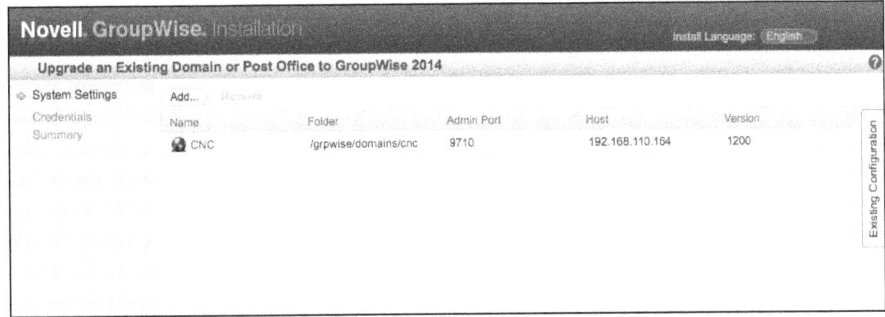

Figure 4-3: Domain to be Upgraded

This lists the path of our domain, the Admin Port has been assigned as the default of 9710, the IP address or host name is listed, and the version shows as 1200.

2. With your domain properly listed in the upgrade section, click Next.
3. If this is the Primary Domain, you will be required to set an administrator and password for your GroupWise system. This is a very important user and password, and should not be forgotten. This is neither a GroupWise nor an eDirectory/AD user. This userid is written to the domain database and is used when you launch The Administration Console.

   It's our recommendation that you use a user specific to this task here. Just as we used gwinstall for our installation user in our **install.cfg**, we'd use something like gwadmin here to differentiate it from other administrative accounts you might have.

   If you choose a "weak" password, Novell will alert you, but you can continue to use the password even if you are told it is weak.

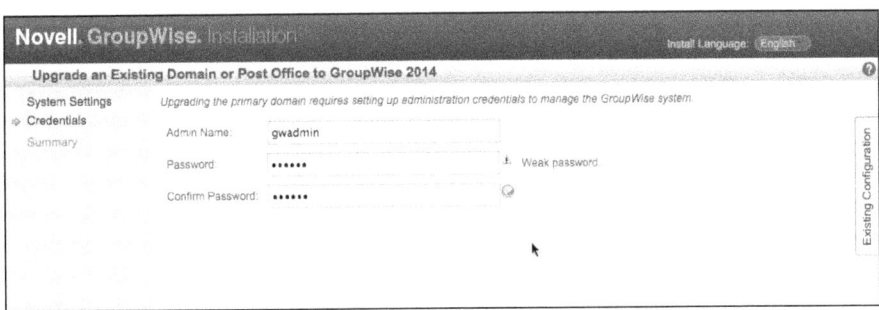

Figure 4-4: Defining the Super Admin userid and password

Set your administration user name and password and click Next.

If this is a secondary domain, you will not see the above figure that prompts you to create a new admin user and password. Rather, you will be prompted for location and credentials of your Primary Domain admin service.

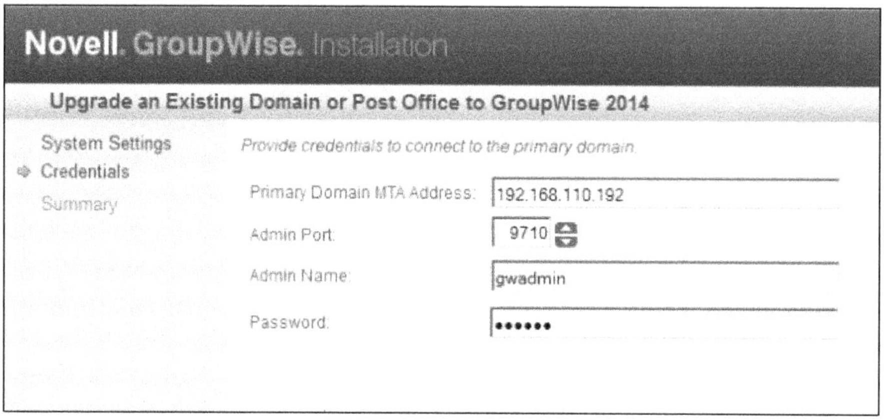

50 | Upgrading GroupWise Domains

Figure 4-5: Connecting to the Primary Domain to complete an upgrade

4. You will now see a summary screen. In our case, our GroupWise system is called "Beta", so you see the name of the system, the domain to upgrade, and the settings for the domain.

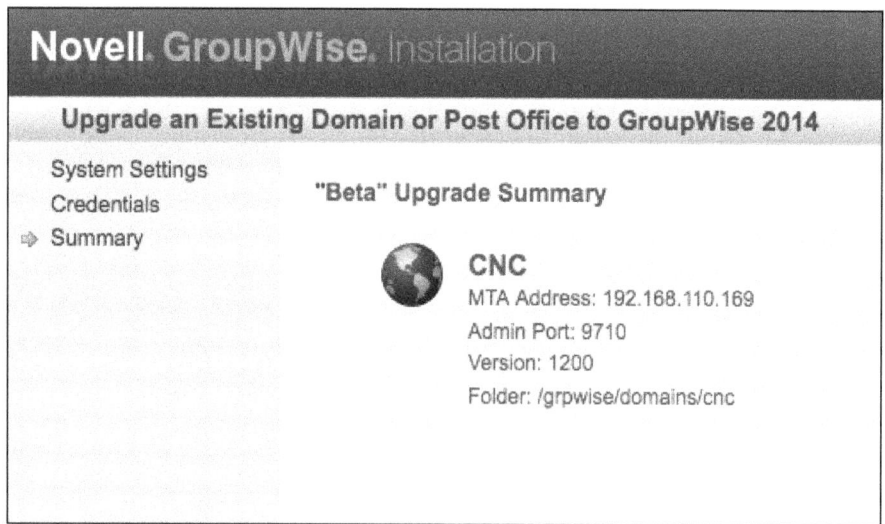

Figure 4-6: Upgrade Summary

5. Click Finish to complete the upgrade. In the background, the Administrative Service will prepare the domain for upgrading and launch the MTA to complete the process.

The Admin Service, MTA and POA all have the ability to upgrade the pertinent databases. The process for upgrading is thus: in the Installation Console, you choose the databases to be upgraded. The installation process then copies the 2014 dictionary (dc) files to the pertinent directories, and instructs the Admin Server to proceed to upgrade. The dc file is essentially a text file that contains the database schema for creating a GroupWise 2014 database. The **gwdom.dc** shows the version number at the very top line as #VERSION=1400. This version number at the top of the file verifies that you have the GroupWise 2014 dc file in your domain directory. The Admin Service looks at the databases and sees if they are eligible to upgrade (i.e., it's either a Primary Domain which can upgrade simply by being told "upgrade", or a Secondary

Domain or Post Office that has been granted the right to upgrade). If the domain is eligible to upgrade, the Admin Service will launch a recovery of the database, effectively converting the domain to GroupWise 2014. You will see a notice to restart your MTAs and POAs, and a link to access your Administration Console. In our experience, a restart is not required.

Geek note: the MTA and POA still have the ability to upgrade the databases as well, but it's a job that's been officially delegated to the Admin Service.

You will see a notice to restart your MTAs and POAs, and a link to access your Administration Console. In our experience, it's not actually necessary to restart anything at this point.

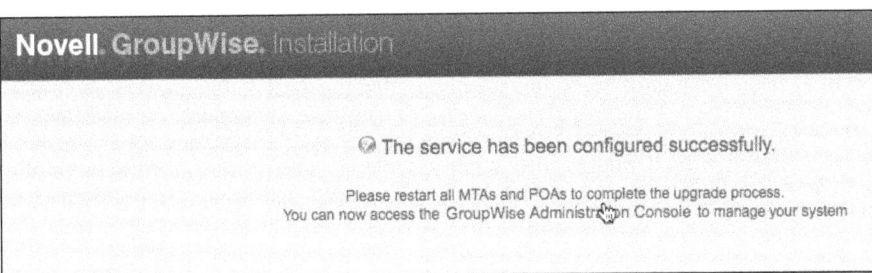

Figure 4-7: Upgrade Complete

If you are watching during the upgrade procedure, you will see the **creating.dbb** and **recover.dbb** files described above temporarily in the domain directory.

```
-rw-r--r--  1 root root  39983 Jan 27 14:15 0127gwbk.001
-rw-r--r--  1 root root 301056 Feb  5 15:37 creating.ddb
-rw-r--r--  1 root root    877 Feb  5 15:37 dzrec.log
-rw-r--r--  1 root root  21737 Jan 23 09:37 gwdom.dc
-rw-r--r--  1 root root  21284 Jan 23 09:37 gwpo.dc
.
.
-rw-r--r--  1 root root 784384 Feb  5 15:37 recover.ddb
-rw-r--r--  1 root root      4 Sep 27 14:11 uid.run
drwxr-xr-x 10 root root   4096 Feb  5 15:37 wpcsin
drwxr-xr-x  5 root root   4096 Sep 27 14:23 wpcsout
-rw-r--r--  1 root root 301056 Feb  5 15:38 wpdomain.db
-rw-r--r--  1 root root  11561 Jul  6  2005 wpdomain.dc
drwxr-xr-x  7 root root   4096 Sep 27 14:30 wpgate
-rw-r--r--  1 root root  10942 Jul  6  2005 wphost.dc
drwxr-xr-x  2 root root   4096 Feb  5 15:37 wpoffice
drwxr-xr-x  2 root root   4096 Sep 27 14:39 wptemp
```

To verify that the domain is in fact version 14, you will launch the Administration Console and check the version in the properties of the domain. We'll do this below in the *"Verifying the Upgrade"* section below.

Domain With Post Office (GWIA optional)

As we saw above, any time you upgrade a domain that owns a GWIA, the GWIA is automatically upgraded for you. Thus in this section, if a GWIA is on the server you are upgrading, the only real difference from the prior section will be will be upgrading the post office simultaneously with the domain

Before we begin, you should read the chapter on *"Upgrading GroupWise Post Offices"* on page 135, through the section on *"Preparing the Post Office Database"* on page 137. Once you have performed all of the tasks delineated prior to the section entitled *"Preparing the Post Office Database"*, return here.

Since all agents on the same server must be upgraded together, a domain that owns a GWIA will have the GWIA upgraded transparently during the upgrade procedure. You will not be prompted for anything regarding the GWIA during the upgrade. If changes need to be made (for example, changing the IP address if this is a move/migration), you can make those after the upgrade.In our figure below, when we click on the "Upgrade" option, we see our domain called CNC and our Post Office called Caledonia.

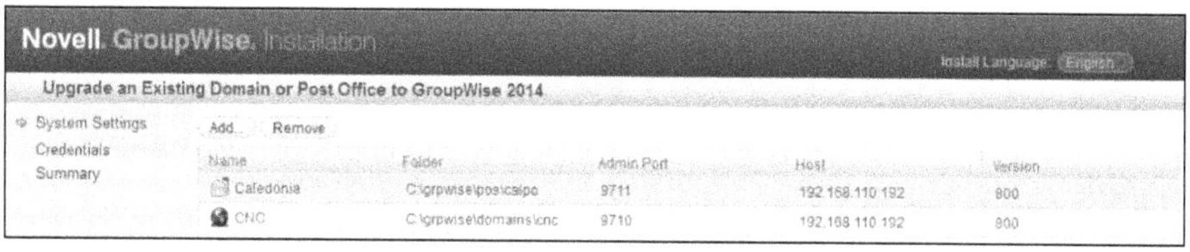

Figure 4-8: Objects to upgrade

This lists the path of our objects, the Admin Ports that have been assigned, the IP address or host name of the server is listed, and the version shows as 800.

1. With your domain and post office properly listed in the upgrade section, click Next.
2. If this is the Primary Domain, you will be required to set an administrator and password for your GroupWise system. This is a very important user and password, and should not be forgotten. This is neither a GroupWise nor an eDirectory/AD user. This userid is written to the domain database and is used when you launch The Administration Console.

   It's our recommendation that you use a user specific to this task here. Just as we used gwinstall for our installation user in our **install.cfg**, we'd use something like gwadmin here to differentiate it from other administrative accounts you might have.

   If you choose a "weak" password, Novell will alert you, but you can continue to use the password even if you are told it is weak.

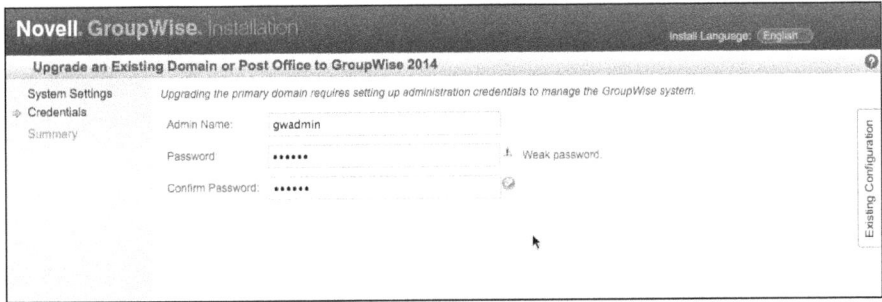

Figure 4-9: Defining the Super Admin userid and password

Set your administration user name and password and click Next.

If this is a secondary domain, you will not see the above figure that prompts you to create a new admin user and password. Rather, you will be prompted for location and credentials of your Primary Domain admin service.

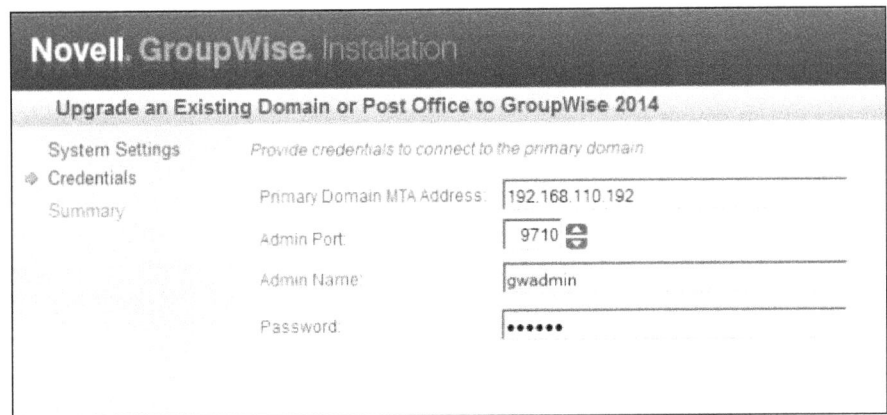

Figure 4-10: Connecting to the Primary Domain to complete an upgrade

3. You will now see a summary screen. In our case, our GroupWise system is called "Beta", so you see the name of the system, the domain and post office to upgrade, and the settings for the domain and post office.

54 | Upgrading GroupWise Domains

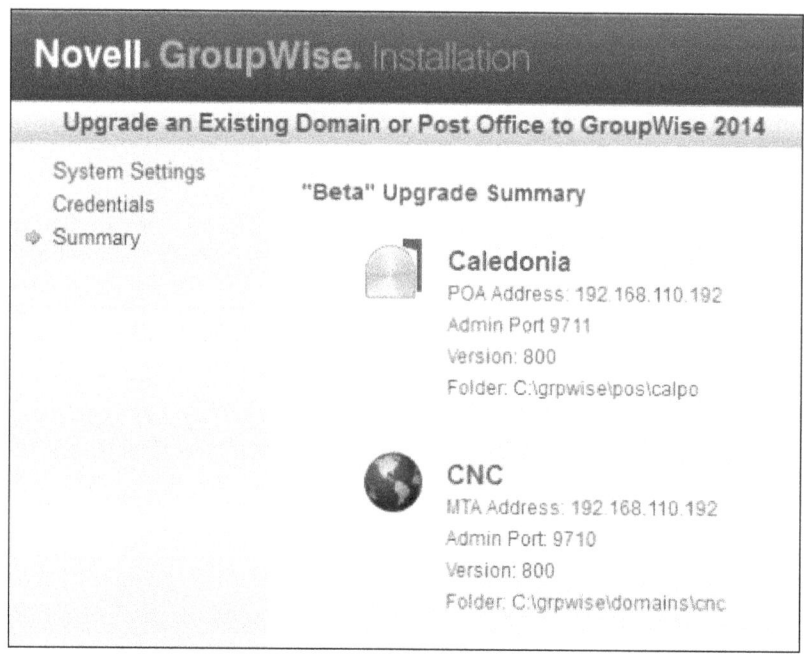

Figure 4-11: The Upgrade Summary Screen

Click Finish to complete the upgrade. In the background, the Administrative Service will prepare begin the upgrade process of the domain and post office and launch the MTA and POA.

The Admin Service, MTA and POA all have the ability to upgrade the pertinent databases. The process for upgrading is thus: in the Installation Console, you choose the databases to be upgraded. The installation process then copies the 2014 dictionary (dc) files to the pertinent directories, and instructs the Admin Server to proceed to upgrade. The dc file is essentially a text file that contains the database schema for creating a GroupWise 2014 database. The **gwdom.dc** shows the version number at the very top line as #VERSION=1400. This version number at the top of the file verifies that you have the GroupWise 2014 dc file in your domain directory. The Admin Service looks at the databases and sees if they are eligible to upgrade (i.e., it's either a Primary Domain which needs no further permission, or a Secondary Domain or Post Office that has been granted the right to upgrade). If the domain database is eligible to upgrade, the Admin Service will launch a recovery of the database, effectively converting the domain to GroupWise 2014. Then the process will happen for the Post Office. You will see a notice to restart your MTAs and POAs, and a link to access your Administration Console. In our experience, a restart is not required.

Geek note: the MTA and POA still have the ability to upgrade the databases as well, but it's a job that's been officially delegated to the Admin Service.

If you are watching during the upgrade procedure, you will see the **creating.dbb** and **recover.dbb** files described above temporarily in the domain and post office directories. Here's an example

```
-rw-r--r--  1 root root  39983 Jan 27 14:15 0127gwbk.001
```

```
-rw-r--r-- 1 root root 301056 Feb  5 15:37 creating.ddb
-rw-r--r-- 1 root root    877 Feb  5 15:37 dzrec.log
.
.
-rw-r--r-- 1 root root 784384 Feb  5 15:37 recover.ddb
-rw-r--r-- 1 root root      4 Sep 27 14:11 uid.run
```

To verify that the domain is in fact version 14, you will launch the Administration Console and check the version in the properties of the domain. We'll do this below in the *"Verifying the Upgrade"* section below.

Verifying the Upgrade

When you completed your upgrades in the sections above, there was a link to the Administration Console in the "upgrade completed". There is also an icon on your server desktop. To go there manually, type this URL in your browser:

https://yourserver:9710/gwadmin-console

Since the installation created a self-signed certificate, you will be prompted to accept the untrusted certificate. Once you have done that, you will be at the Administration Console login screen.

Figure 4-12: Login Screen for the Administration Console

56 | Upgrading GroupWise Domains

Log in with the username and password you created above.

You will now see the Administration Console Dashboard. We will not go into great detail about this screen here, but will make a few comments.

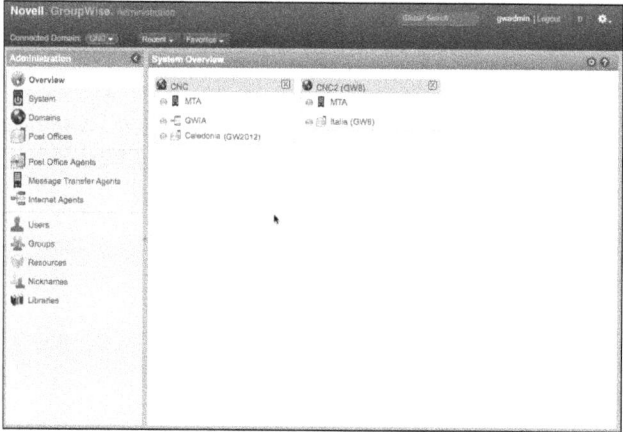

Figure 4-13: Administration Console

Here we see that our system has two domains, two post offices and a GWIA. Any domain or post office that is NOT GroupWise 2014 will show the version number next to its object. For example, in our figure, the Caledonia PO is still at 2012, and the CNC2 Domain and Italia PO are GroupWise 8.

To verify that our CNC domain is indeed version 2014, we can click on the name CNC, which is a link to the domain properties.

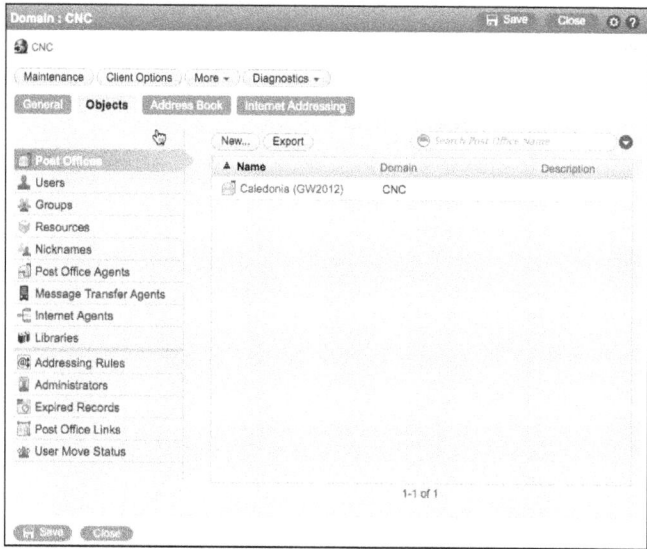

Figure 4-14: Domain Objects Properties

You will first see the "Object" screen shown above. Just click on the General Tab to see the details for the domain.

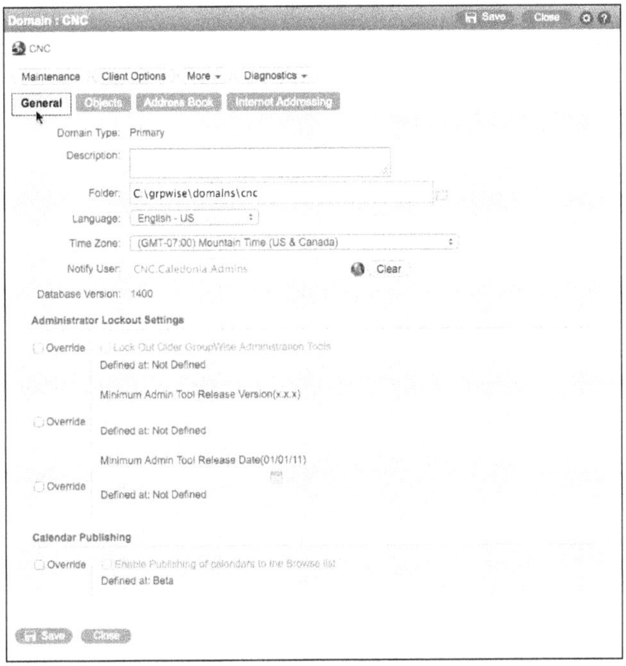

Figure 4-15: Domain General Properties

Notice that our domain shows version 1400 on the General Tab, so we have in fact upgraded our primary domain.

Follow the same instructions for the Post Office to check the version.

Since this was an in-place upgrade, there should be no major issues, like MTAs not talking properly to POAs and the like. If the system was communicating prior to the upgrade, it should really have no difficulties continuing to communicate.

To verify that all of your agents are loaded, the simplest way is to access the HTTP monitors for each agent upgraded. You should have verified back in *"Enabling the HTTP Monitor for Your Agent"* on page 11 that your HTTP monitors were operational. The default paths for these monitors are:

- MTA: http://yourserver:7180
- POA: http://yourserver:7181
- GWIA: http://yourserver:9850

If you cannot connect to your monitors, verify on the server that the agents are actually running:

- On Linux, go to a terminal prompt and type **rcgrpwise status**
- On Windows, go to the Services monitor (Start|Administrative Tools|Services) and look for "GroupWise" services to see if they are running.

Additional Post Office Steps

If you have upgraded a Post Office in tandem with its Domain, you should check the steps in *"Upgrading GroupWise Post Offices"* beginning with *"Configuring and Verifying a DVA for your Post Office"* on page 141.

Where to from here?

Depending on the size and complexity of your system, and your overall upgrade plan, there are a number of "next steps" that you can take. The main rule of thumb is that you must upgrade ALL components of GroupWise that reside on the same server. Let's look at a couple of very common configurations that you might be looking at.

Single Server

Sites with a single GroupWise server have everything in one place. This is acceptable for very small sites, although we always DO recommend that a site have a second domain as a fail safe measure. That said though, today we're upgrading, not redesigning your system, so we'll work with what we have. Single servers in very small organizations often house the following components:

MTA for the Primary Domain

POA for a single Post Office

GroupWise Internet Agent

GroupWise WebAccess Agent (GroupWise 8 and older)

GroupWise WebAccess Application

GroupWise Monitor

GroupWise Calendar Publishing Host

If this scenario fits your situation, then your Domain, GWIA and Post Office are already upgraded, and all you need to do is upgrade the WebAccess Application (the GroupWise 8 and earlier WebAccess Agent is no longer used). So just jump over to the chapters on upgrading your GroupWise WebAccess, GroupWise Monitor and GroupWise Calendar Publishing Host and Upgrading your GroupWise Clients. You'll be finished in no time!

Multiple Servers

There are as many configurations of multiple server GroupWise systems as there are GroupWise customers it seems!

If your primary domain resides on a server all by itself, you are finished with this server. You can stop here, or move on to upgrading any post offices that belong to this primary domain, upgrading a secondary domain server, etc. It's possible you might wish to go ahead and upgrade your GWIA at this point, but remember that you won't want to do this if you have users in older GroupWise post offices accessing via IMAP4 or POP3 through your GWIA. See the chapter on Upgrading Your GroupWise Internet Agent.

If your system is small, and you will be upgrading all of your post offices over a weekend (for example), and you can afford to have WebAccess down for some users while you upgrade, you might choose to upgrade your WebAccess now. If you can provide for two separate WebAccess Application servers, you can upgrade your WebAccess and make it the default web server for WebAccess while you continue to upgrade your post offices. See the chapter on Upgrading Your GroupWise WebAccess.

Primary Domain and Post Office on the Same Server

It might be that you have a small system with your primary domain and post office on one server, and another server with a secondary domain for your GWIA and web server for WebAccess. In this situation, you will move the second server and perform the domain/gwia upgrade as noted above. Finally, you can proceed to upgrade WebAccess.

Troubleshooting Domain Upgrade Problems

There are very few things that can go wrong during a domain upgrade. If you find that your domain refuses to show as a GroupWise 2014 domain in ConsoleOne, do a couple of things:

- Double-check that the installation actually copied the dc files into the domain directory. Open the gwdom.dc file with a text editor to verify that it is in fact the GroupWise 2014 file.

- If this is a secondary domain, verify that the secondary domain KNOWS that the primary domain is a GroupWise 2014 domain. You can do this by connecting to the secondary domain in ConsoleOne and looking at the properties of the primary domain. It should show as version 1400 (or just 14 since ConsoleOne does not know about GroupWise 2014). If the primary does NOT show as a GroupWise 2014 domain when viewed from the perspective of the secondary domain, you will need to launch the Administration Console in your browser to verify (as described above) that it shows as a GroupWise 2014 domain (look in the properties of the primary). Once you have confirmed that the primary is GroupWise 2014, rebuild the secondary domain. You will need to use the command line utilities for GroupWise 2014 to rebuild the secondary domain database. See the section on *"Command Line Utilities"* on page 128 in the chapter on *"The GroupWise Administration Console"* to see how to accomplish this.

Troubleshooting Post Office Upgrade Problems

There are very few things that can go wrong during a post office upgrade. If you find that your post office refuses to show as a GroupWise 2014 post office in the Administration Console do a couple of things:

- Double-check that the upgrade procedure copied the new dc files into the post office directory. Open the **gwpo.dc** and **ngwguard.dc** files with a text editor to verify that they are in fact the GroupWise 2014 files.

- Double-check that the domain owning this post office is actually a GroupWise 2014 domain (i.e., it shows as version 1400 in the Administration Console).
- Unload and reload the POA to see if this solves the problem.
- It is possible that communications issues have prevented the post office database from receiving the news that its parent domain is a GroupWise 2014 domain and thus is allowed to upgrade. Remember that just loading the GroupWise 2014 agent software is not enough. If all else fails, rebuild the post office database. See *"Validating or Rebuilding a Post Office Database"* in *"The GroupWise Administration Console"* on page 115.

Once you are ready to continue, just turn to the next chapter in your upgrade plan.

5 Directory Integration and Synchronization

In 1996 Novell shipped GroupWise 5.0. It was the first release that had totally been developed under the Novell umbrella (what we know as GroupWise 4.1 had been in beta as WordPerfect Office 4.0b when Novell purchased WordPerfect Corporation). The changes were not terribly huge from a user or basic structure standpoint. However, suddenly you needed to have NDS (Novell Directory Services, now just known as NetIQ eDirectory) to manage GroupWise.

GroupWise was only "loosely" integrated with eDirectory, and this caused no small amount of confusion for the next 18 years. Until Novell added LDAP authentication with GroupWise 6.5, there were truly no operational dependencies on eDirectory at all. In other words, you could set up a GroupWise system on Windows, for example, disconnect the NetWare servers, and so long as you never needed to add a user to your system, GroupWise would hum along just fine. It seemed like a lot of "overhead" to have GroupWise connected to eDirectory in a very loose way, and yet depend so entirely on eDirectory for configuration and maintenance.

GroupWise 2014 will be a welcome change for some administrators, and a vexing step back for others. At it's very core, GroupWise 2014 has the right idea: Remove the dependency of a Directory from the GroupWise system, and yet allow for synchronization of data back and forth between GroupWise and a directory service if desired. So let's look at the benefits and the disadvantages of this new way of GroupWise life. These pros and cons are based on the shipping version of GroupWise, and we expect to see many of the disadvantages addressed in future service packs and releases. As of today, here's where we stand:

Pros:
- GroupWise is no longer tied to eDirectory, so sites that have moved or are moving to an Active Directory environment can use AD for the authentication and integration if they choose.
- GroupWise can be used as a totally standalone system for very small companies that use NO directory service for their access (and before you say they don't exist, let us assure you they do!).
- GroupWise management is no longer tied to management tools not under the control of the GroupWise engineers. Both nwadmin and ConsoleOne were developed by other teams at Novell, and GroupWise had to somehow "fit in". Edicts such as "all Novell products will be managed by iManager" were unrealistic for a product like GroupWise, which being only "loosely" tied to eDirectory could not be properly administered with web based tools that could not effect direct access to the GroupWise databases.
- GroupWise 2014 has a separate Management Console that is uniquely and purposefully designed to be the best "GroupWise" Administration tool without dependencies and limitations of being a snapin or part of a larger administration tool.

Cons:

- At the time GroupWise 2014 ships, there will be no IDM driver available. Sites reliant on IDM for their GroupWise/Directory integration will be required to manage their systems with two sets of tools.
- The iManager and MMC plugins for GroupWise are in their infancy, and provide only limited functionality (adding users to post offices, for example), and sites will be required to have two separate management tools for their networks.
- GroupWise 2014 has a separate Management Console that is uniquely and purposefully designed to be the best "GroupWise" Administration tool without dependencies and limitations of being a snapin or part of a larger administration tool. Hey - wasn't this listed as an advantage above? It's one of those double-edged swords. This also means that sites who were accustomed to one tool being able to handle everything will suddenly be faced with the need for multiple administrative tools pertaining to GroupWise.

The good news though is that GroupWise administration will be totally controlled by the GroupWise development team, and ultimately limited only by their choice of REST as the engine for their management, and their own imaginations. The buck stops there.

When we talk about LDAP and GroupWise, there are really two issues at hand:

- Directory Integration & Synchronization
- Directory Authentication

These topics are not necessarily as straight-forward as you might think, so let's discuss.

What is Directory Integration and Synchronization?

Generally when we think of GroupWise and Directory Integration, we think of eDirectory, because frankly that is the only directory that GroupWise versions 5.0 through 2012 are capable of integrating with. In order to explain Directory Integration in a wider sense, we will use eDirectory as our model.

In GroupWise 2012 and earlier, GroupWise users were by their very nature associated directly with an eDirectory object, either an eDirectory user, or a special GroupWise object called an External Entity. Most administrators never actually knew that it was even possible for a GroupWise user to NOT have an eDirectory association, unless something odd happened in the system, and one day a perfectly normal GroupWise user suddenly appeared in the GroupWise view with a "white shirt".

Our figure below shows two eDirectory users who have GroupWise accounts (Red Shirts), one External Entity (Green Shirt - a GroupWise user who has a special eDirectory object that allows for no access to network resources other than GroupWise access), and one totally unassociated GroupWise user who has no ties to eDirectory at all (White Shirt). Prior to GroupWise 2014, having unassociated users was typically a "mistake", but it did happen occasionally. Interestingly enough, the GroupWise user still functioned okay, so one wonders in retrospect why the External Entity was so important!

Figure 5-1: A variety of GroupWise User Objects

If a disturbance in the Force were to happen, and the eDirectory connection with the GroupWise object was damaged (but not entirely deleted - i.e., the icon did not turn white), the object would become unmanageable - literally! You would receive an error like "replication may be in progress" or other strange error messages, and you would be unable to deal with things like changing user passwords, moving users to new POs, etc. You would first need to fix the "association" before you could continue.

In prior releases of GroupWise, there were eDirectory Schema Extensions available that allowed GroupWise specific objects to be referenced in the tree (Domains, Post Offices, Resources, Distribution Lists, etc.). Without these extensions, many GroupWise functions could not be properly managed in ConsoleOne. GroupWise 2014 no longer needs any Directory extensions to function. In fact, the only information that GroupWise "writes" to the Directory is the email address for users, via LDAP.

GroupWise 2014 takes away the "direct" eDirectory link, and relies instead on LDAP for all Directory integration functions. In this first iteration of GroupWise 2014, the directory types are limited to eDirectory and Active Directory. One can envision a day when OpenLDAP would also be supported, allowing GroupWise to be integrated into just about any networking system available.

During a GroupWise upgrade, assuming certain criteria have been met, your system will be automatically integrated with eDirectory (see *"Preparing Your LDAP System"* on page 14).

So, in a nutshell, when we speak of Directory Integration (at least in this guide) we are referring to the association between a GroupWise user and a user in eDirectory or AD.

If a user is properly integrated with a Directory (in GroupWise terminology we say the user is "associated" with a Directory), then the changes made in the Directory can synchronize to GroupWise through an LDAP connection.

Directory Rights Requirements

As you configure directory objects in this chapter, you will be asked for an LDAP user to use as the synchronization agent user. It is best practice to create a user specifically for this task.

eDirectory

In order to be able to Synchronize information from eDirectory to GroupWise, the account that you specify for the LDAP Sync must have Browse objects rights to users in the eDirectory Tree. There are also specific Attribute Rights that are required in order to Publish users' e-mail addresses back to the directory. The LDAP account specified for syncing requires Read and Write to the *eMailAddress* and *mail* attributes.

Additionally if the System is upgraded from GroupWise 8 or 2012 the user will need read and write to these additional attributes.

- nGWFileID
- nGWGroupWiseID
- nGWObjectID
- nGWPostOffice
- nGWVisibility
- nGWAccountIDn
- GWMailboxExpirationTime

Active Directory

In order to synchronize information to Active Directory, the LDAP account must have write rights to the *mail* and *proxyAddress* attributes in AD.

What Is Directory Authentication?

When Novell introduced LDAP authentication with GroupWise 6.5, it was seen as primarily a way to accomplish a couple of things:

- Extend the functionality of GroupWise passwords to enforce password restrictions such as length and expiration policies.
- Provide a single-signon solution for GroupWise users at all points of entry.

Administrators had long lamented that GroupWise passwords were too simple, and there was no way to force a user to change a password on a schedule. Additionally, while it was possible to allow users to avoid having to put in their password from their Windows workstation if the user was already logged into eDirectory, the GroupWise specific password was needed for WebAccess, IMAP and the like. Only the Windows client could benefit from a "single login" to authenticate to GroupWise. Additionally, because GroupWise passwords were separate from the eDirectory password, users frequently didn't even know the GroupWise password if they were relying on the eDirectory authentication at the desktop.

Utilizing LDAP passwords for authentication solved both of these problems. Users only needed one password, the password length and duration could be defined by the administrator, and the GroupWise password itself became unimportant.

GroupWise 2014 still allows for either LDAP authentication or native GroupWise passwords for authentication.

You should not confuse the idea of LDAP authentication with Directory Integration and Synchronization. You can turn on LDAP authentication at the Post Office and not have any Directory Integration for the system. We've had many AD shops do just this in older versions of GroupWise. These sites used their AD LDAP server as their "Authentication" servers. It was not necessarily a simple setup. It required entering the LDAP login information in the LDAP Authentication field for each user. That said, it was possible even with older versions of GroupWise to use Active Directory as the authentication source, even though the users were actually "associated" with users in the eDirectory tree.

Launching the New Administration Console

First you must log into your Administration Console from your Web Browser. There was a link to the Administration Console at the end of your Primary Domain upgrade. You can also launch the Administration Console either by using the Icon on your Server Desktop (which is actually just a shortcut for your browser), or navigate directly to your Console by navigating to:

https://yourserver.com:9710

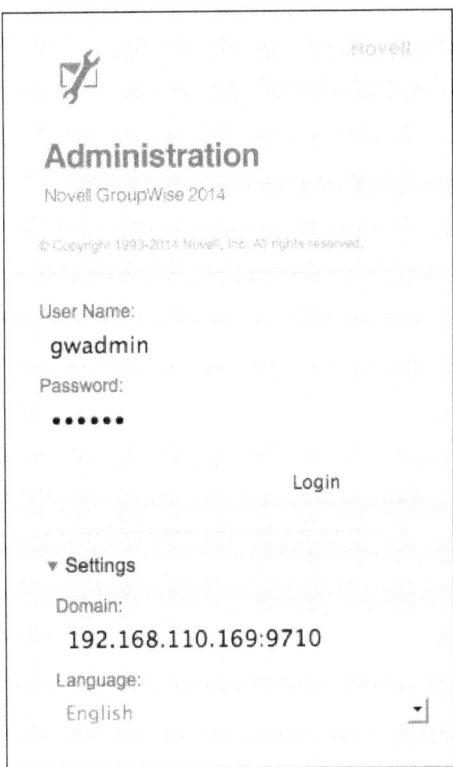

Figure 5-2: The Administration Console Login Windows

Figure 5-3 shows the main GroupWise Administration Console screen. This is the default "Overview" or "Dashboard" view when you open the Administration Console.

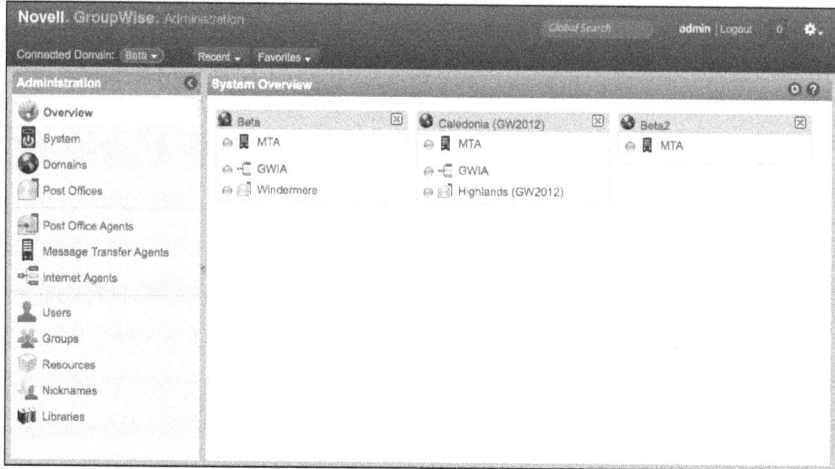

Figure 5-3: The GroupWise Administration Console Dashboard

We will discuss the Administration Console in more detail in the next chapter. For now we have some business to attend to with Directory Services.

The Initial Directory Integration

In *"Preparing Your LDAP System"* on page 14, we showed you how to configure your GroupWise system prior to upgrading to GroupWise 2014. During the upgrade of your Primary Domain, if your LDAP system is setup properly as described in the aforementioned sections, your new GroupWise 2014 system should be automatically integrated with eDirectory.

If after your upgrade you see a red box in the top right corner of the Administration Console, the likelihood is that your Directory Integration failed.

Figure 5-4: Error notification in Administration Console

When you click on the red box, you will see any errors that are being reported by the Administration Console.

Figure 5-5: Initial Directory Configuration Error

We will look at how to correct this in *"Correcting a Failed Directory Integration"* below. First, let's see how this looks if the initial Directory Integration is successful.

Let's start by looking at our test system.

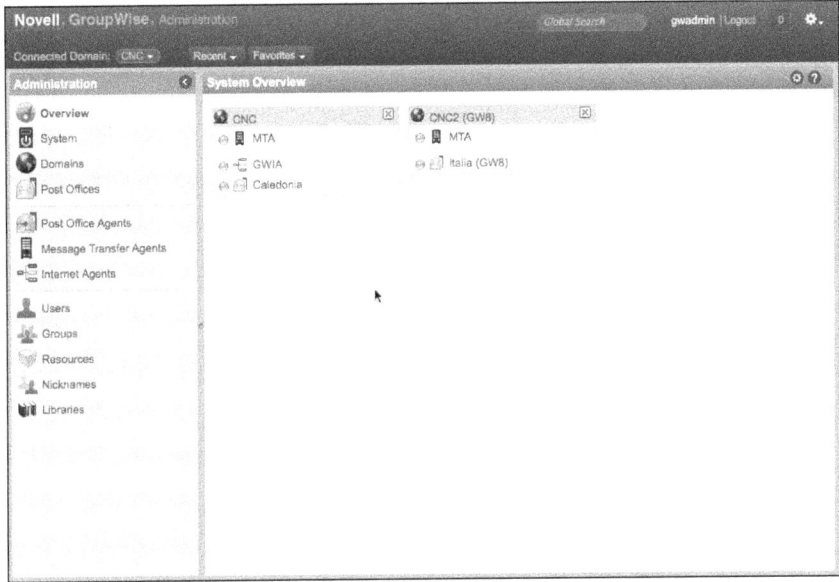

Figure 5-6: GroupWise Test System

In this system, we have upgraded our GroupWise Primary domain to GroupWise 2014. This domain also has a GWIA and Post Office. We have a Secondary Domain that is still at GroupWise 8 version.

Click on Users, so that we can see what our users look like in our upgraded system.

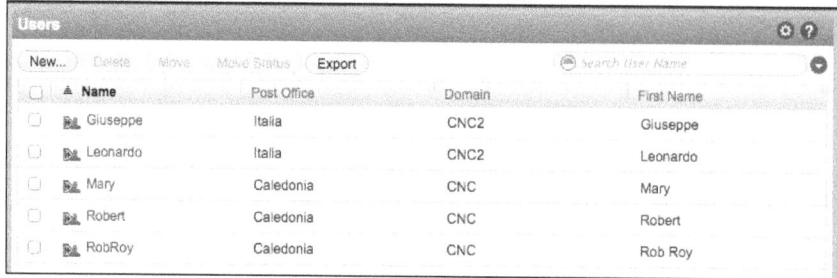

Figure 5-7: Users in our upgraded system

Compare this to another system below.

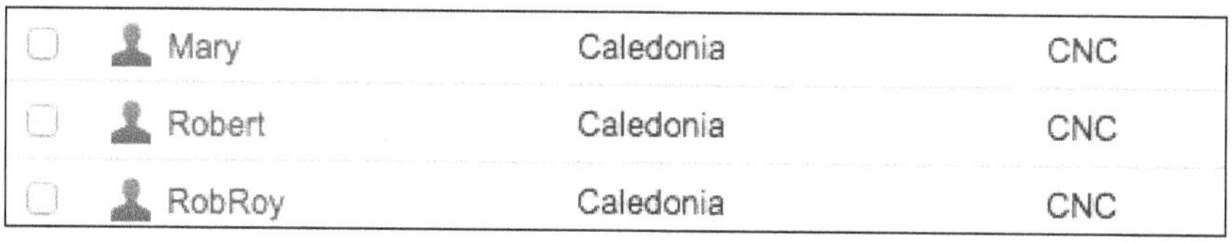

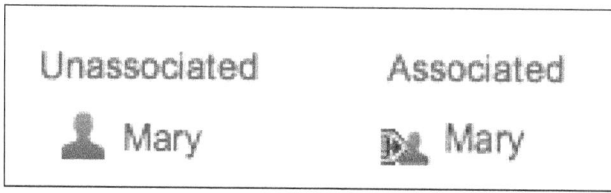

Figure 5-8: Unassociated Users

If you look closely, you will see that there are two separate icons for GroupWise users. One indicates that a user is associated with a directory, and one indicates that the user is a "stand-alone" groupwise user.

Figure 5-9: Unassociated vs. Associated Users

Since our system came from a prior version of GroupWise, which required eDirectory, you should only see the Unassociated icon if you had users in eDirectory that had lost their eDirectory Association (see the "White Shirt" in Figure 5-1 above).

NOTE: Even if your LDAP servers and eDirectory Synchronization was not properly configured before the upgrade, your GroupWise users will show an "Associated" icon. This can be misleading, and we will discuss that later in this chapter.

Associated Users

When we look at the General Details for an Associated User, we see the following:

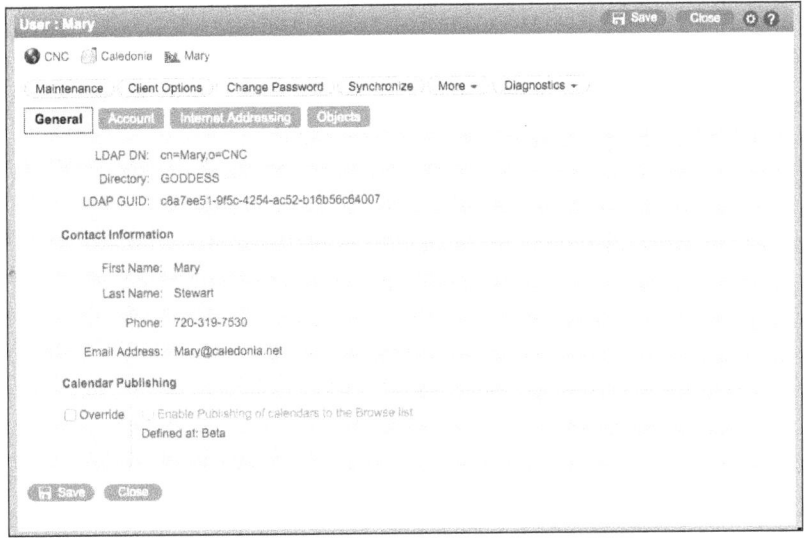

Figure 5-10: A user associated with eDirectory

Notice the LDAP information for the user

LDAP DN: cn=Mary,o=CNC
Directory: GODDESS
LDAP GUID: c8a7ee51-9f5c-4254-ac52-b16b56c64007

This information is read-only. The only information on this window that can be changed is the calendar publishing information. All other information, including phone numbers, physical address, department and the like are defined in the LDAP directory.

By contrast if we were to look at an Unassociated User, all information can be manipulated within the GroupWise Administration Console directly. Unassociated Users receive no information from any directory source. Thus, if you were to choose to dissociate your users from eDirectory and make them all Unassociated users, changes made in eDirectory (or Active Directory, if that is your Directory of choice) would not filter down to the GroupWise system. Very small systems with no need for either eDirectory or Active Directory would probably choose this method.

Unassociated Users

Below we see an Unassociated User.

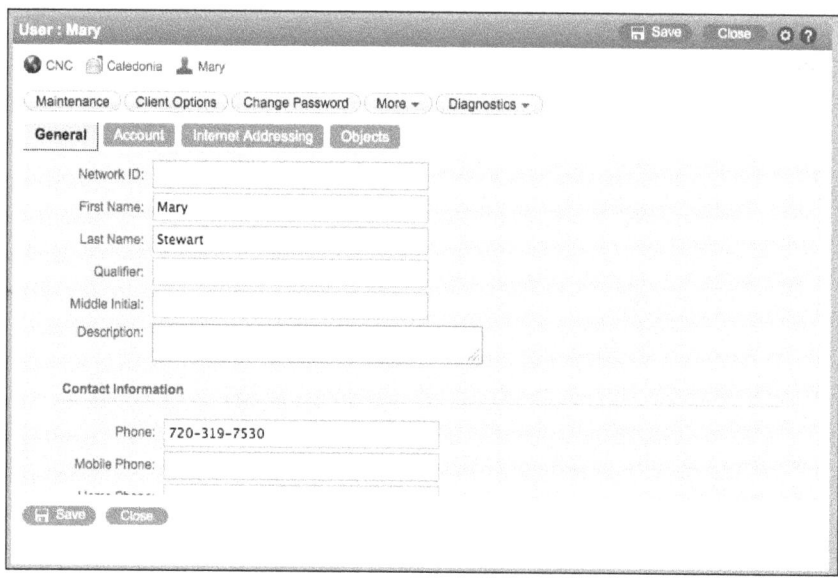

Figure 5-11: An Unassociated User has all information stored in the GroupWise System

Unassociated Users are managed entirely within the GroupWise Administration Console. All updates to user name, address, phone number, department and the like are entered directly into the GroupWise database through the Administration Console.

Non-Associated Users

In our chapter on *"Preparing Your GroupWise System"*, it was mentioned that if LDAP and eDirectory Synchronization are not properly configured in your pre-upgraded GroupWise system, the automatic Integration with eDirectory will not occur. This results in a special situation where the users are not Associated with eDirectory, and yet they also are not considered Unassociated Users. For our purposes in describing these users, let's call them "Non-Associated". Notice in our figure below, Giuseppe has the "Associated User" icon, and the information for Giuseppe is read-only in the General tab. Yet there is no LDAP DN and GUID information present. In this state, Giuseppe is somewhat in limbo. Changes in the Directory will not propagate to Giuseppe's object in GroupWise, but the Administrator is also unable to edit the information directly. Giuseppe is stuck in a state between Associated and Unassociated. This is very similar to situations in ConsoleOne where you might attempt to edit a user object only to be warned that "replication" was in progress, and the user was not accessible. Certainly you can still do some routine maintenance tasks on this Non-Associated user. You can change the password, run GWCheck, create Nicknames, etc. You simply cannot change the "address information" typically found in the General tab.

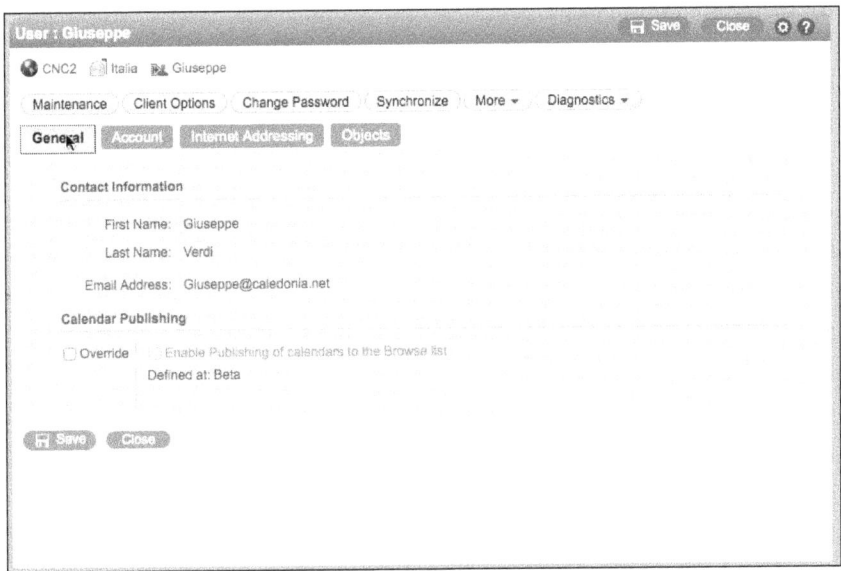

Figure 5-12: A Non-Associated User

We'll show you how to fix synchronization issues such as this below.

The Directory Object

When we look more closely at our LDAP Servers in the sections below, you will note that there are two types of objects: The Directory and the LDAP Server. We'll discuss those now.

The Directory Object (in our case in named Goddess) will represent either eDirectory or Active Directory, and is what we will call a "Master LDAP Server". Many of the settings in the Directory Object will flow down to any additional LDAP Servers that are subordinate to the Directory.

The Directory is used for two purposes:

- The Directory provides the facility to synchronize LDAP users to their GroupWise counterparts.
- The Directory serves as an LDAP Authentication source for users logging into GroupWise using LDAP credentials.

When you verify or create the Directory objects below, you will be providing both of these functions to your system.

The LDAP Server Object

Subordinate to the Directory Object can be one or more LDAP Server objects. In our upgraded system, our LDAP Server, defined as CNC and listed in *"Preparing Your LDAP System"* on page 14, provides only Authentication Services. It is not in charge of any synchronization.

72 | Directory Integration and Synchronization

Multiple LDAP servers can be defined if you have multiple eDirectory or AD Domain Controller servers. This can provide redundancy for your users to ensure that if one LDAP server is down, users can continue to log into GroupWise. However, since the Directory object itself is also an Authentication source, you really only need to define LDAP servers if you have more than one LDAP server that can server as an authentication source.

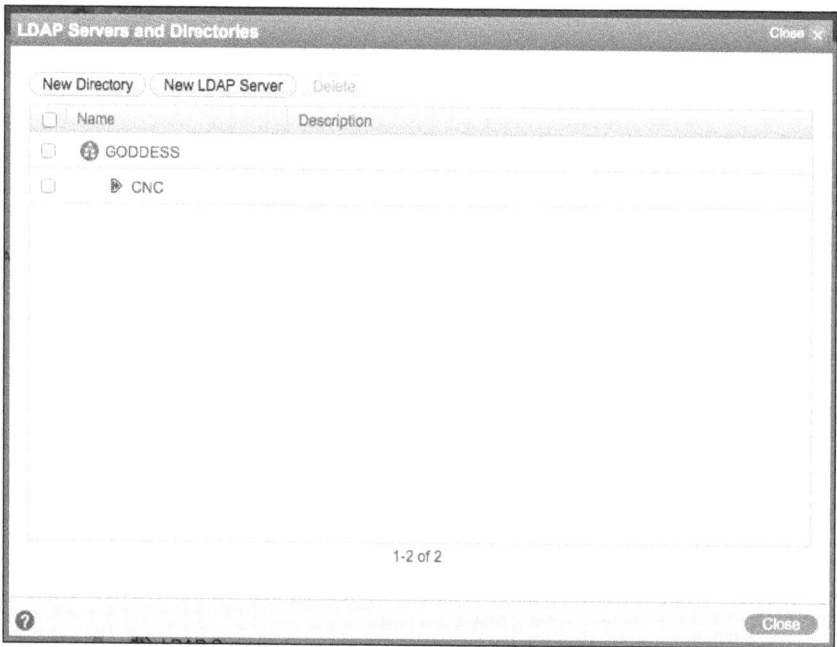

Figure 5-13: Our LDAP System

For the rest of this chapter, we will be focusing on the following scenarios:
- *"Verifying a Successful Directory Integration"*
- *"Correcting a Failed Directory Integration"*
- *"Integrating Active Directory into Your GroupWise System"*
- *"Removing eDirectory Associations to become Stand-Alone"*

The likelihood is that you only need deal with one of these scenarios. We have duplicated a lot of the content so that you can read the section that pertains to you, and avoid a lot of jumping around.

If you goal is to remove eDirectory altogether and immediately either integrate your entire system with Active Directory, or remove all Directory Associations, there is little need for you to go through the steps of verifying or correcting your current configuration. You can skip down to the section that pertains to your situation.

Verifying a Successful Directory Integration

If you received no Directory Integration errors (shown in Figure 5-4 and Figure 5-5 above), we can assume that your Directory integrated properly. That said, we will want to verify the installation, and generally just show you how it should look. Also, we have seen instances where systems were set up for eDirectory synchronization properly, but had one or more domains not actually synchronizing. We'll want to look at the system to make sure it is in order.

Verifying the Directory

First, click on System in the Administration Console. This choose LDAP Servers.

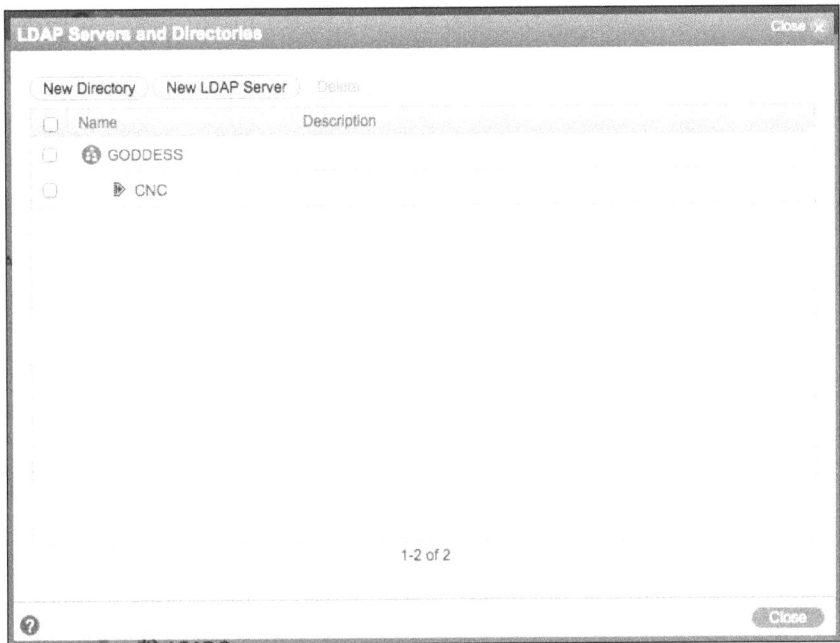

Figure 5-14: Our LDAP System

Here our imported LDAP Directory and Server is from eDirectory. The name of the Tree is Goddess. We had defined an LDAP server in ConsoleOne and named it CNC. This information came over during the upgrade with no prompt for intervention. In other words, if the system was correct before the upgrade, it should be correct here. If you had issues with the eDirectory Synchronization prior to the upgrade, you will continue to have those problems after the upgrade!

Let's look at our Directory named Goddess. Simply click on the name of the Directory to open the details page.

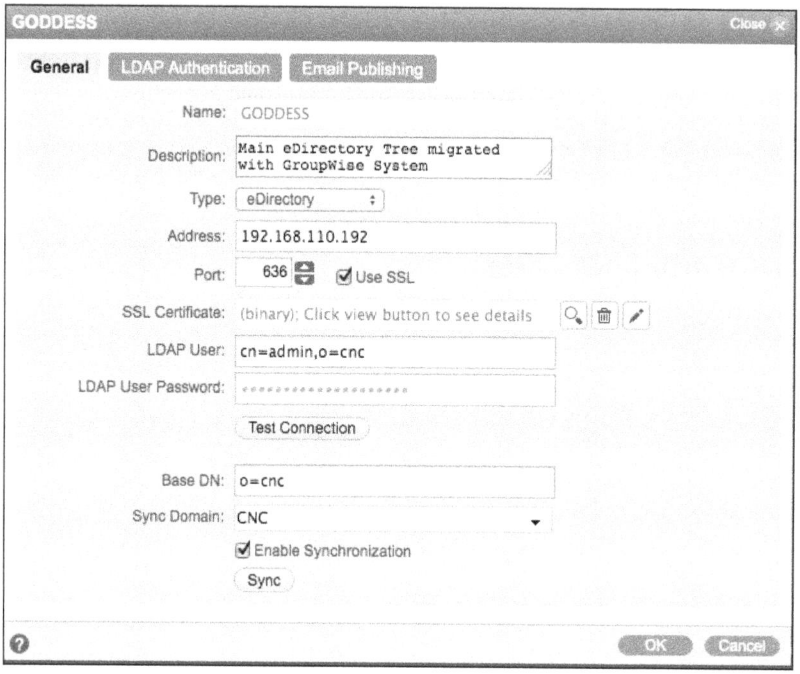

Figure 5-15: Our migrated eDirectory "Directory"

The General tab of the Directory shows the tree name, Directory type (in an upgrade this will always be eDirectory) and the location of the Directory. Verify all settings here, enter the LDAP user password, and click Test Connection to ensure that the Directory is properly configured.

> **NOTE:** If you come back to this screen at a later time to test, and the LDAP password is greyed out as in the figure, you will be required to put the password in again in order to complete a successful test.

The Base DN is the "starting point" for your LDAP search. A migrated Directory will not have any value listed in the Base DN. For synchronization purposes, this is not an issue, as the Synchronization queries a specific LDAP GUID to compare property values. However, if you will be authenticating via LDAP you will want to set a Base DN. In our example above, we have a very small tree, and users are in the "O" container. Larger organizations generally have OUs based on type of object, or company organization, etc. You do not want your Base DN too high in your tree, as that would require the LDAP search to look through too many records. By the same token though, you want to make sure that all user objects you wish to manage in this directory are found below this Base DN designation.

Note the Sync Domain. As with prior versions of GroupWise, it is really only required that one MTA be configured to do synchronization for the entire system. Choose the Domain whose MTA should perform the sync for this Directory. The MTA must have a Scheduled Event for Directory Synchronization enabled for Directory Synchronization to actually occur automatically. We will go through the steps to verify the synchronization in *"Testing Directory Synchronization"* at the end of this chapter.

The Directory is also serves as the default LDAP authentication source. Here you define the LDAP settings for your LDAP authentication. Click on the LDAP Authentication tab to see the current, migrated settings.

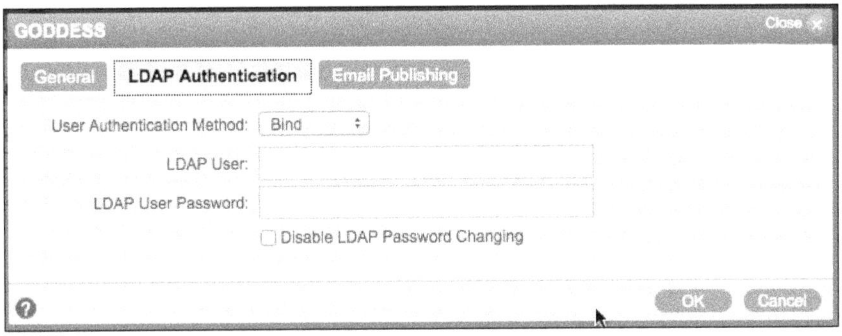

Figure 5-16: LDAP Authentication Settings

We can also look at the Email Publishing settings here. Now that GroupWise has been decoupled from eDirectory, the only changes GroupWise ever makes to the directory (whether eDirectory or Active Directory) are related to the email addresses of your users.

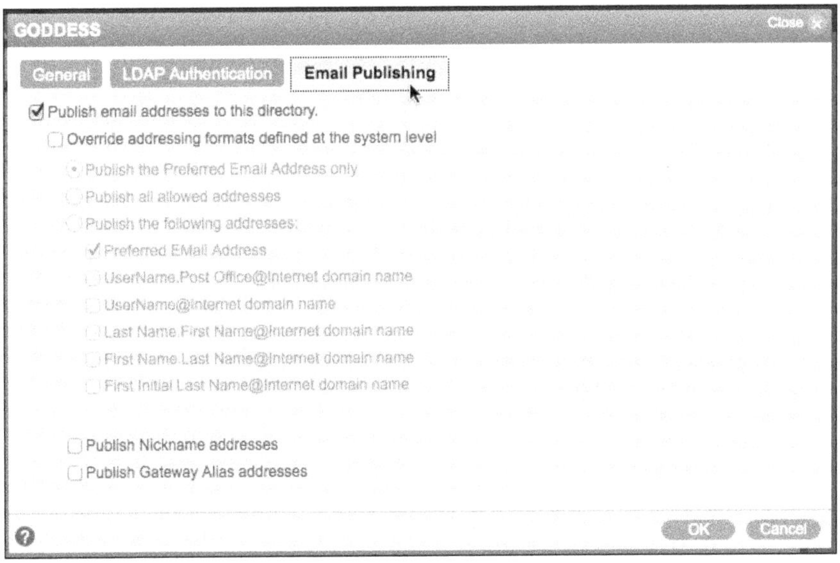

Figure 5-17: The Email Publishing Settings

You can change these settings to meet the needs of your organization. These settings are defined in System|Internet Addressing. You can modify them there for the entire system, or you can changed them here by clicking on the "Override" box and choosing the options you desire.

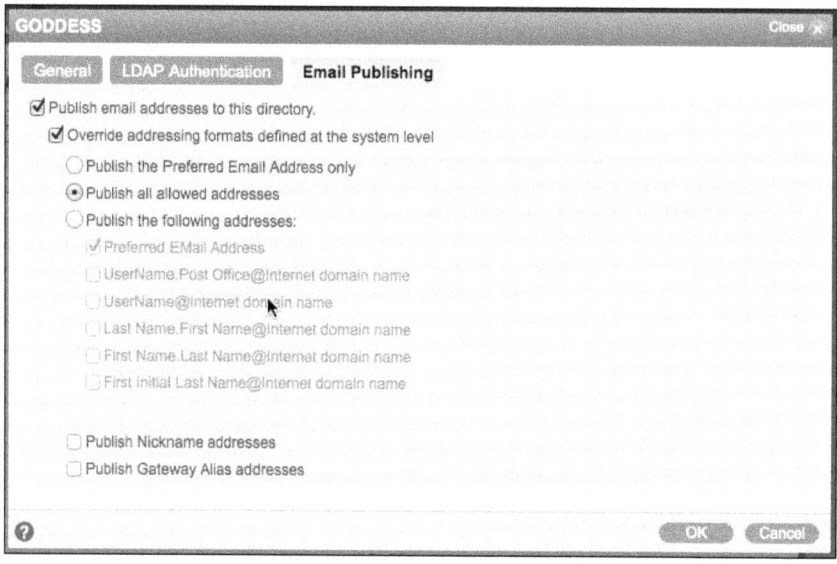

Figure 5-18: Modified email publishing settings

You can choose to publish all allowed addresses, only certain types of addresses, even nicknames. The eDirectory email field is multi-valued and can accept more than one email address. If you are using the LDAP server to provide address lookup for a smart host (perhaps an anti-spam appliance in front of your GroupWise system), you would need to decide which addresses are allowed. In some cases, this is necessary in order to keep costs down. For example, if your anti-spam provider treats each email address as a "user", danitaz, danita, danita.zanre, and zanre.danita could start to get expensive.

Verifying the LDAP Server

In Figure 5-14 under the Directory you also see our LDAP server (named CNC). When we click on the link for the LDAP server, we see the following window.

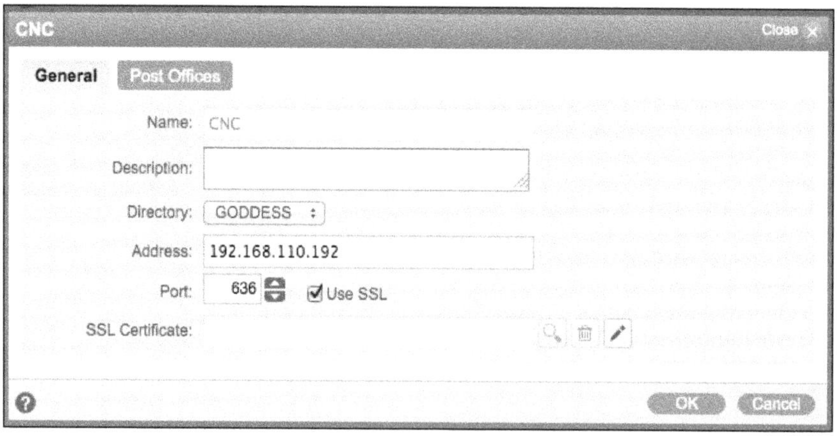

Figure 5-19: LDAP Server Configuration

This is pretty straightforward. The contains the information for the LDAP server to which users will authenticate for access to GroupWise (if you have LDAP authentication enabled). You can create multiple LDAP servers here for failover and redundancy in case one server is down when a user attempts to log into GroupWise.

The Post Offices tabs lists each GroupWise Post Offices that will use this LDAP server as its primary authentication source. If this LDAP server is down, and other LDAP servers have been configured, the POA will step through the listed servers to find an available authentication source.

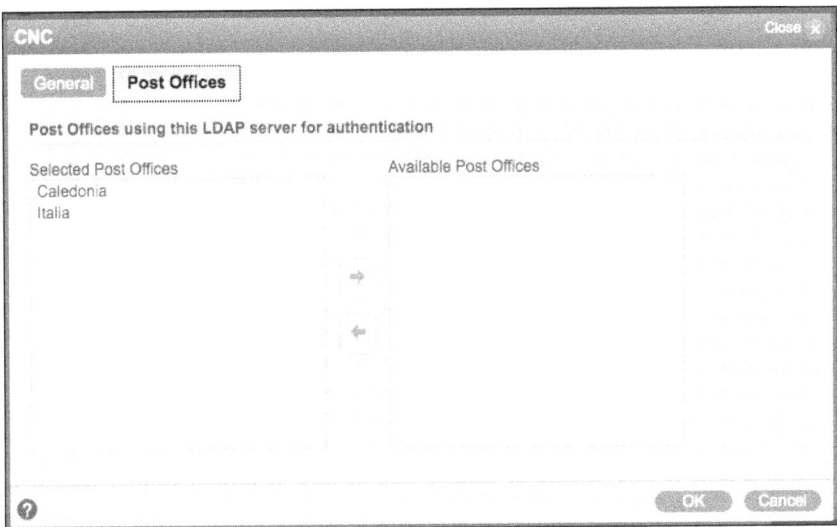

Figure 5-20: Assigning Post Offices to LDAP servers for authentication.

These settings enable your LDAP server to be used as authentication for your users. However, to actually be in effect, you must activate it in the Post Office Security settings.

It is beyond the scope of this upgrade guide to discuss LDAP server layout and system design. Make certain that the servers you had defined in your former GroupWise system are correct and operational here.

Verifying User Associations

As we saw in Figure 5-10 above, when users are properly associated with the Directory, you will be able to tell readily by looking at the General tab for the user in question. It would, however, be tedious to look through every user in your system! We can do a quick check to see which users are integrated, and which (if any) are not.

First, click on Users in the list to the left. Now click into the search field (not Global Search) in the upper right.

Type in

directory=null

You will see a list of all unassociated users in your system.

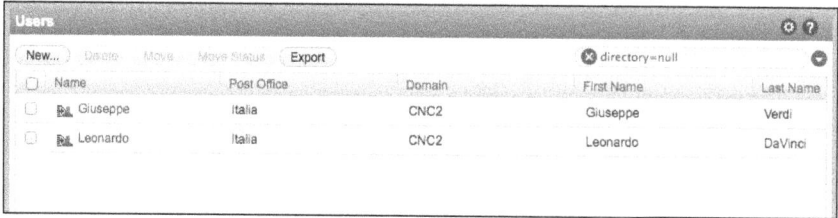

Figure 5-21: A listing of unassociated users

By the way, if you are curious, you can also type

directory=directoryname

Our Directory was named Goddess (imported from our eDirectory tree), so we could type

directory=goddess

and see the resultant user list.

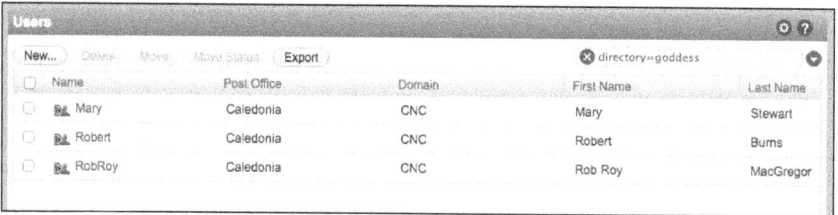

Figure 5-22: Listing of all users in our directory

In our case, upon further inspection, we found that in our eDirectory Synchronization in ConsoleOne, the CNC2 domain had not been configured for synchronization. Thus, those users have been brought into the upgrade GroupWise system in what we have termed "Non-Associated" states (this is not a Novell term, but we felt we needed a designation for these types of objects). It could be that you will have no users in this state. It could be that you will have many!

Depending on how many users you have who are unassociated, and where they reside in your system, you may choose to associate them en masse at the post office, domain or system level.

At the Domain or Post Office level, click on More and choose Directory Associations.

The Caledonia Upgrade Guide for GroupWise 2014 In-Place Upgrade | 79

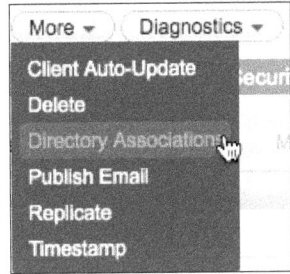

Figure 5-23: Choosing Directory Associations

If you wish to do all of the users at once, go to System|Directory Associations.

Regardless of the method, you will next see the following screen.

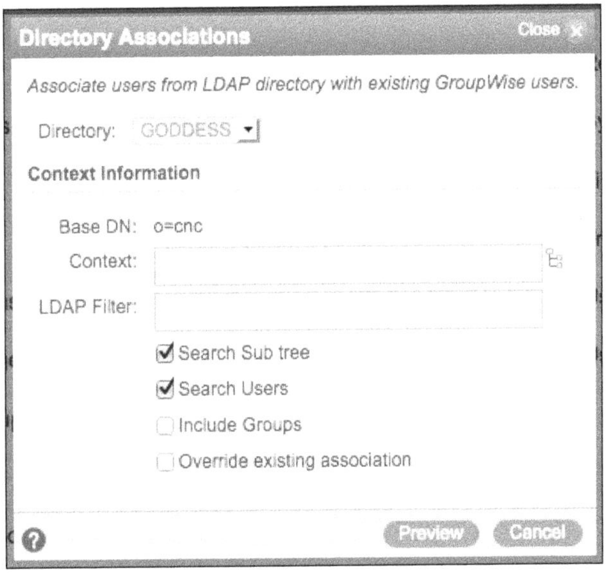

Figure 5-24: Accessing the Directory Associations

You may be asked for the LDAP password here.

Once you click Preview you will see the list of users that have been matched in eDirectory.

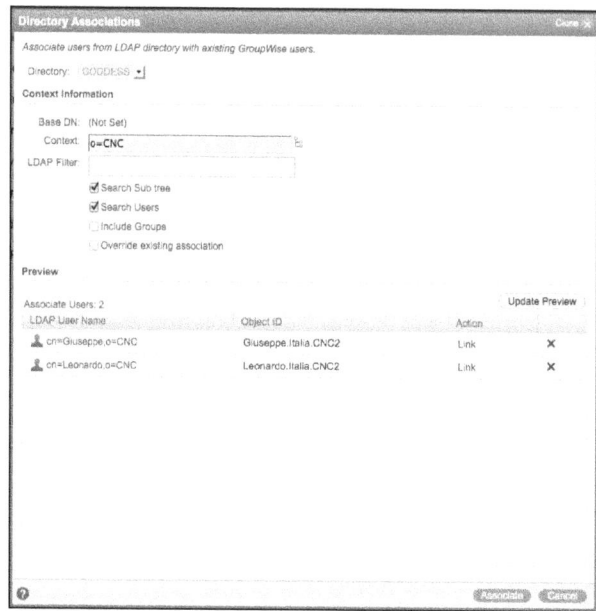

Figure 5-25: Matched Users

If for some reason you did not want to associate a particular user, you could click on the "X" to the far right of the name.

If you know or suspect that you have duplicate userids throughout your tree, double check that the proper GroupWise user is matched with the appropriate eDirectory user. If you see an incorrect association, click the X and make note of the user. You can associate this user manually after you finish the mass association.

Once you have verified all of the associations, click Associate.

At the Success window, click Close.

Earlier in Figure 5-12 we showed you our user Giuseppe Verde who was in what we've termed a Non-Associated state. If we look at Giuseppe's details now, we see that he has an LDAP GUID and has been associated with our Goddess Directory.

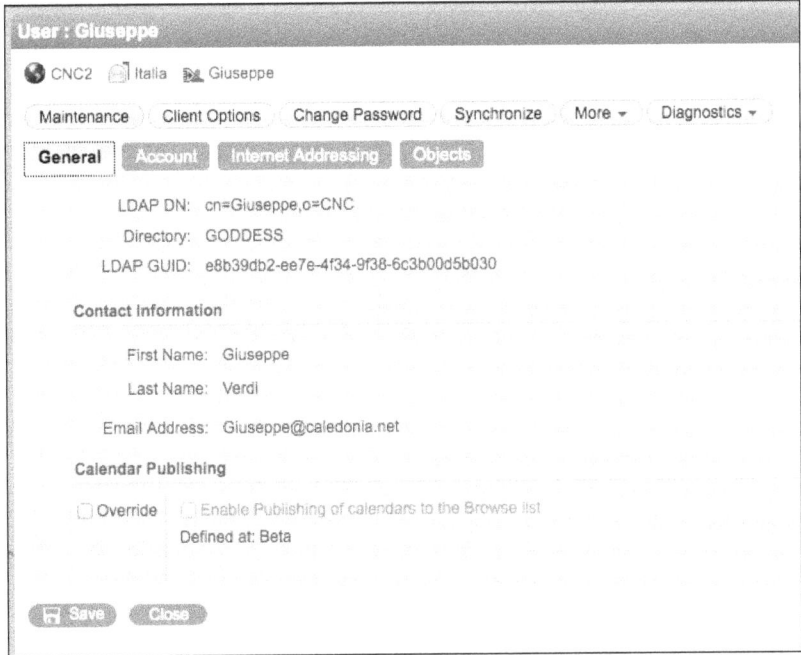

Figure 5-26: Our newly associated user.

Correcting a Failed Directory Integration

The very first time you logged into the Administration Console after upgrading your Primary Domain, you may have seen an error notification in the top right corner of the Administration Console. While this does not always mean that Directory Integration failed, that is the most likely scenario.

Figure 5-27: Error notification in Administration Console

When you click on the red box, you will see any errors that are being reported by the Administration Console.

82 | Directory Integration and Synchronization

Figure 5-28: Initial Directory Configuration Error

This means that either you were unable to configure your eDirectory Sync on your prior system (for example, you are migrating from NetWare, or your Windows server is GroupWise 7 or earlier, or even your entire system is GroupWise 6 or earlier!). We will now go through the steps required to integrate your directory.

Verifying the Directory

In the Administration Console, go to **System|LDAP Servers**. Here our imported LDAP Directory and Server is from eDirectory. The name of the Tree is Goddess. We had defined an LDAP server in ConsoleOne and named it CNC. This information came over during the upgrade with no prompt for intervention. You will at a minimum see the eDirectory object after the upgrade, and if you had defined LDAP servers, they will be here as well.

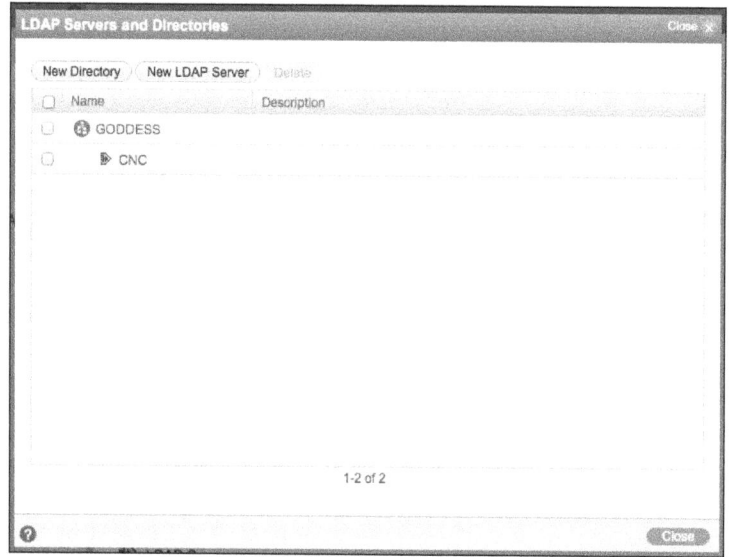

Figure 5-29: Our LDAP System

It's possible that you will only see a Directory listed, as in the following figure.

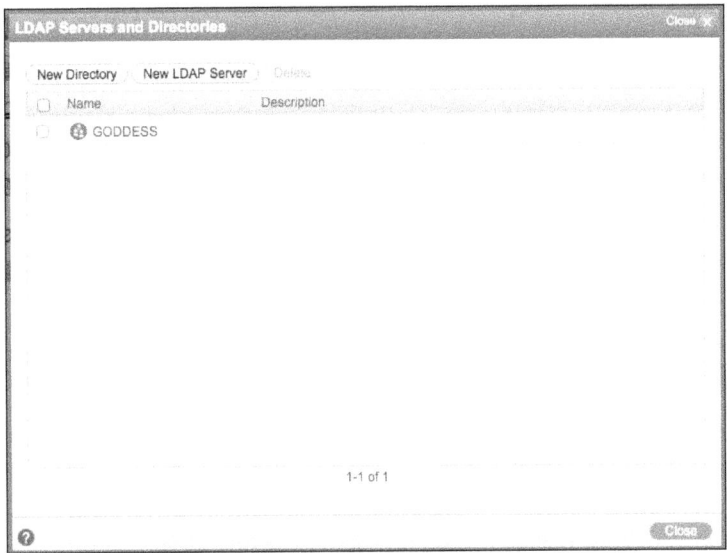

Figure 5-30: A Directory with no LDAP Servers

GroupWise systems that do not use LDAP Authentication, and were not set up properly for eDirectory Synchronization as per our instructions in *"Preparing Your LDAP System"* on page 14, will only have a Directory listed, representing the eDirectory tree where the GroupWise system resides. This of course includes all systems migrated from NetWare, as well as older systems that did not meet our minimum requirements in that section.

Let's look at our Directory named Goddess. Simply click on the name of the Directory to open the details page.

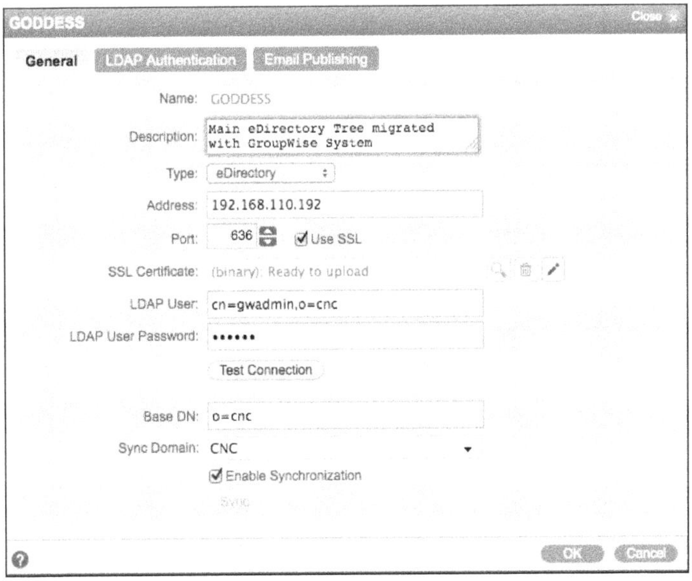

Figure 5-31: Our migrated eDirectory "Directory"

84 | Directory Integration and Synchronization

The General tab of the Directory shows the tree name, Directory type (in an upgrade this will always be eDirectory) and the location of the Directory. If your integration failed you may find that you need to fill out these details. Enter the IP address of your Directory, LDAP port and whether it is SSL. If SSL you will need to upload the SSL certificate for the LDAP server. See *"Exporting Trusted Root Certificates"* later in this chapter for information on exporting the trusted root certificate for this purpose.

The Base DN is the "starting point" for your LDAP search. A migrated Directory will not have any value listed in the Base DN. For synchronization purposes, this is not an issue, as the Synchronization queries a specific LDAP GUID to compare property values. However, if you will be authenticating via LDAP you will want to set a Base DN. In our example above, we have a very small tree, and users are in the "O" container. Larger organizations generally have OUs based on type of object, or company organization, etc. You do not want your Base DN too high in your tree, as that would require the LDAP search to look through too many records. By the same token though, you want to make sure that all user objects you wish to manage in this directory are found below this Base DN designation.

Note the Sync Domain. As with prior versions of GroupWise, it is really only required that one MTA be configured to do synchronization for the entire system. Choose the Domain whose MTA should perform the sync for this Directory. The MTA must have a Scheduled Event for Directory Synchronization enabled for Directory Synchronization to actually occur automatically. We will go through the steps to verify the synchronization in *"Testing Directory Synchronization"* at the end of this chapter.

Once you have all settings entered, click Test Connection. If all is well, you will receive a green banner at the top of the screen indicating success!

NOTE: If you come back to this screen at a later time to test, and the LDAP password is greyed out as in the figure, you will be required to put the password in again in order to complete a successful test.

The Directory is also where you define the settings for LDAP authentication for this directory. Click on the LDAP Authentication tab to see the current, migrated settings. While an LDAP server configuration in GroupWise 2014 is only required if you wish to use LDAP Authentication, the pertinent settings for how LDAP Authentication will be configured are in the Directory Object.

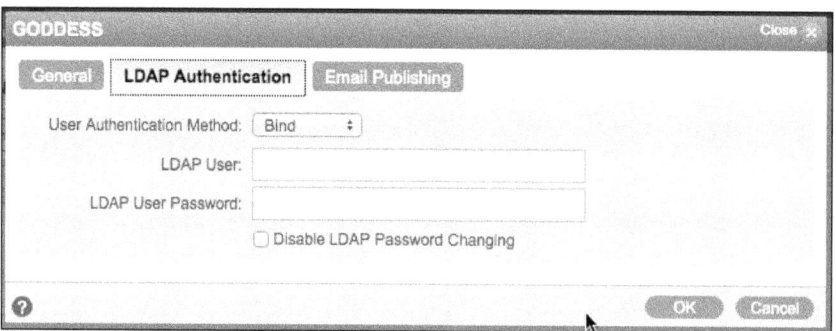

Figure 5-32: LDAP Authentication Settings

We can also look at the Email Publishing settings here. Now that GroupWise has been decoupled from eDirectory, the only changes GroupWise ever makes to the directory (whether eDirectory or Active Directory) are related to the email addresses of your users.

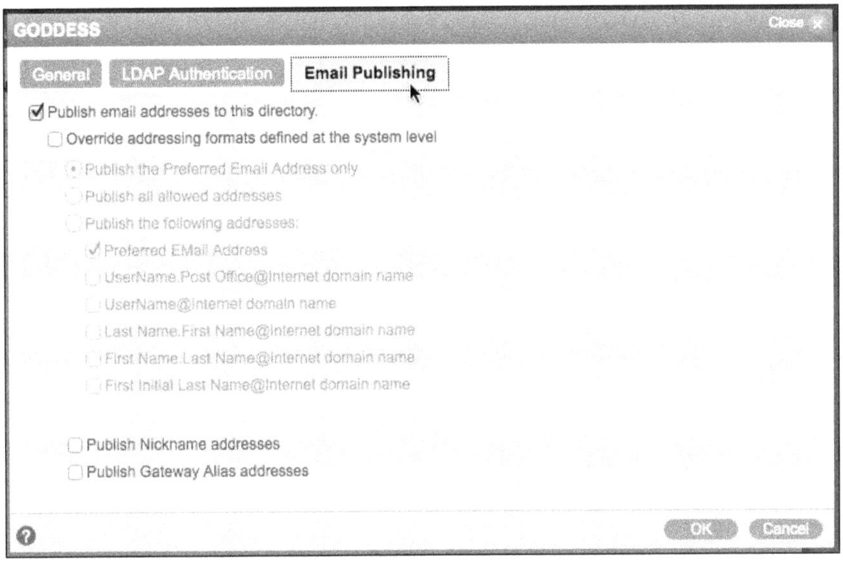

Figure 5-33: The Email Publishing Settings

You can change these settings to meet the needs of your organization. These settings are defined in **System|Internet Addressing**. You can modify them there for the entire system, or you can changed them here by clicking on the "Override" box and choosing the options you desire.

86 | Directory Integration and Synchronization

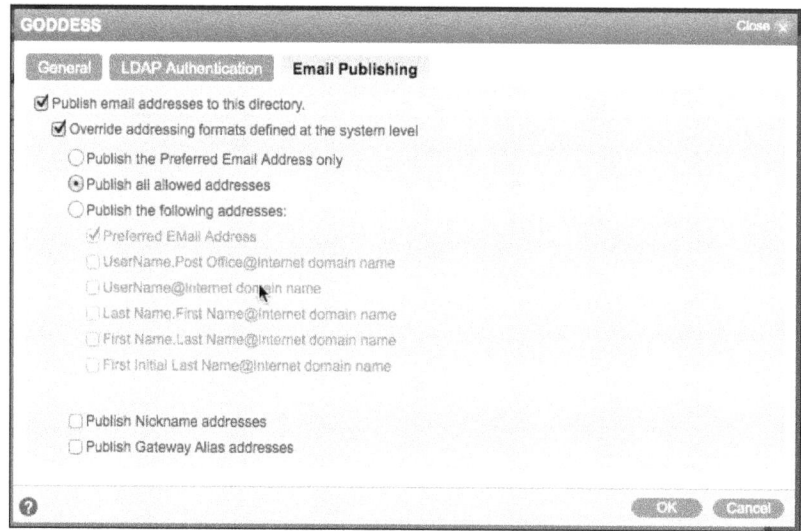

Figure 5-34: Modified email publishing settings

You can choose to publish all allowed addresses, only certain types of addresses, even nicknames. The eDirectory email field is multi-valued and can accept more than one email address. If you are using the LDAP server to provide address lookup for a smart host (perhaps an anti-spam appliance in front of your GroupWise system), you would need to decide which addresses are allowed. In some cases, this is necessary in order to keep costs down. For example, if your anti-spam provider treats each email address as a "user", danitaz, danita, danita.zanre, and zanre.danita could start to get expensive.

Verifying User Associations

As we pointed out in Figure 5-10 above, when users are properly associated with the Directory, you will be able to tell readily by looking at the General tab for the user in question. It would, however, be tedious to look through every user in your system! While it may be that none of your users are Associated, we've seen some instances where merely fixing the Directory server causes an Integration to complete when you save the Directory settings (you may receive a popup question asking if you wish to update the information for all users in the system). If you would like to check the state of your user integrations before attempting the Directory Associations, follow the steps below.

1. First, click on Users in the list to the left.

2. Notice the search field in the upper-right of the user list. Click into that field.

    Type in

    directory=null

You will see a list of all unassociated users in your system.

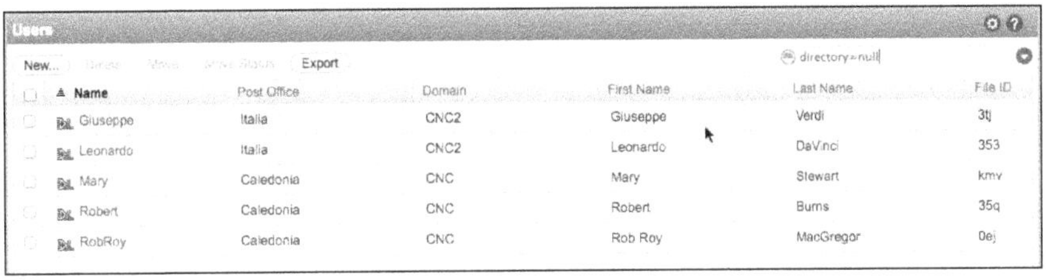

Figure 5-35: A listing of unassociated users

Depending on how many users you have who are unassociated, and where they reside in your system, you may choose to associate them en masse at the post office, domain or system level.

At the Domain or Post Office level, click on More and choose Directory Associations.

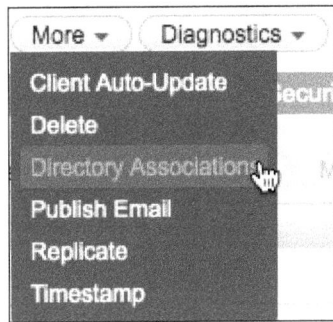

Figure 5-36: Choosing Directory Associations

If you wish to do all of the users at once, go to **System|Directory Associations**.

Regardless of the method, you will next see the following screen.

88 | Directory Integration and Synchronization

Figure 5-37: Accessing the Directory Associations

You may be asked for the LDAP password here.

Once you click Preview you will see the list of users that have been matched in eDirectory.

Figure 5-38: Matched Users

If for some reason you did not want to associate a particular user, you could click on the "X" to the far right of the name.

If you know or suspect that you have duplicate userids throughout your tree, double check that the proper GroupWise user is matched with the appropriate eDirectory user. If you see an incorrect association, click the X and make note of the user. You can associate this user manually after you finish the mass association.

Once you have verified all of the associations, click Associate.

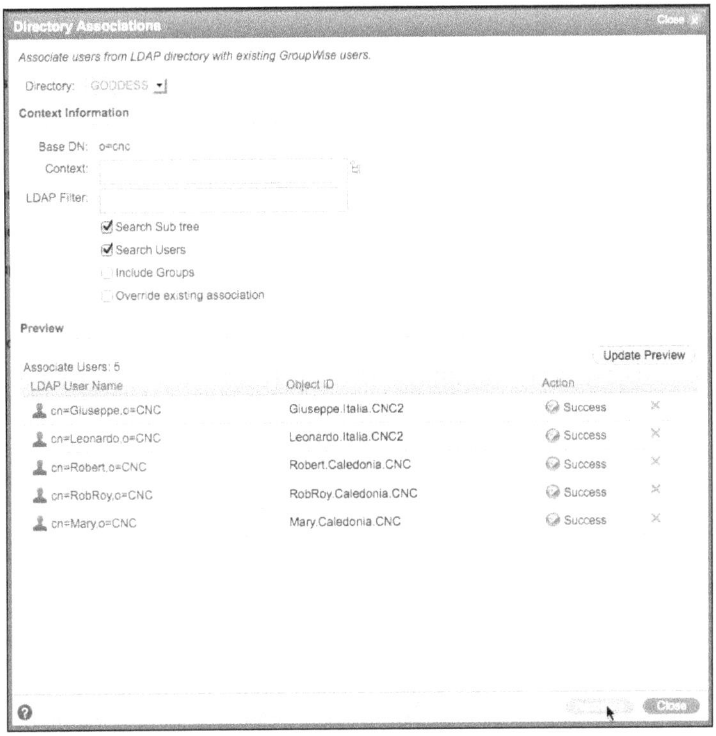

Figure 5-39: Successful Association

At the Success window, click Close.

Earlier in Figure 5-12 we showed you our user Giuseppe Verde who was in what we've termed a Non-Associated state. If we look at Giuseppe's details now, we see that he has an LDAP GUID and has been associated with our Goddess Directory.

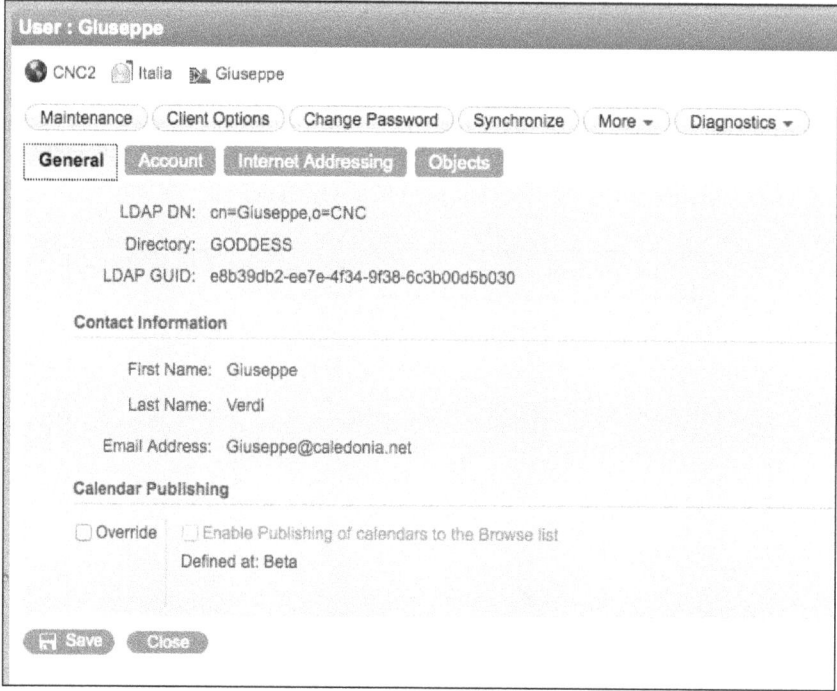

Figure 5-40: Our newly associated user.

Verifying the LDAP Server

While the Directory object is required to synchronize your Directory to GroupWise, and acts as an authentication source, the purpose of the LDAP Server is to provide redundancy as an additional authentication source for the GroupWise Client. It is technically not required if you are not using LDAP Authentication. That said, even if you have never used LDAP Authentication before, it is not a wasted exercise to verify and/or create an LDAP server for your system. If you have more than one LDAP server available in your network, you may wish to configure additional LDAP servers here.

1. To create an LDAP Server for authentication, first click on **System|LDAP Servers**.

2. If you have an LDAP server listed under your Directory, click on it to open the properties. If you do not have an LDAP server for authentication, click New LDAP Server.

3. Fill in the information for your LDAP server. You may wonder why there is no authentication information here, but remember that was defined for the entire Directory in the Directory object.

Figure 5-41: Creating the LDAP Server

4. Click on the Post Offices tab and move all post offices that should use this LDAP server as their primary authentication source from the right to the left. If this LDAP server is down, and other LDAP servers have been configured, the POA will step through the listed servers to find an available authentication source.

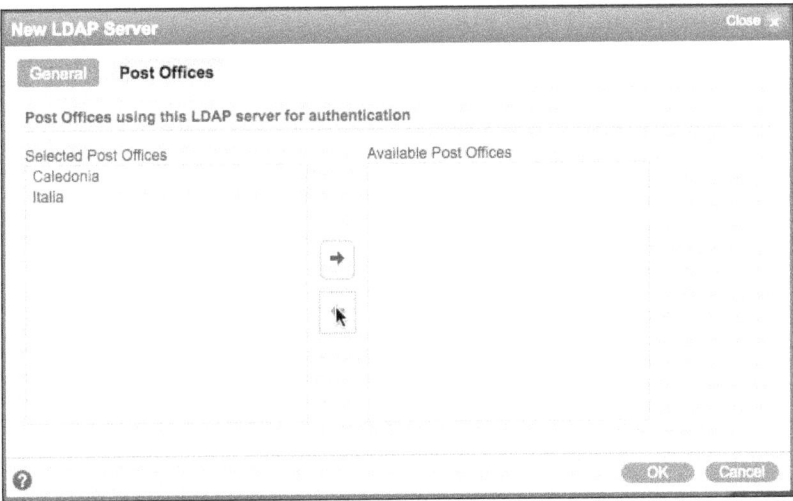

Figure 5-42: Post Office associations for LDAP Server

5. These steps enable your LDAP server to be used as authentication for your users. However, to actually be in effect, you must activate it in the Post Office Security settings.

Once you have successfully associated your users, you can jump to *"Testing Directory Synchronization"* below.

Integrating Active Directory into Your GroupWise System

One of the new features of GroupWise 2014 is the ability to Integrate directly with Active Directory in lieu of, or in conjunction with, eDirectory. Some of the reasons for this might be your organization has moved to an AD environment and currently only uses eDirectory for GroupWise. Or you might have some users in an AD environment, and others in eDirectory, all sharing a GroupWise system. Thus, you may have a need or desire to associate some or all of your users to AD.

If you are moving immediately to Active Directory, and will not need eDirectory at all after your upgrade to GroupWise 2014, there is really little reason to follow the steps above to check and verify your integrations with eDirectory. If you will be moving users slowly to AD, then you should first ensure that your current eDirectory system is also functional by following the steps in the sections above pertaining to verifying your Integrations.

The first thing that must be done when planning an integration with Active Directory is of course to create the Directory Object in the GroupWise Administration Console. Follow these steps:

1. In the Administration Console, click on System and then on LDAP Servers.

2. You should see your current eDirectory tree listed as in the figure below.

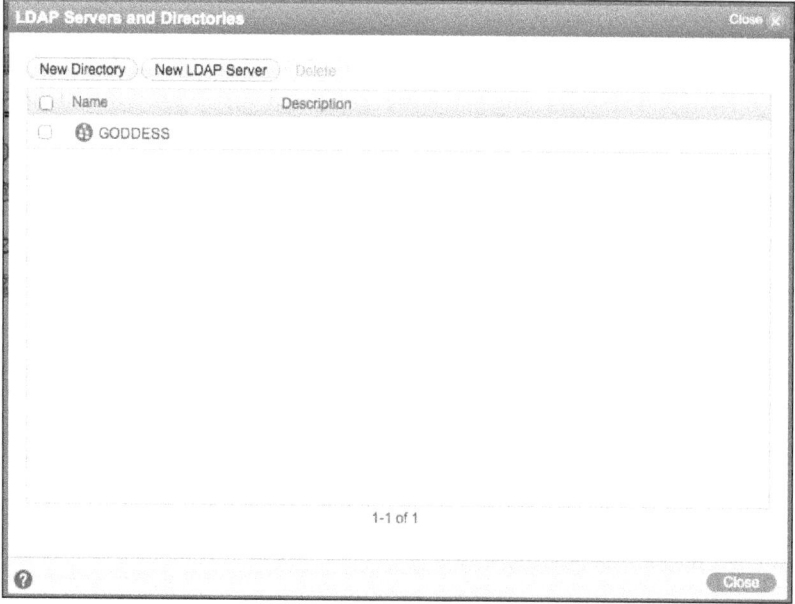

Figure 5-43: The eDirectory listing

3. Click New Directory

4. Fill in the Directory creation window with information about your Active Directory LDAP server.

5. If your Domain Controller LDAP server is enabled for SSL, you will need to export the certificate for importing into this Directory setup. See *"Exporting Trusted Root Certificates"* later in this chapter for details on how to accomplish this.

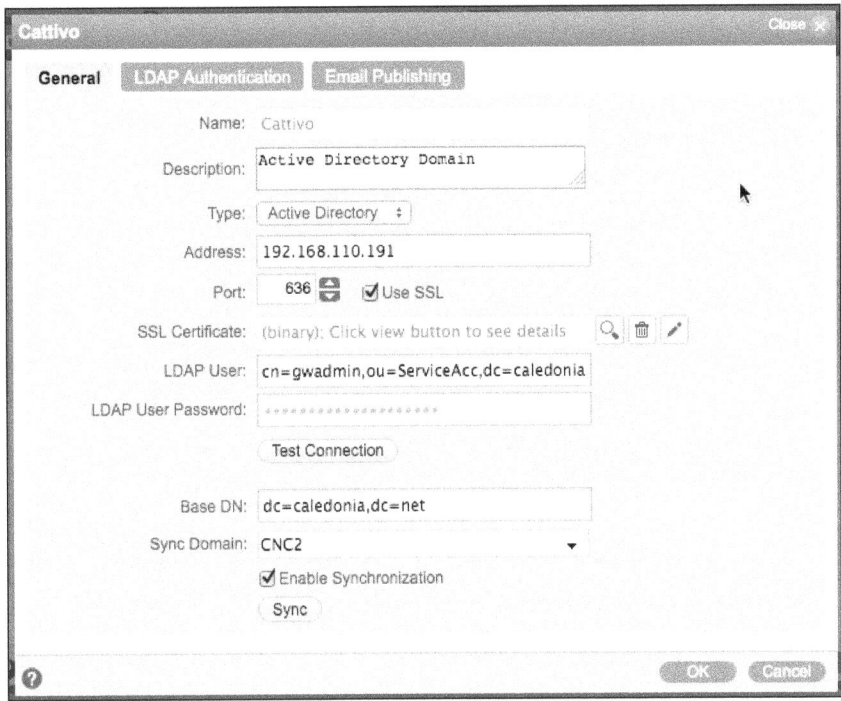

6. Click Test to ensure that you have everything entered correctly

> **NOTE:** If you come back to this screen at a later time to test, and the LDAP password is greyed out as in the figure, you will be required to put the password in again in order to complete a successful test.

7. The Base DN is the "starting point" for your LDAP search. All users who should be managed by this directory must reside under this Base DN. You do not want your Base DN too high in your tree, as that would require the LDAP search to look through too many records. By the same token though, you want to make sure that all user objects you wish to manage in this directory are found below this Base DN designation. In our testing, the Base DN for Active Directory must be above the OU for your users. The query does not appear to look directly in the level of the Base DN.

8. Choose your Sync Domain. This is the Domain whose MTA will perform Directory Synchronization for this Directory. The MTA must have a Scheduled Event for Directory Synchronization enabled for Directory Synchronization to actually occur automatically. You will test this Synchronization in *"Testing Directory Synchronization"* below.

We can also look at the Email Publishing settings here. Now that GroupWise has been decoupled from eDirectory, the only changes GroupWise ever makes to the directory (whether eDirectory or Active Directory) are related to the email addresses of your users.

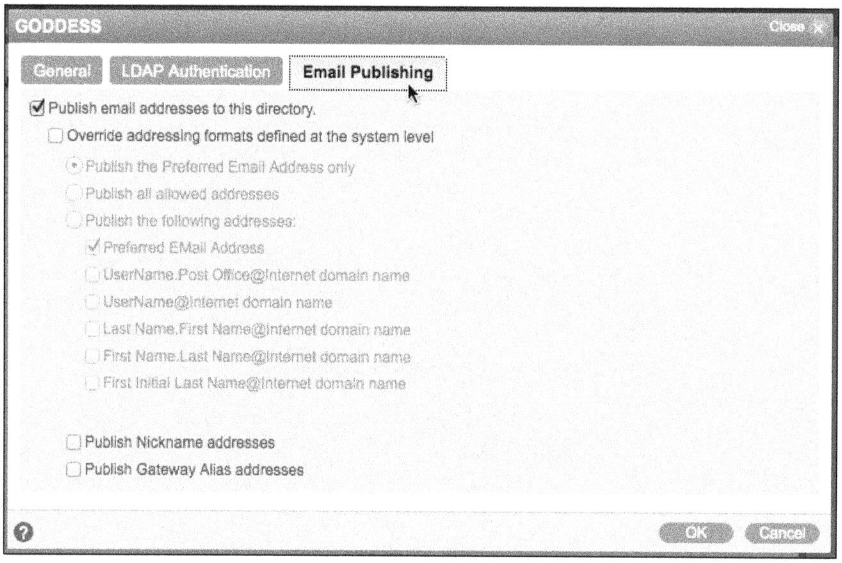

94 | Directory Integration and Synchronization

Figure 5-44: The Email Publishing Settings

You can change these settings to meet the needs of your organization. These settings are defined in **System|Internet Addressing**. You can modify them there for the entire system, or you can changed them here by clicking on the "Override" box and choosing the options you desire.

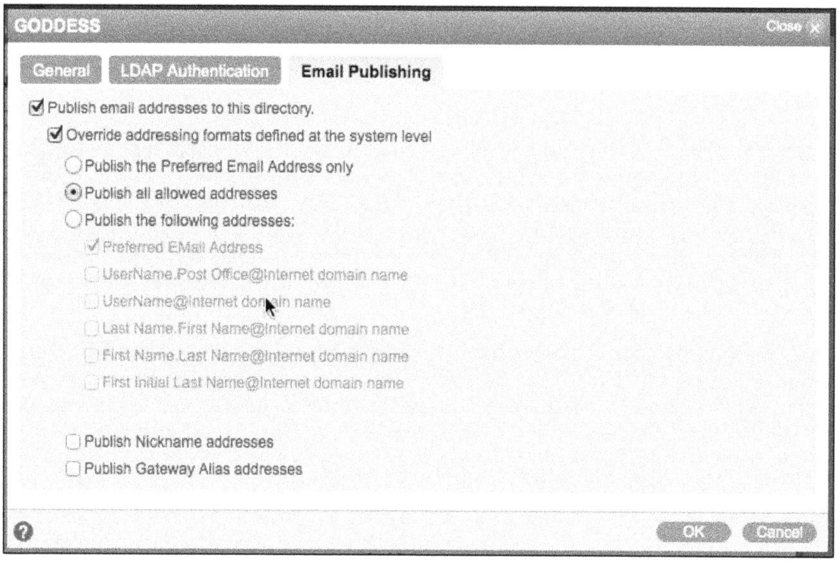

Figure 5-45: Modified email publishing settings

You can choose to publish all allowed addresses, only certain types of addresses, even nicknames. With AD, the preferred ID is written to the mail attribute and the others are written to the proxyAddresses attribute as follows:

- primary email address is written to the mail attribute, and also to the proxyAddresses as SMTP:user@domain (SMTP uppercase)
- other email addrs are written as smtp:user@domain (smtp lowercase)

This can be viewed by going into the AD Users and Computers, go to View and select Advanced Features. Then in the user properties there is an Attribute Editor tab that will show all the LDAP attributes/values. Look for the proxyAddress line to view all Email addresses

If you are using the LDAP server to provide address lookup for a smart host (perhaps an anti-spam appliance in front of your GroupWise system), you would need to decide which addresses are allowed. In some cases, this is necessary in order to keep costs down. For example, if your anti-spam provider treats each email address as a "user", danitaz, danita, danita.zanre, and zanre.danita could start to get expensive.

Associating GroupWise Users with Active Directory

You can Associate your GroupWise users with Active Directory users individually, by Post Office, by Domain or entire system. If you plan on associating a large number of users at once, it's best practice to do the association procedure during a slow time on the network, perhaps evening or weekend.

Depending on whether your users were properly associated with eDirectory or not, you may have some or all of your users as Associate Users, Unassociated Users, or even our "Non-Associated" designation.

Associating Individual Users

If you choose to associate individual users to Active Directory, you must actually dissociate the user first, and then associate to the new directory (of course, if the user is not associated to eDirectory at this point, you only need associate the user to the new Directory).

1. In the Administration Console, find the user. You can click into the Global Search field and type the user's name to quickly access the user.
2. Open the user properties and under More, click Dissociate.
3. If the More button says Associate, then the user is not associated with any Directory. After the user is Dissociated, click More again. This time choose Associate.
4. You will see the below figure. Make sure your AD Directory is listed, and browse the tree for the user.

96 | Directory Integration and Synchronization

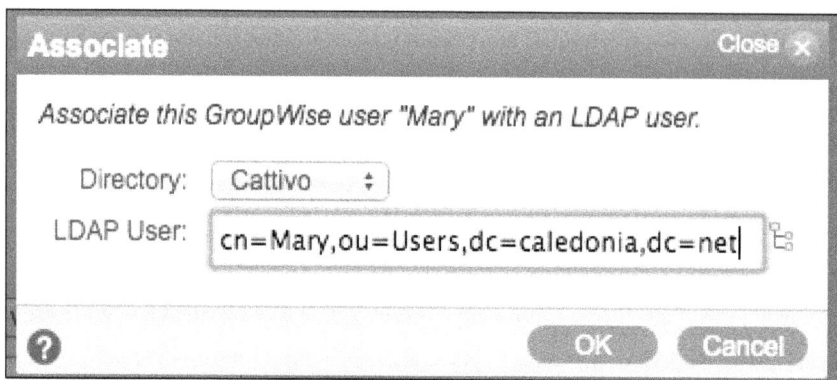

Figure 5-46: Associating Individual Users

5. Click OK to Associate.
6. Now if we look at the General Tab for Mary, we will see that she is associated with the Cattivo (Active Directory) Domain.

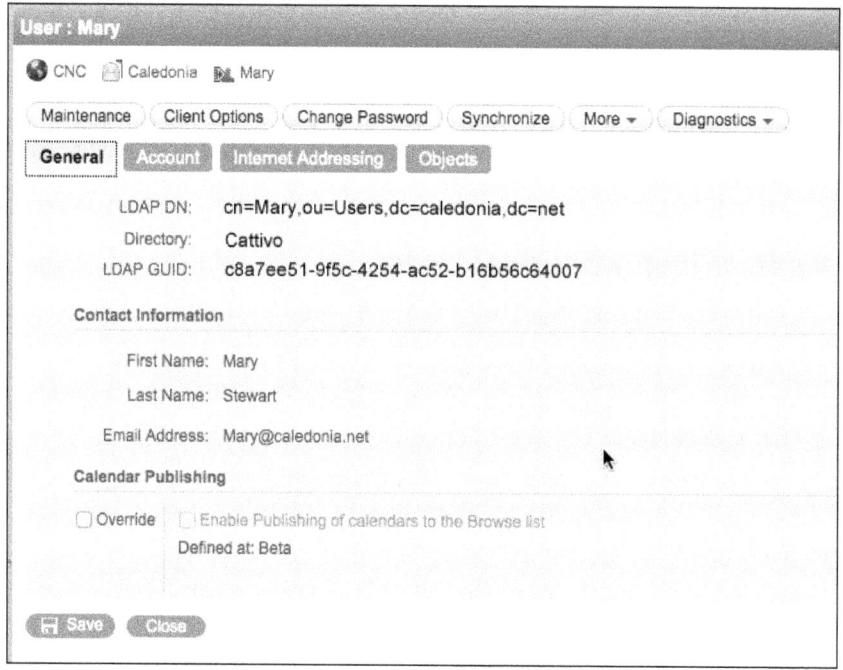

Figure 5-47: User Associated with Active Directory

Associating Users En Masse

You can also associate users to Active Directory en masse. In order to do so, your GroupWise object id must match the AD samAccountName. Otherwise, the matching cannot occur.. If you wish to associate your users to Active Directory by post office or by domain, open the object in question, and under More choose Associate.

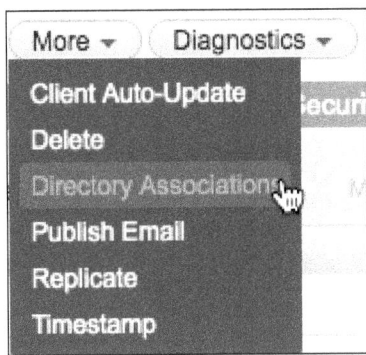

Figure 5-48: Choosing Directory Associations

If you wish to make the change for the entire system, click on System and then Directory Associations.

You can make the switch in one step, rather than having to attempt to dissociate users and then associate them with AD.

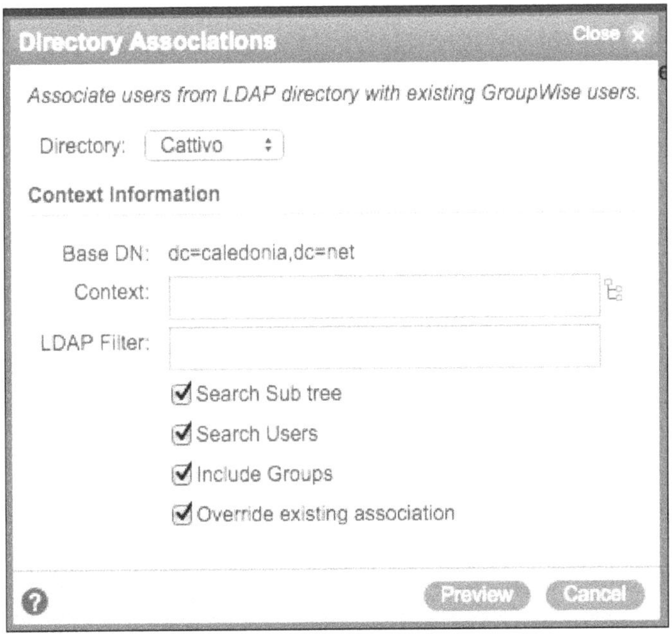

Figure 5-49: Associate users to Active Directory en masse

The important setting for associating your users without first needing to dissociate them is to check the box that says "Override existing association". This will allow users in any state (associated, unassociated, or even our special "non-associated") to change to the new Active Directory association in one step.

After you click Preview, review the users and when you are ready, click Associate.

If you know or suspect that you have duplicate userids in your Active Directory Domain, double check that the proper GroupWise user is matched with the appropriate AD user. If you see an incorrect association, click the X and make note of the user. You can associate this user manually after you finish the mass association.

Creating the LDAP Server

While the Directory object is required to synchronize your Directory to GroupWise and act as the default authentication source for LDAP authentication, the purpose of the LDAP Server is to provide additional authentication sources for the GroupWise Client. It is technically not required if you are not using LDAP Authentication. That said, even if you have never used LDAP Authentication before, it is not a wasted exercise to verify and/or create an LDAP server for your system. If you have more than one LDAP server available in your network, you may wish to create additional LDAP servers.

1. To create an LDAP Server for authentication, first click on System|LDAP Servers
2. If you have an LDAP server listed under your Directory, click on it to open the properties. If you do not have an LDAP server for authentication, click New LDAP Server.
3. Fill in the information for your LDAP server. You may wonder why there is no authentication information here, but remember that was defined for the entire Directory in the Directory object.

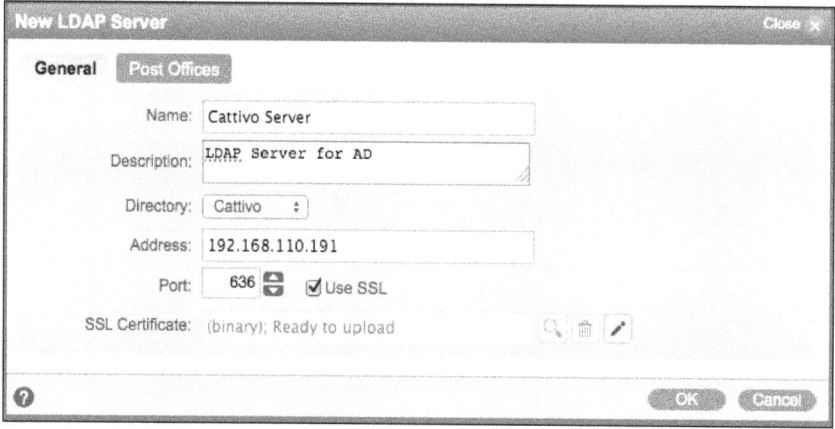

Figure 5-50: Creating the LDAP Server

4. Click on the Post Offices tab and move all post offices that should use this LDAP server as the primary authentication source from the right to the left. If this LDAP server is down, and other LDAP servers have been configured, the POA will step through the listed servers to find an available authentication source.

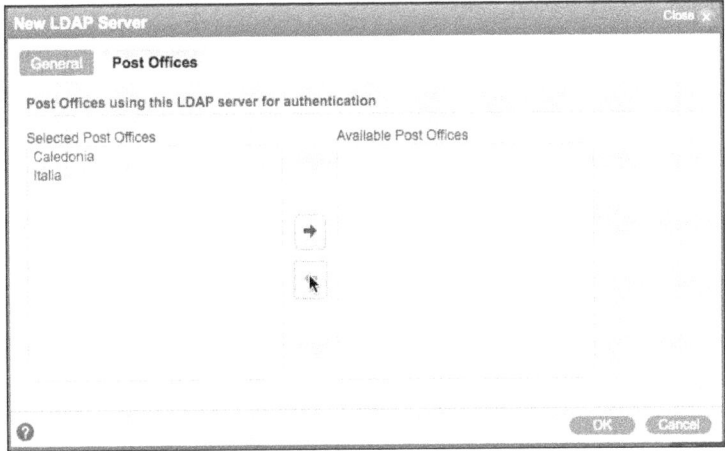

Figure 5-51: Post Office associations for LDAP Server

5. These steps enable your LDAP server to be used as authentication for your users. However, to actually be in effect, you must activate it in the Post Office Security settings.

Removing eDirectory Associations to become Stand-Alone

If you are planning on removing integrations from your existing eDirectory tree and turning GroupWise into a "stand-alone" system, the steps are fairly simple.

1. In the GroupWise Administration Console, click on System, and then LDAP Servers.
2. Check the box next to your eDirectory tree.

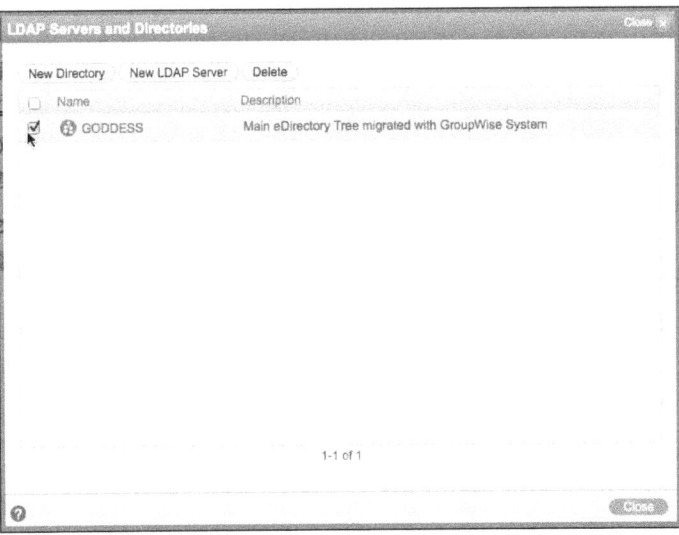

Figure 5-52: Preparing to delete your Directory

100 | Directory Integration and Synchronization

3. Click on Delete at the top of the window.
4. You will receive a warning that this action cannot be undone (although it would not be a huge undertaking in the relative scheme of the Universe to recreate the Directory!).
5. Click Okay.
6. Click Users in the left pane of the Administration Console
7. Voila! All of your users are now Unassociated.

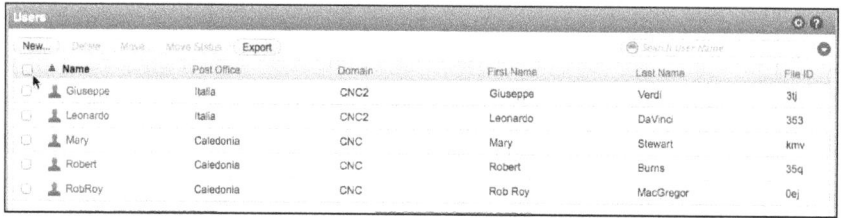

Testing Directory Synchronization

Once you have confirmed your Directory settings (whether eDirectory, AD or both), you can test to ensure updates are happening.

1. Use iManager or ConsoleOne without any GroupWise snapins, or MMC if this is AD to change something that needs to synchronize to GroupWise. For example, a phone number.
2. Go back to System and click on LDAP Servers.
3. Click on the name of your Directory to open the details
4. At the bottom of the window, click Sync.
5. Go look at your MTA log (in verbose mode) and you should see a synchronization event.

   17:51:03 18B8 Synchronizing Directory Goddess
   17:51:03 18B8 Connecting to LDAP server at 192.168.110.192 for Directory Goddess
   17:51:03 18B8 Checking CNC.Caledonia.Mary
   17:51:03 18B8 Checking CNC.Caledonia.Robert
   17:51:03 18B8 Checking CNC.Caledonia.RobRoy
   17:51:03 18B8 Checking CNC2.Italia.Giuseppe
   17:51:03 18B8 Checking CNC2.Italia.Leonardo
   17:51:04 18B8   Update Telephone Number:720-319-7530
   17:51:04 18B8 Disconnecting from LDAP server for Directory Goddess
   17:51:04 18B8 Synchronization complete for Directory Goddess

Once you have verified that Synchronization is occurring, check your Scheduled Event to ensure that synchronization occurs regularly.

1. In the Administration Console, click on Message Transfer Agents in the left column, and then click on the MTA for the domain you defined in your Sync Domain in the Directory configuration.

2. Click on Scheduled Events.

3. Regardless of whether you had eDirectory Synchronization configured before, you will no doubt have one or more NDS and/or eDirectory Synchronization events. Various version of GroupWise changed the events, even creating a new "eDirectory" event when the name changed, but leaving the NDS event behind. You can have multiple events configured here if you desire to have an update more than once a day. Or you can choose to delete any extraneous events you find here, and have only one scheduled event for synchronization.

4. Click on the Event you wish to edit. The default for this event is 1:00 a.m. local time. Set it to any time you choose.

5. If you wish to have synchronization occur more than once a day, you will need to create multiple events and set them for different times.

6. Click Okay, and make certain that the event is enabled (checked).

External Entities

External Entities are interesting objects going forward. They cannot be modified in ConsoleOne without GroupWise Snapins. External Entities may be edited in iManager, and thus are "associated users". However, there is no way to create new External Entities in iManager. Going forward, eDirectory synchronized users must be full eDirectory users, or be managed as unassociated users in the GroupWise Administration Console.

If you want to dissociate your External Entities and treat them as unassociated users, you will need to manage the dissociations one at a time. There is no method to mass dissociate at this time. In order to dissociate an External Entity, do the following:

1. In the Administration Console, click on Users.

2. Find the user in your list. External Entities are not listed separately. They will look like any other user.

3. Click on the External Entities to view the properties.

4. Under More, click Dissociate.

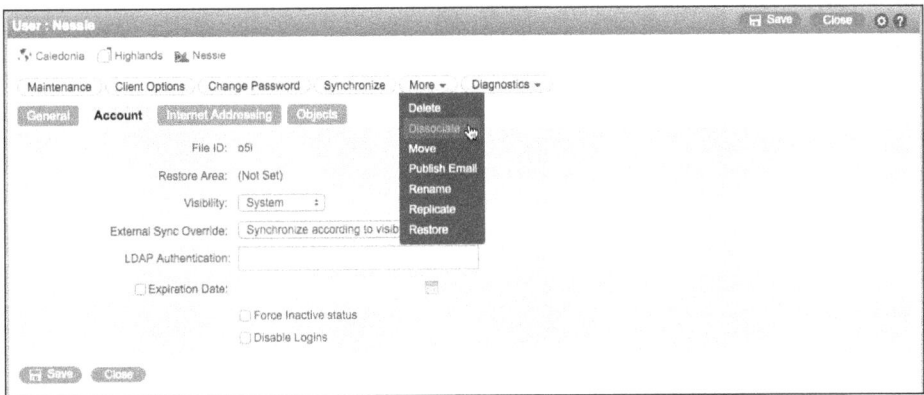

Figure 5-53: Dissociating External Entities

Exporting Trusted Root Certificates

iManager

To export your Trusted Root Certificate for a Linux server with iManager, see

https://www.novell.com/support/kb/doc.php?id=7013142

Instructions for ConsoleOne can be found at

http://www.novell.com/coolsolutions/tip/19360.html

Windows

SSL is not enabled automatically for LDAP on Windows. It is beyond the scope of this guide to design and configure SSL for your LDAP environment. We point you to this Microsoft TechNet document for guidance.

http://social.technet.microsoft.com/wiki/contents/articles/2980.ldap-over-ssl-ldaps-certificate.aspx

Directory Plugins

There are Directory plugins for eDirectory via iManager and Active Directory through Microsoft Management Console (MMC). The first iterations of these plugins have some basic functionality for adding users to GroupWise as they are added to the Directory itself. We expect there will be additional functionality as GroupWise 2014 and this new Administration Model progress. For now, here is how to install and utilize these plugins.

Installing the iManager Plugin

iManager Plugins are npm files. The GroupWise Plugin will typically be named **GroupWisePlugins-<build>.npm**.

Download the npm file from download.novell.com or your Novell Customer Care Portal. Then follow these instructions.

1. Log into iManager (for example https://192.168.110.210/nps/servlet/webacc).
2. Click Configure at the top of the window

Figure 5-54: Accessing Role Configuration

3. Click on Plugin Installation
4. Click Available Plugin Modules

5. Click Add

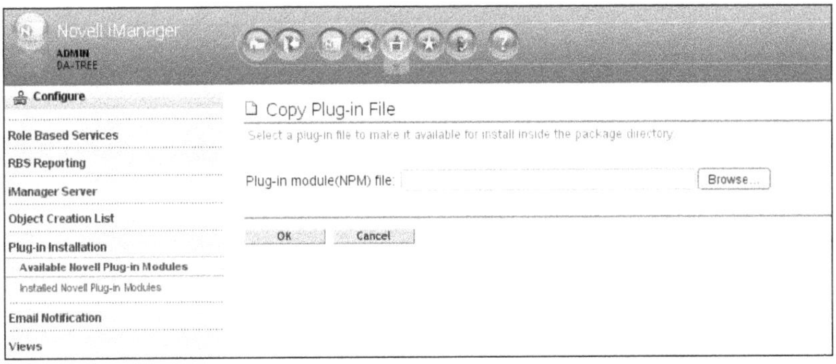

Figure 5-55: Adding a new plugin

6. Browse for the npm file you downloaded
7. Click OK
8. You will be returned to the plugin list. Find the GroupWisePlugins listing, check it and click Install at the top.

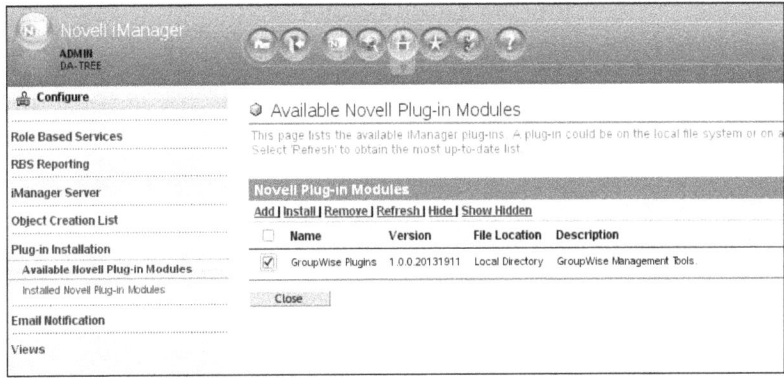

Figure 5-56: Installing the new Plugin

9. After the installation is completed, click Close.
10. You are instructed to restart Tomcat on your eDirectory server running iManager

    For Linux, run

    /etc/init.d/novell-tomcat6 start (OES)

    or

    /etc/init.d/tomcat6 start (SLES)

    On Windows, click Start > Administrative Tools > Services. Then right-click Tomcat 6, and click Restart.

    The plugin has been installed.

104 | Directory Integration and Synchronization

11. Log back into iManager, then click the Configure button again (Figure 5-54).
12. Select Role-Based Services > RBS Configuration.
13. Notice that we have uninstalled modules

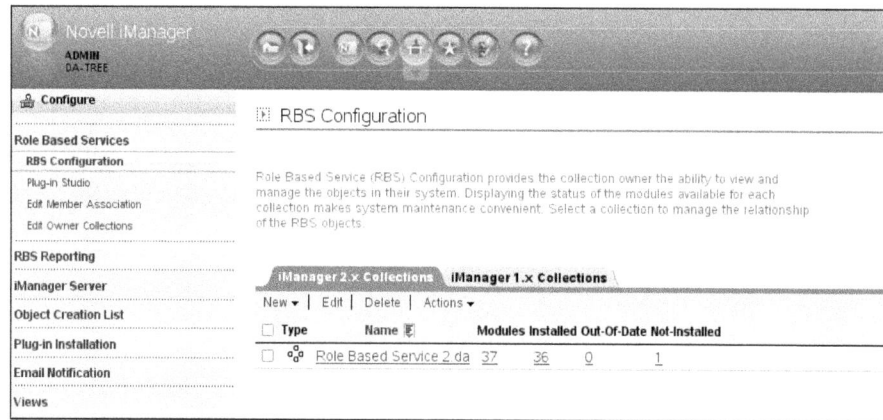

Figure 5-57:

14. Click on the number under uninstalled
15. Click on GroupWise and choose Install

Figure 5-58: Add GroupWise Module

After the module is installed, return to Roles & Tasks.

After the module has been installed, it must first be configured before it can be used. To do so, do the following in iManager.

1. Click Users and then Modify User

2. Browse to any user (Admin, your own - we're not making changes, just activating the plugin).

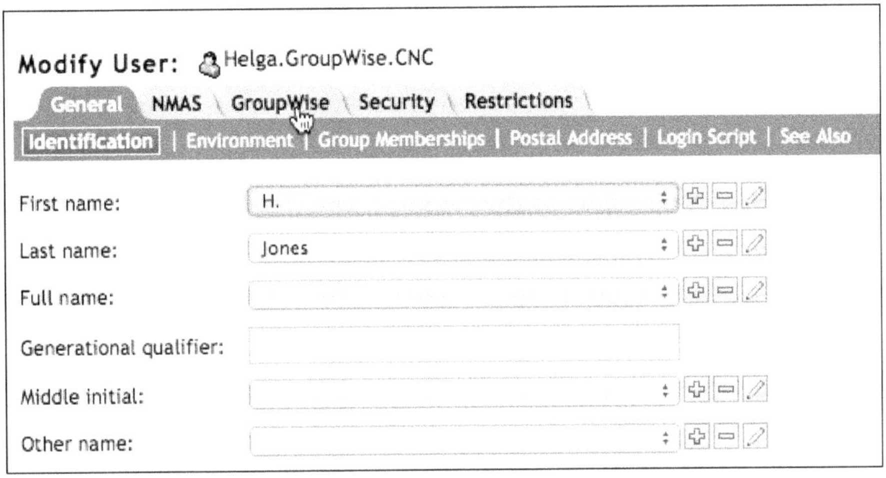

Figure 5-59: The new GroupWise Tab

3. When you click on the GroupWise tab for the first time you will see the following:

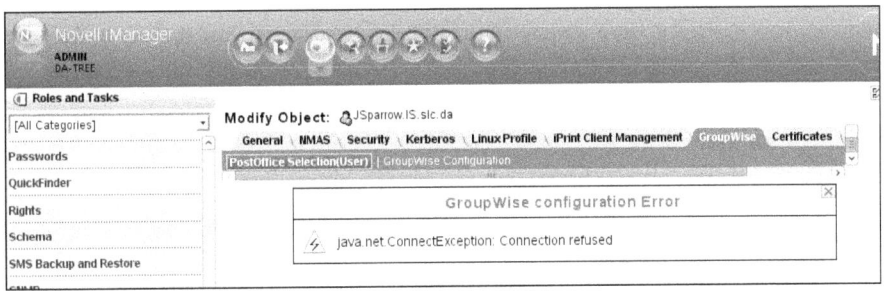

Figure 5-60: Notice that the GroupWise Plugin is not configured

4. Click on GroupWise Configuration above the error notice.
5. Next you must fill out your LDAP server information for your tree.

Figure 5-61: LDAP Server Configuration

- Enter GroupWise Admin Service URL: IP address or Host name of service
- Enter GroupWise Admin Service Port: 9710 by default
- Enter LDAP server ID: Directory Name
- Enter GroupWise Admin Username: gwadmin (per our installation)
- Enter GroupWise Admin Password: admin service password

Using the iManager Plugin

Now that your plugin has been successfully configured, let's see how it works. We will create a new user, add the user to GroupWise, and then modify an existing user.

1. In iManager Roles, click on Users and then Create User
2. Create the User in the same way you create all of your users, including using any user templates, setting home directories, etc.

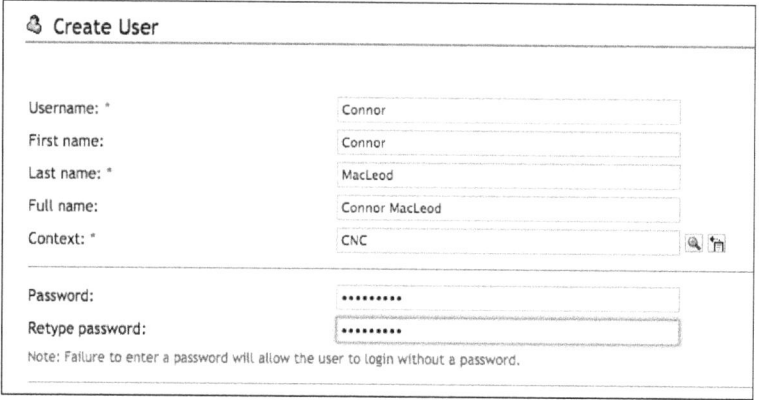

Figure 5-62: Creating a new User

3. You will be at the following screen. Click Modify (not OK).

The Caledonia Upgrade Guide for GroupWise 2014 In-Place Upgrade | 107

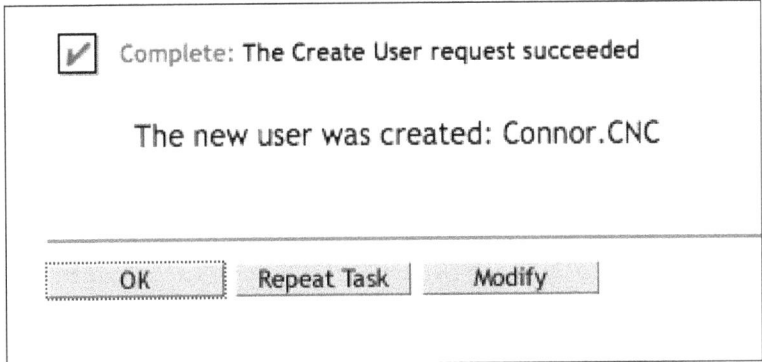

Figure 5-63: Click Modify at the Successful User Creation

4. Click on the GroupWise Tab. Since this is a new User who does not belong to a GroupWise Post Office, you will see the following informational notice, and a dropdown for choosing the Post Office for the user.

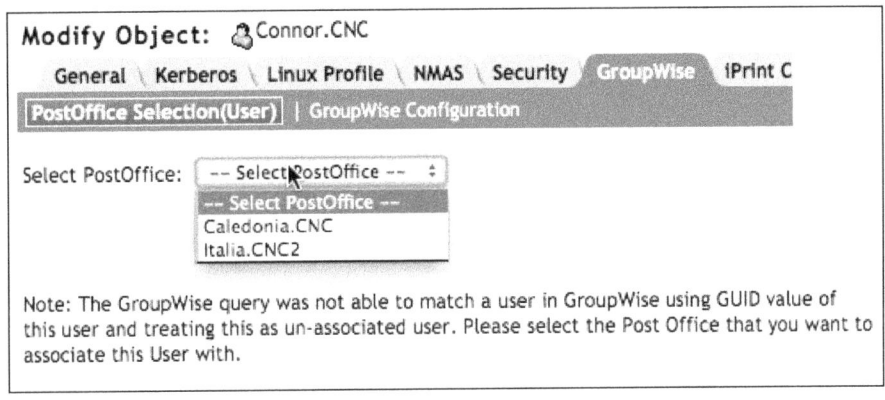

Figure 5-64: New User who does not belong to a post office

5. Choose the post office for this user. We'll put Connor MacLeod in the Caledonia Post Office.
6. You will receive a success notification, and the user is now in the Caledonia Post Office.

We can check this status by going to the GroupWise Administration Console. Follow the instructions in *"Launching the New Administration Console"* earlier in this chapter.

1. Click on Users
2. Find your user, in our case Connor.
3. On the General Tab for Connor, you will see that he has an LDAP GUID and has been added properly to the Post Office.

108 | Directory Integration and Synchronization

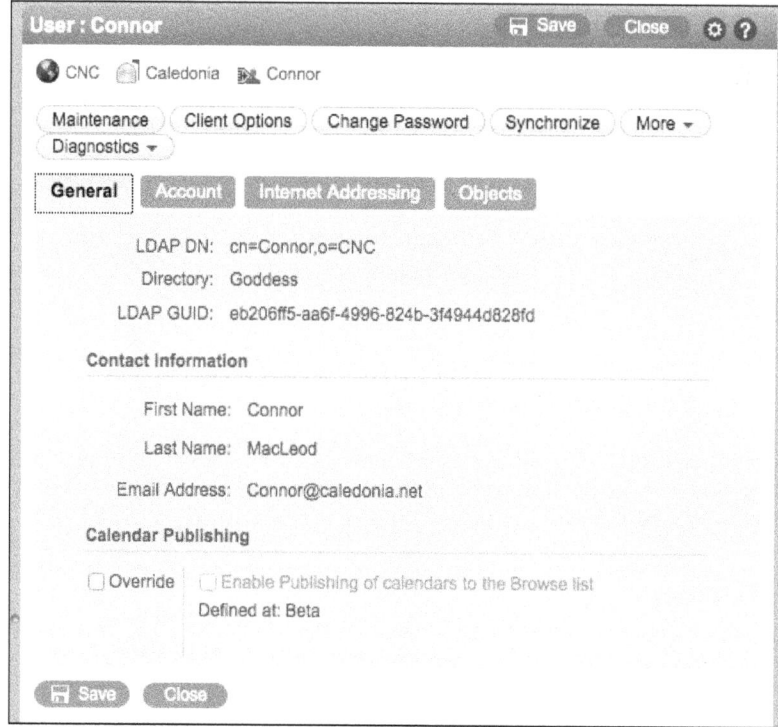

Figure 5-65: Our user, added from iManager

In addition to modifying a new user in order to add to a post office directly after creation, the only other functionality of the iManager plugin is to modify existing users who do not already have a GroupWise account. Simply follow the instructions above, but rather than clicking Create User choose Modify User. Find the User to Modify, and click on the GroupWise tab.

You will either see the window in Figure 5-13 above, and you can proceed to adding the user to a post office, or you will see the following, indicating that the user is already a member of a GroupWise Post Office.

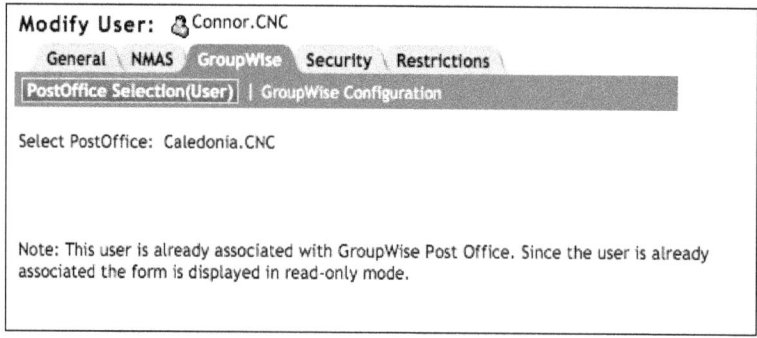

Figure 5-66: User already belongs to a post office.

There is currently no other functionality of the GroupWise iManager Plugin. For example, deleting a user in iManager will not delete the associated GroupWise User.

MMC Plugin

The GroupWise MMC Plugin installation is launched from **<installationfiles>\setup.exe**.

Follow the instructions below to install the plugin.

1. After launching **setup.exe**, choose GroupWise MMC Plugin,

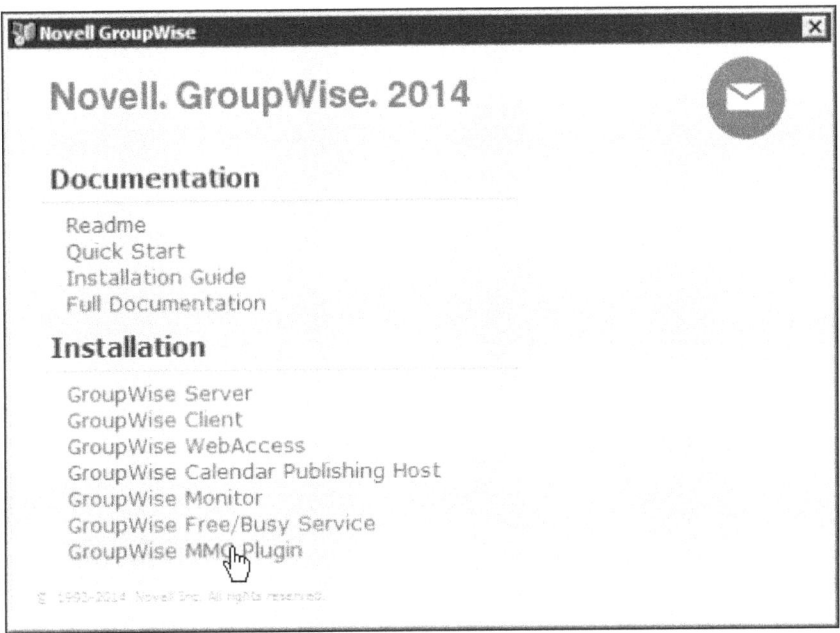

Figure 5-67: Launching the MMC Plugin Setup

2. Some redistributable runtimes will install. This can take a few minutes.
3. When prompted, select your language for installation.
4. Click next at the welcome screen.
5. Accept the license agreement
6. At the next screen you will see the installation options for the MMC plugin, which really are only whether you will actually install it, and the directory location for the installation. Click Next.

110 | Directory Integration and Synchronization

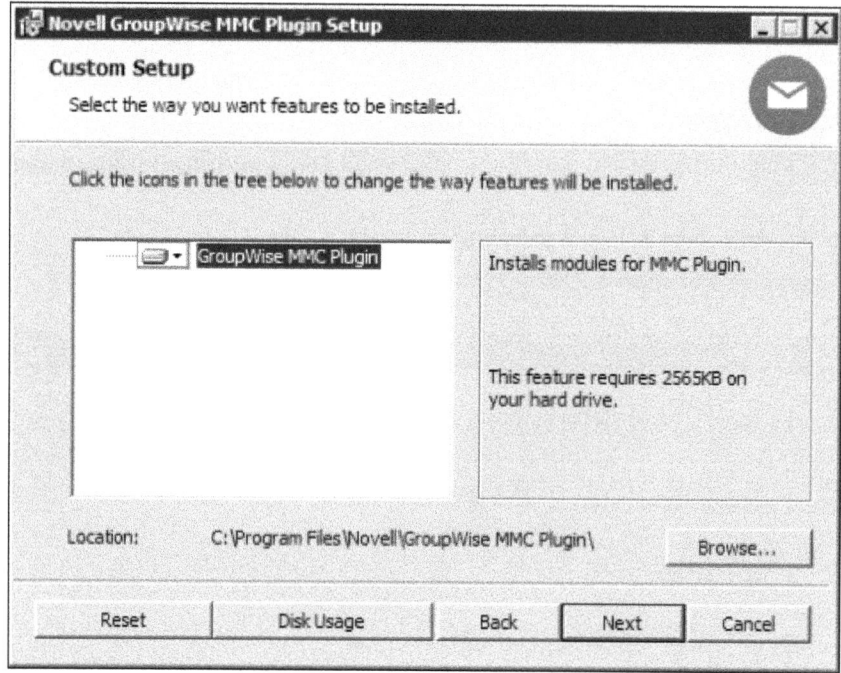

Figure 5-68: Custom Setup Screen

7. At the next screen click Install.
8. You will be at the completion screen. Keep the "Configure" box checked in the lower left, and click Finish.
9. At the next screen (you will configure your LDAP connection from MMC to the GroupWise Administration Service.

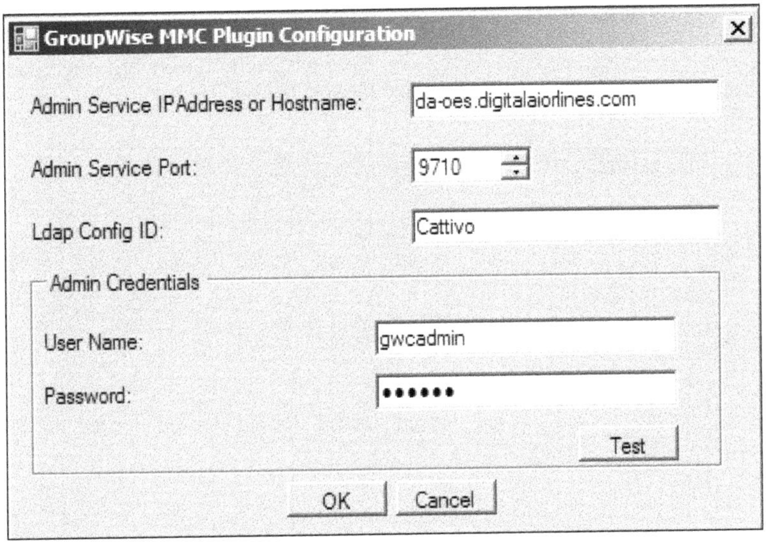

Figure 5-69:

- Enter GroupWise Admin Service URL: IP address or Host name of service
- Enter GroupWise Admin Service Port: 9710 by default
- Enter LDAP server ID: Directory Name
- Enter GroupWise Admin Username: gwadmin (per our installation)
- Enter GroupWise Admin Password: admin service password

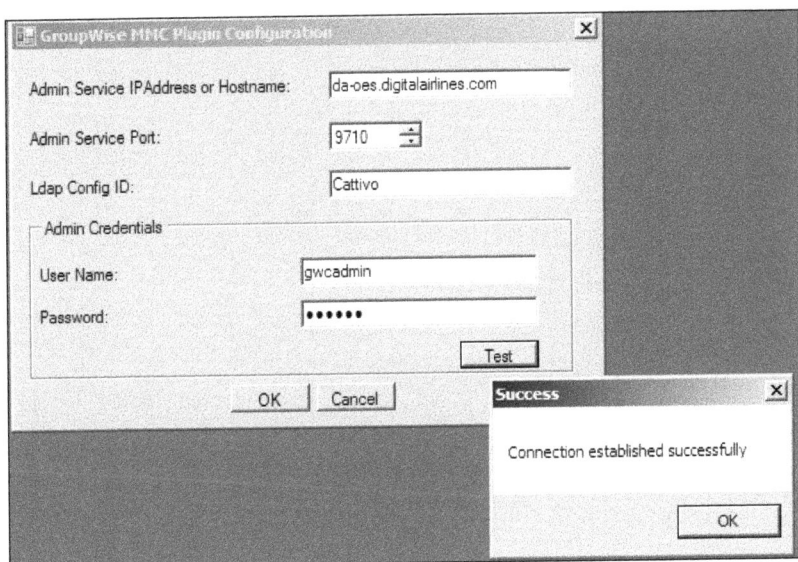

Figure 5-70: Successful Configuration

Using the MMC Plugin

In MMC, create your user as usual. Once you have passed the Password page you will be presented with the Select GroupWise Post Office Dialog below.

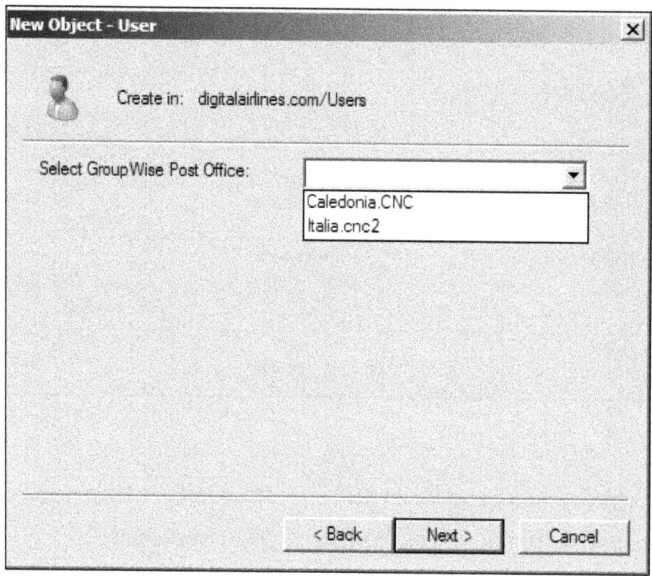

Figure 5-71: Adding User to Post Office

Once the user is added, you will receive a confirmation window telling you that the addition was successful.

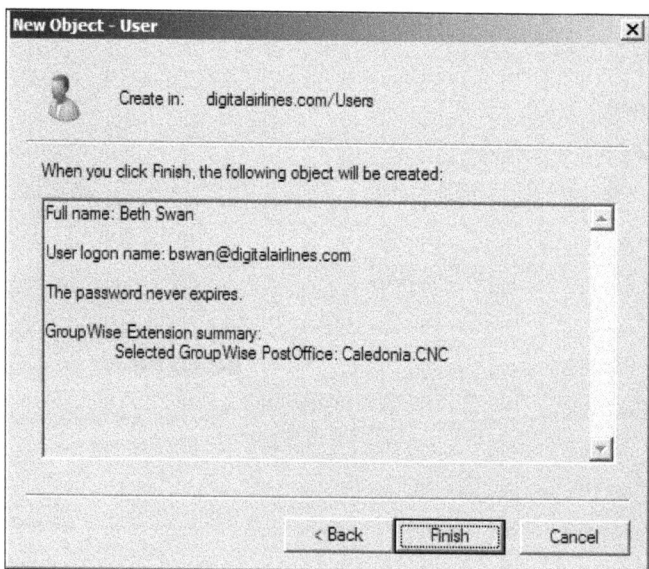

Figure 5-72: New Object Added

We can check this status by going to the GroupWise Administration Console. Follow the instructions in *"Launching the New Administration Console"* earlier in this chapter.

1. Click on Users
2. Find your user, in our case bswan.
3. On the General Tab for bswan, you will see that she has an LDAP GUID and has been added properly to the Post Office.

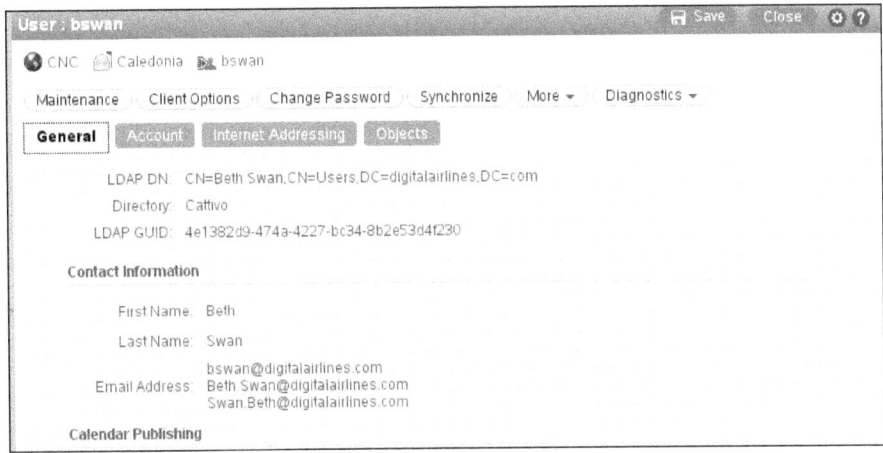

Figure 5-73: User Successfully Added to GroupWise Post Office

Cleaning up eDirectory

At some point in the future, far enough ahead that you know that you will no longer need ConsoleOne for anything GroupWise, you can do some cleanup. PLEASE do these steps in iManager or a copy of ConsoleOne with no snapins. (If we could make a PDF flash a warning, we would now). If you are attached to a GroupWise domain in ConsoleOne when deleting these objects, ConsoleOne will attempt to delete the object in the GroupWise system itself, and not merely from the eDirectory tree.

There are many GroupWise Only objects that can be removed from your eDirectory tree when you are confident that you will no longer need them. A few months from now, when you are in a tidying mood, you can delete any of the following:

- GroupWise Domains
- GroupWise Post Offices
- GroupWise MTAs
- GroupWise POAs
- GroupWise WebAccess Objects (more detail is given in the WebAccess chapter)
- GroupWise Distribution Lists
- GroupWise Resources
- GroupWise Libraries
- GroupWise External Entities

6 The GroupWise Administration Console

If you are familiar with the GroupWise Upgrade Guides that have been produced by Caledonia in the past, you will know that we generally only cover "upgrade" items. However, the new administration model for GroupWise 2014 is such a departure from what we as administrators have been accustomed to, that it really is important to discuss the administrative changes in much more detail than we ever have in the past. This is not an Administration Guide though, so we will not get into a lot of detail on routine GroupWise Administration. We simply wish to familiarize you with the look and feel of the new administration model, and point out some interesting new options.

First let's look at the components that are involved in the new GroupWise 2014 Administrative Model. They are:

- GroupWise Admin Service
- GroupWise Administration Console
- GroupWise Command Line Utilities
    - gwadmin-ipc
    - gwadminutil
    - gwcheck
- Redesign of some GroupWise related directory structures

Now we will look at these components in more detail

The GroupWise Admin Service

In prior versions of GroupWise, administration was accomplished through ConsoleOne (or even NWAdmin or ad.exe if we go back far enough). The administrator needed direct file access to a domain database in order to do domain level administration (configure system, create objects, perform directory maintenance), and also required direct file access to a post office database in order to perform post office or user level maintenance (run stand-alone GWChecks, document properties maintenance, etc.).

As ConsoleOne became deprecated in all other Novell products, largely being replaced by iManager, the need for direct file access kept GroupWise tied tightly to ConsoleOne. The need to access databases directly made the idea of a web based tool very difficult to accomplish.

Enter HTTP REST (Representational State Transfer). Now, the inner workings of REST go far beyond the scope of this guide. However, in a nutshell, Novell's implementation of REST for GroupWise 2014 allows instructions to be transmitted from the administrator's web browser to the admin service of a GroupWise agent. The REST service has a direct file connection to the database, similarly to how ConsoleOne accessed the database. The Administration Console sends information through REST to be written to the database.

For writing instructions such as creating users, configuring links, defining Internet Addressing and the like, the connection by the Admin Console is to the "Admin Service Port" of the MTA. For functions such as restarting an agent, the connection by the Admin Console is to the Admin Service Port for the POA or GWIA in question. Thus, as you configure your GroupWise 2014 system, each agent that you configure will receive a unique "admin port". The default ports for a given agent are:

- MTA: 9710
- POA: 9711

Thus, in addition to needing to configure things such as the MTP and HTTP ports for an MTA, you will also need an Admin port. The same goes for POAs. Like all other ports on a server, you can opt to not use the default ports, but really only should change them if you have a conflict.

The GroupWise Admin Service gathers the configured Admin ports for the agents on a given server, and feeds this information into the Admin Console to effect a connection between the administrator's web browser and the agents on the servers where the databases actually reside. In this way, GroupWise administration can be accomplished from any web browser that has access to the admin ports in question. Direct file access and mapped drives is, for the most part, no longer necessary.

Take for example, the act of rebuilding a secondary domain database. In ConsoleOne, the Administrator needed a mapped drive to both the location of the primary domain database and that of the secondary domain database. If this was impractical, the administrator could rebuild the secondary's domain database to a local drive and then somehow copy or transport it to the remote location. In GroupWise 2014, the Admin Service for the primary domain knows the IP addresses and port (location) of the Secondary Domain's Admin Service. The Primary Domain Admin Servers communicates the necessity to rebuild the Secondary Domain, and Admin Service at the remote location completes the task. In this example, the administrator may or may not be aware of the exact physical location of the post office. That really is of little concern in this situation, as the process is being completed by the Admin Services, and not a utility connected via mapped drives to both locations.

While it would be possible to nat through to these admin ports even from the Internet at large, it is recommended that sites use a VPN and LAN access for accessing GroupWise administration.

The GroupWise Administration Console

Be gone ConsoleOne! Music to some administrators' ears no doubt! Certainly, while Danita has played around a bit using ConsoleOne against a GroupWise 2014 domain, it is neither recommended nor supported by Novell. Once your GroupWise domain is upgraded to GroupWise 2014, you should no longer use ConsoleOne to manage those domain's objects. In fact when you install the GroupWise 2014 "server" on a Linux server, the GroupWise administration snapins are removed from ConsoleOne on that server. The Windows snapins stay, not because it's okay to use them on Windows, but because GroupWise snapins are not registered as an "installed" program in Windows and cannot be removed automatically during the installation.

Logging Into the Administration Console

First you must log into your Administration Console from your Web Browser. You can do that either by using the Icon on your Server Desktop (which is actually just a shortcut for your browser), or navigate directly to your Console by navigating to:

https://yourserver.com:9710

Figure 6-1: The Administration Console Login Windows

Figure 6-2 shows the main GroupWise Administrative Console screen.

Figure 6-2: The GroupWise Administration Console Dashboard

This guide is not a full GroupWise administration manual. That said, we want to make sure you can find your way around, and so we will point out instances where something has moved that might not be obvious.

Much of the Administration Console is hyperlinked so that you can move around from one location to a logical "next step" without having to "back out" to a new window. So, for example, if you are looking at a User (RobRoy in the image), there will be "breadcrumbs" at the top of the window that allow you to jump to the user's Post Office (in our case Caledonia) or the Domain (here CNC).

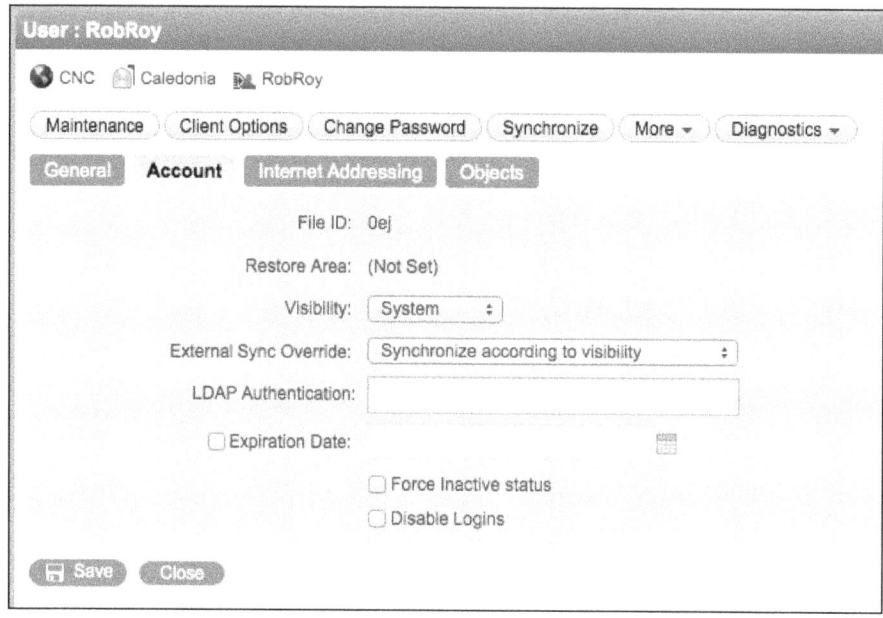

Figure 6-3: Navigating through the Administration Console

Check every opportunity you get to see if the name of an object is a link to assist in navigation.

For the rest of this chapter, we'll show you how to access items that might not seem so obvious.

Accessing Objects from the Dashboard

From the main Console Dashboard, you can click on any of the objects you see (domains, post offices, GWIAs) to be taken directly to that object. In the case of a Post Office, clicking on the Post Office name will take you to the Post Office settings, whereas clicking on the "status light" and then clicking the word POA will take you to the POA settings. Also, clicking on the indicator circle next to the object will link you directly to the http monitor for the agent.

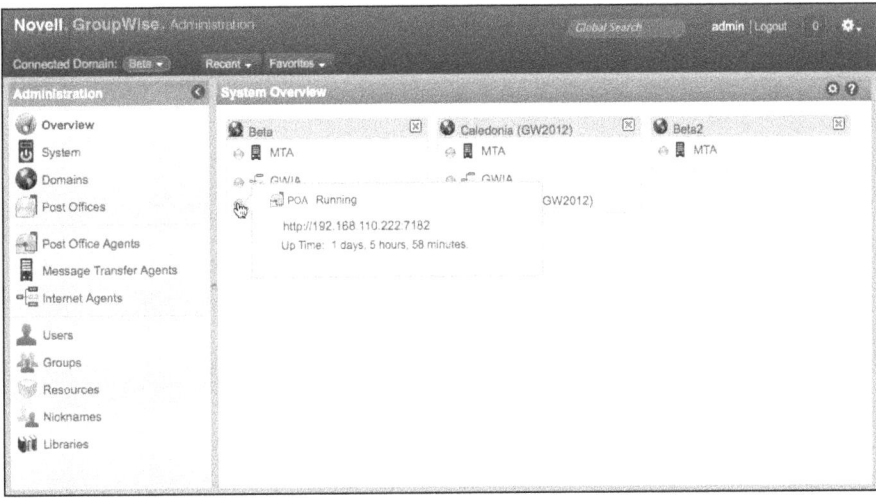

Figure 6-4: Access the HTTP Monitors directly from the Dashboard Overview

In a large GroupWise System, you may have more domains on this dashboard than you are interested in seeing. You can remove them by clicking the X in the grey bar associated with each domain. To restore a domain that you have removed, you can click the cog icon in the System Overview line.

Figure 6-5: Adding Domains to the Dashboard

You can also get to the Post Office or Post Office Agent settings, for example, by clicking on the desired object type in the left column, and then choosing the object in the resultant list. There are many, many ways to move about the Administration Console. No longer do you need to exit out of a range of windows only to need to open another set of windows to reach your destination. Of course, if you attempt to leave a window before saving a change, you will be reminded first!

Global Search

The Global Search field allows you to search for objects by name without the need to click through the menus. Search for a user, a post office, a group.

Context Specific Search

When accessing lists, such as Users or Post Offices or Groups, there is a context specific search box to the right above the list.

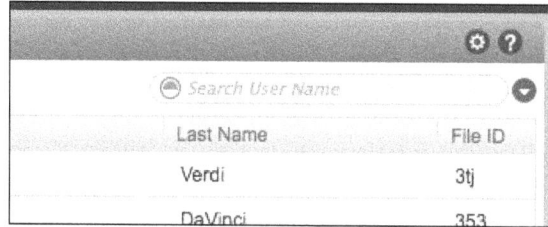

Figure 6-6: A Context Search Field.

Here you can type a single letter, part of a name, etc. to narrow down the list. There are, however, many more things you can do from this field.

Type Control-Space while in this field, and a popup appears to show you variables that can be searched.

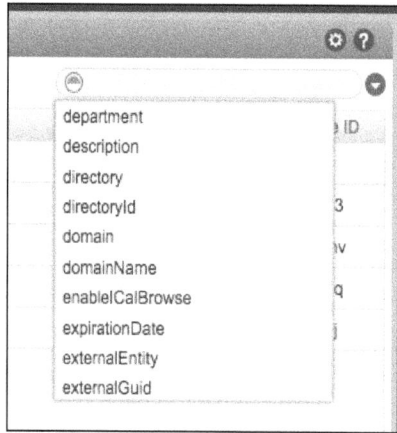

Figure 6-7: Context search popup

Thus you could search for the user with a specific FID, or find all Post Offices with client lock-out dates.

Export

Any list type of view can be exported to csv. You can add columns to the list by clicking on the cog icon above the search field (See Figure 6-6 above). Thus, you could export a list of users, including last login date, or mailbox size. Or a list of post offices, with time zone listings. No longer must you use complicated log parsing to let a list of valuable information.

Quick Lists

At the top of the Administration Console, you will find a list of recent used items, as well as a favorites list you can build to get to your most needed items quickly.

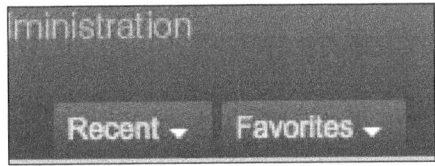

Figure 6-8: Accessing Useful Lists

System Settings

In ConsoleOne, the System Settings were found under Tools|GroupWise System Operations. In the Administration Console, they are simply under System. Additionally, many entries that were under Tools|GroupWise Utilities have also been relocated the System Settings.

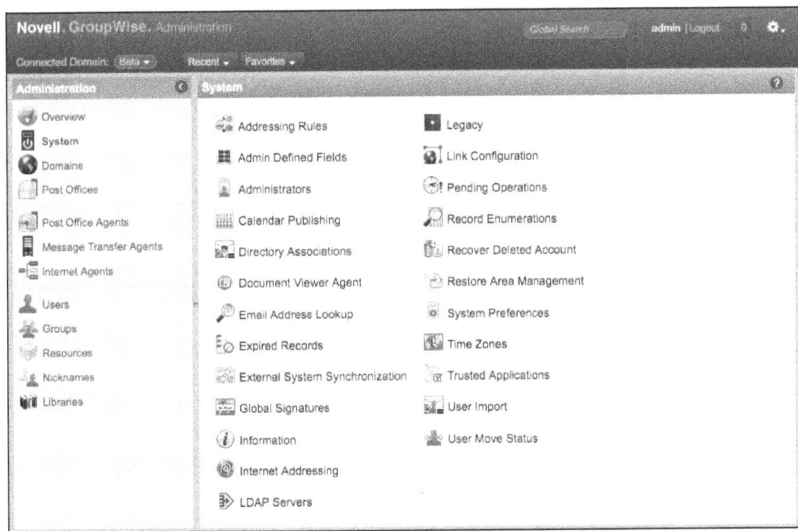

Figure 6-9: GroupWise System Settings

Most of the items you found under GroupWise System Operations in ConsoleOne can be found here, as well as some new items. We will not go over each of these items. Most of them will be obvious if you compare them with ConsoleOne. Let's look at a few of the newer and/or relocated items.

Administrators

When you upgraded your Primary Domain, you were prompted to create a GroupWise Administrator for your system. We suggested that you name this user something like gwadmin.

Here you can assign any GroupWise user to be a System level administrator. This is the similar in eDirectory to giving a user "Admin" equivalence. The System level administrator has all rights to the system as the original administrator your created during your upgrade.

Any administrator you assign uses his or her GroupWise credentials to authenticate.

Directory Associations

This is a new entry for facilitating mass association of Directory users (eDirectory or Active Directory) and GroupWise users. This is discussed in detail in *"Directory Integration and Synchronization"* on page 61.

Document Viewer Agents

In GroupWise 2014, Document Viewer agents become system objects that can then be assigned to Post Offices. When you upgraded your GroupWise Post Offices, if Document Viewer Agents were found on the Post Office servers, they continue to be utilized. If, however, you upgraded a Post Office that did not have a GWDVA installed, no GWDVA was configured, and you must manually create the object and attach it to your POA. We discuss this in *"Configuring and Verifying a DVA for your Post Office"* on page 141.

Email Address Lookup

This option allows you to enter an email address in the search field, and quickly find out which user this belongs to. At present, however, if the result is a nickname, you cannot quickly see here who the nickname belongs to

Legacy

This location contains Gateway objects (such as WebAccess Agents) and Software Distribution Directories. Once you no longer have any need for these objects, you can delete them here.

Link Configuration

In ConsoleOne, Link Configuration included Post Office Links. Post Office Links have been moved to the Domain settings, and will not be found here.

User Import

This setting allows you to import GroupWise users from an LDAP directory. Choose the users from the Directory for whom you wish to create accounts, and voila!

Domain Settings

When you click on Domains, you can see all of the Domains in your system. There are a couple of items under Domains that will seem new to you.

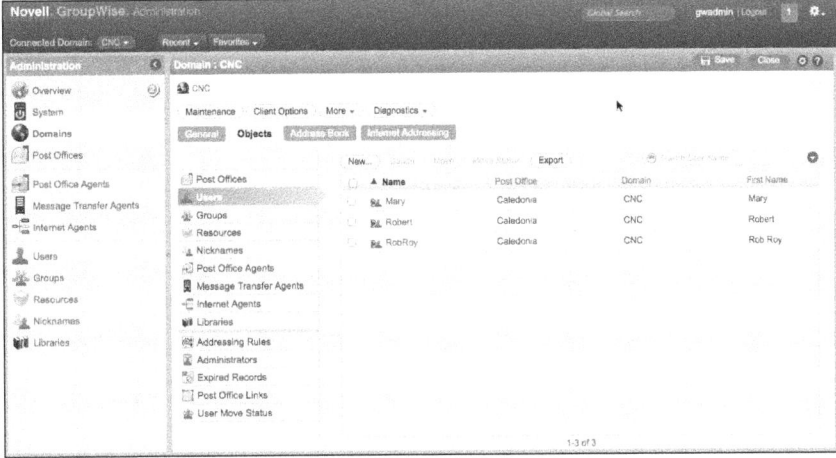

Figure 6-10: Domain Items

Administrators

You can assign any GroupWise user to be a domain administrator. This allows the user to manage all aspects of the Domain.

Post Office Links

In ConsoleOne, Post Office Links were found under "Link Configuration". These links are defined now under the Domain object.

Maintenance

In ConsoleOne, you accessed Maintenance in a separate Window. All Domain maintenance is now available right from the Domain object.

Client Options

In addition to the Client Options that you are familiar with, the new settings for Client Auto-Update are also accessed here. We discuss Client Auto-Update settings in *"Upgrading GroupWise Clients"*.

Message Transfer Agents

You should be able to find your way around the MTA settings without too much difficulty. There are some new options here.

General

In the General Tab, you have the ability to control the agent (Start/Stop) and also launch directly into the HTTP Monitor from this screen.

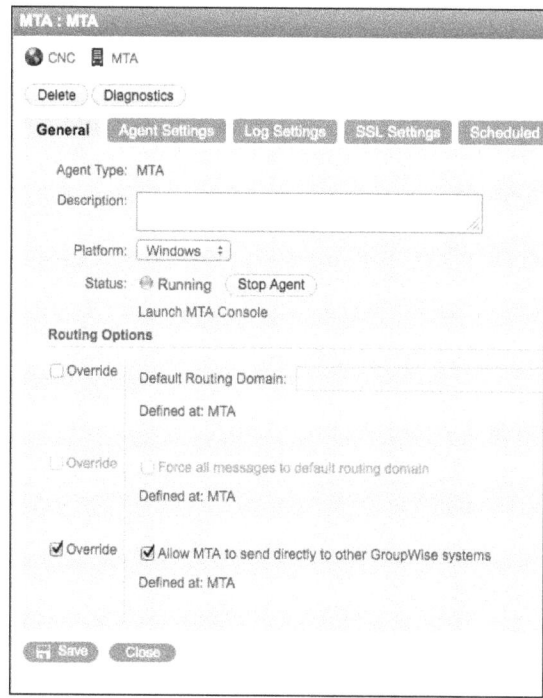

Figure 6-11: The MTA General Tab

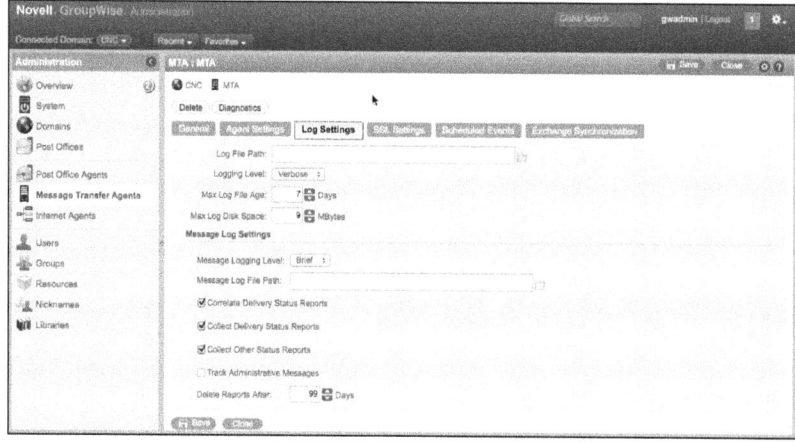

Figure 6-12: MTA Log Settings

Post Office Settings

Items are laid out a bit differently in the Post Office settings, but should not be difficult to navigate.

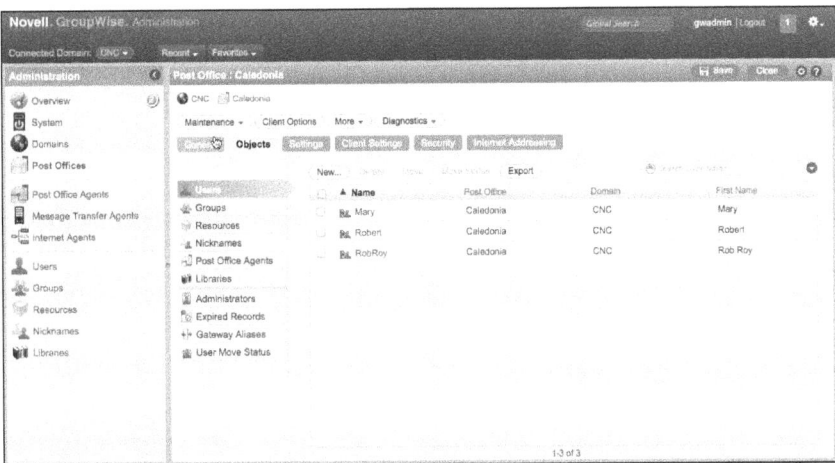

Figure 6-13: Post Office Settings

Administrators

You can assign any GroupWise user to be a post office administrator. This allows the user to manage all aspects of the Post Office.

Maintenance

In ConsoleOne, you accessed Maintenance in a separate Window. All Post Office maintenance is now available right from the Post Office object. This includes both Post Office database maintenance, and Mailbox/Library Maintenance for the entire Post Office.

Client Options

In addition to the Client Options that you are familiar with, the new settings for Client Auto-Update are also accessed here. We discuss Client Auto-Update settings in *"Upgrading GroupWise Clients"*.

Replicate (Formerly Synchronize)

As you move through the objects of your GroupWise system, one of the options you will see under **More** is **Replicate**.

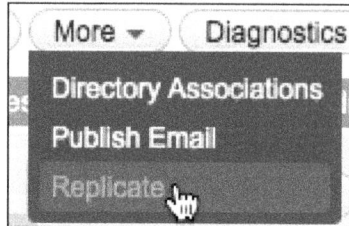

Figure 6-14: The Replicate function

This is not a new function. It's simply the former "Synchronize" renamed. This will take the information for the object and replicate it through the GroupWise system, just as the former Synchronize command did. This function name was changed to avoid confusion with the new "Directory Synchronization" for integration with eDirectory and Active Directory.

Post Office Agents

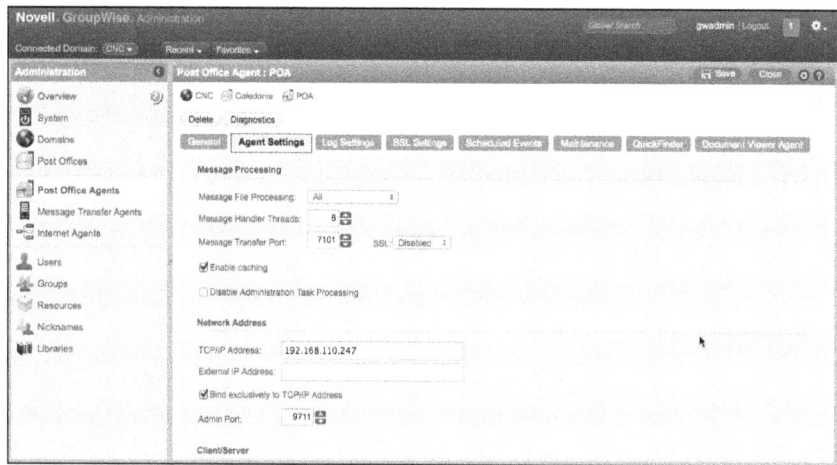

Figure 6-15: Post Office Agent Settings

General

From the General Tab of the Post Office Agent, you can start and stop the agent (just click on the Stop/Start Agent button). From here you can also launch directly into the POA HTTP Monitor.

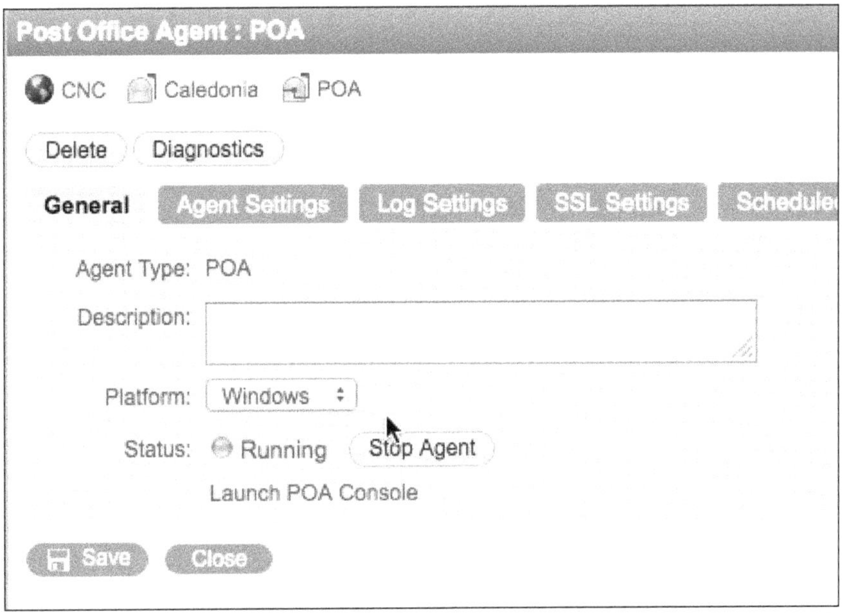

Figure 6-16: The POA General Tab

Agent Settings

While the Post Office Agent settings are easy to maneuver, you will notice that the Network Address for the agents has moved to the Agent Settings tab.

Document Viewer Agents

The Document Viewer Agent tab allows you to assign DVAs to your Post Office, and better load balance the indexing and rendering of agents. We discuss the Document Viewer Agent settings in more detail in *"Configuring and Verifying a DVA for your Post Office"* on page 141.

Groups

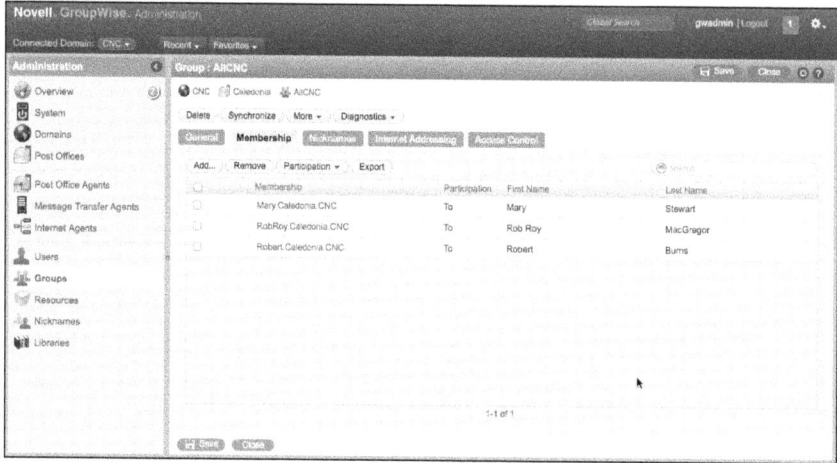

Figure 6-17: Group Settings

GroupWise Distribution Lists have been changed back to simply "Groups", which they were before the merging with eDirectory with GroupWise 5.0.

Clicking the Access Control Tab of Groups allows to you limit who can send to a particular Group, and also assign users to administer the Group.

Command Line Utilities

Of all of the changes for GroupWise 2014, the command line utilities are the most unexpected for some. Since the beginning of GroupWise (really all the way back to the beginnings of WordPerfect Office), we've had direct database access in one form or another. From GENOFF to AD.EXE to NWADMIN to ConsoleOne, there was a direct link from the administration tool to the database in question. Granted GENOFF was a command line tool itself, so one could say we've come full circle with GroupWise 2014!

The web based Administration Console has been long awaited and much clamored for. Not that it is here, it poses some particular problems when dealing with many of the database functions for GroupWise 2014. The Administration Console connects to the domain database through a REST connection, which allows it to generate commands directly to the database it is controlling. This does allow for database maintenance for objects that are controlled by a REST process. For example, a GroupWise 2014 Post Office database can be rebuilt from the Administration Console, but a GroupWise 2012 or older Post Office database owned by a 2014 domain requires rebuilding from the command line. During your upgrade especially, but also in some special administrative situations, you will be required to perform actions at the command line using one of various command line utilities available. We'll go over these now. Please note: This is not an Administration Guide. We're not attempting to cover every single aspect of GroupWise Administration here. We simply wish to show you the new functionality of the command line and point out where things are different than you might expect. If you need further information there are great resources such as:

- Novell GroupWise Documentation (http://novell.com/documentation/groupwise2014)

- The Caledonia GroupWise Power Administrator Resource (http://caledonia.net/register)

So, on to the command line utilities. If you navigate to your **<serverfiles>/admin** directory you will see the following objects:

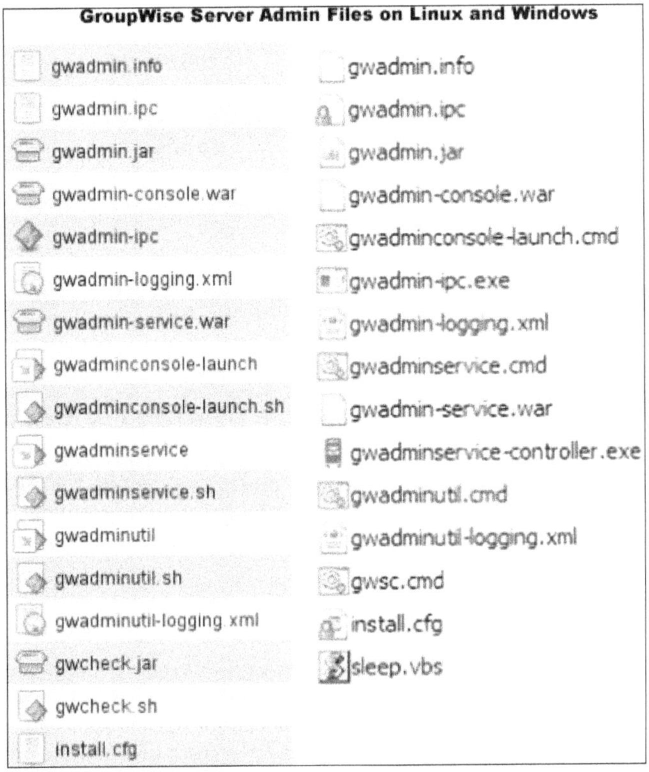

GroupWise Server Admin Files on Linux and Windows	
gwadmin.info	gwadmin.info
gwadmin.ipc	gwadmin.ipc
gwadmin.jar	gwadmin.jar
gwadmin-console.war	gwadmin-console.war
gwadmin-ipc	gwadminconsole-launch.cmd
gwadmin-logging.xml	gwadmin-ipc.exe
gwadmin-service.war	gwadmin-logging.xml
gwadminconsole-launch	gwadminservice.cmd
gwadminconsole-launch.sh	gwadmin-service.war
gwadminservice	gwadminservice-controller.exe
gwadminservice.sh	gwadminutil.cmd
gwadminutil	gwadminutil-logging.xml
gwadminutil.sh	gwsc.cmd
gwadminutil-logging.xml	install.cfg
gwcheck.jar	sleep.vbs
gwcheck.sh	
install.cfg	

Figure 6-18: The Server Admin Directory

We will explain the important utilities here, as they relate to your Upgrade and how they might differ from prior administration. Remember also that some of these functions are also available within the Administration Console (i.e., validating databases and the like). We will go over them here from the command line as well, for thoroughness.

gwadminutil

gwadmintuil is used for all of the functions that were in Tools|GroupWise Utilities|System Maintenance in Console One. This includes rebuilding databases, merging systems, releasing domains, etc. In order to see all of the functions available with **gwadminutil**, simply type **gwadminutil** at the command line:

windermere:/opt/novell/groupwise/admin # ./gwadminutil.sh

GroupWise Admin Command Line Utility (14.0.0.114855)

Usage: gwadminutil <command>

Commands:

validate	**setadmin**
recover	**upgrade**
reclaim	**ca**
reindex	**certinst**
rebuild	**dbinfo**
sync	**installcfg**
convert	**services**
release	**config**
merge	

All of the command line utilities have a modicum of instructions built in by simply invoking the command. For example, to find out usage for a rebuild, simply type **gwadminutil rebuild** will explain that the usage is:

example: **gwadminutil rebuild -d /gw/dom1 -n Dom1.Po1 -o /tmp/po1 -cd**

This will rebuild Po1, belonging to Dom1 (which is located at **/gw/dom1**). It will rebuild the post office to **/tmp/po1** and create the necessary directory structure for the PO, including the dc files. The path **/tmp/po1** must exist. In other words, this would essentially create a new post office directory for a severely damaged PO.

Rebuilding a Secondary Domain Database

During your upgrade we instruct you to validate your Secondary Domain database. The can be done in ConsoleOne, connected to the Secondary Domain. If the validation fails, you must rebuild the Secondary Domain from the Primary. You cannot run the rebuild from ConsoleOne, and you cannot rebuild a database lower than version 2014 from the Administration Console. Thus you must run the rebuild from the **gwadminutil** utility on the Primary Domain server. If you have the ability to connect to both servers at the same time (map a drive from the Primary Domain server to the Secondary Domain server in Windows, or mount the volume containing the Secondary Domain from the Primary Domain Linux server), you can rebuilt "in place". Otherwise you can rebuild the Secondary Domain database to a temporary location on the local drive of the Primary Domain server, and copy the resultant **wpdomain.db** file to the Secondary Domain location. The command to rebuild the Secondary Domain is, for example:

gwadminutil rebuild -d /grpwise/domains/cnc -n cnc2 -o /tmp/cnc22

Once you have the new **wpdomain.db** file in **/tmp/cnc2**, you can copy that file to the actual directory for the domain CNC. The **/tmp/cnc2** folder must exist.

Validating or Rebuilding a Post Office Database

Similarly to rebuilding a domain database above, you may be called upon during your upgrade to rebuild a post office database.

During your upgrade we instruct you to validate your post office database. If the domain and post office are on the same server, we suggest that you check them both at the same time from ConsoleOne. Even if the domain and post office are on different servers, this can often be done prior to upgrading the domain, provided that you do not intend to wait very long between the upgrades.

If you must validate and possibly rebuild the post office database after the owning domain is already at version 2014, it becomes more complicated. You either need to have access to both the domain and post office directories at the same time, or you can copy the **wphost.db** file to a temporary directory on the domain server. To validate a post office, run the following command:

gwadminutil validate /path

This will of course be either the actual path, if you have access to it from the domain server, or a temporary path where you have copied the **wphost.db** file.

If the validation fails, you will need to rebuild the database. If you have the ability to connect to both servers at the same time (map a drive from the Domain server to the Post Office Domain server in Windows, or mount the volume containing the Post Office from the Domain Linux server), you can rebuilt "in place". Otherwise you can rebuild the Post Office database to a temporary location on the local drive of the Domain server, and copy the resultant **wphost.db** file to the Post Office location. The command to rebuild the Post Office is, for example:

gwadminutil rebuild -d /grpwise/domains/cnc2 -n cnc2.italia -o /tmp/italia

Once you have the new **wphost.db** file in **/tmp/italia**, you can copy that file to the actual directory for the post office Italia. The **/tmp/italia** folder must exist.

Checking Your Database Version

During the upgrade we generally tell administrators to look at the database version of their domains and post offices in the Administration Console. You can also do this with **gwadmintul**.

gwadminutil dbinfo /grpwise/domains/beta

returns

System Name: CNCMAIL

System GUID: EC08E830-FE29-0097-B7C3-02608CA65E03

Name: Beta

Database Version: 1400

Admin Service: 192.168.110.222:9999

gwadmin-ipc

In the chapter on *"Installing the GroupWise Administration Service"*, we used **gwadmin-ipc** a number of times to authenticate the installation token. Should this file be missing or damaged, you would not be able to access the Installation Console. Some other functions of the **gwadmin-ipc** include:

a. gwadmin-ipc query to give you status of gwadmin services;

```
gwlinux:/opt/novell/groupwise/admin # ./gwadmin-ipc query
151.155.136.215:9713=>Italia.CNC2(/grpwise/pos/italia)
151.155.136.215:9710=>CNC(/grpwise/domains/cnc)
151.155.136.215:9712=>CNC2(/grpwise/domains/cnc2)
151.155.136.215:9711=>Caledonia.CNC(/grpwise/pos/calpo)
```

b. can use it to manually add/remove an adminservice listener. This is mostly for clustering.

/opt/novell/groupwise/admin/gwadmin-ipc start utah cluster

gwcheck.sh

The **gwcheck.sh** has not changed from prior versions. You can still launch mailbox/library maintenance from the Administration Console on individual users or entire post offices. You can also use **gwcheck.sh** as a command line tool. We like using the command line version for specific tasks:

- watching for a specific expected error to occur, rather than waiting for a log file to be emailed.
- checking a specific database (for example, msg201.db)
- scripting gwcheck

The remaining utilities in the **<serverfiles>/admin** folder are used the by the admin service itself and are rarely accessed by mere mortals.

Connecting to other Domain Administration Consoles

In ConsoleOne, we frequently would need to "Connect" to a different Domain database. You would simply right-click on a Domain and choose "Connect". You might do this to compare settings to make sure that address book listings were the same from all domains.

The "domain database" connection in GroupWise 2014 is not through direct access to a database as it was in ConsoleOne. Rather it is through the Admin Service running on the Domain server.

If you wish to connect to a different domain's Admin Service, you simply follow these steps:

Click on the dropdown list at the top of your Administration Console, and choose the Domain's Admin Service. You will only see GroupWise 2014 domains in the list. If you need connect to a database prior to GroupWise 2014 (perhaps to check directory synchronization or other listings), you must use ConsoleOne for your connection.

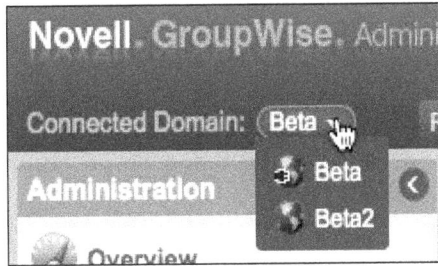

Figure 6-19: Changing the Domain

Reinstalling ConsoleOne Snapins on Linux

While we've cautioned against using ConsoleOne for day-to-day administration, you may find yourself in a situation where you really need to access the GroupWise system via ConsoleOne. The Administration Service installation does not remove the snapins on Windows, but it does on Linux. Should you find yourself in a bind, and you really need them, you must install them manually with the rpm. This is very simple!

This assumes you have kept ConsoleOne on your server. If not, you will need to first go to your /consoleone directory of your older GroupWise software and install ConsoleOne.

With ConsoleOne installed on the server, change to the /admin folder of your older GroupWise media. you will see a novell-groupwise-admin-<version>.rpm file. To install type this:

rpm -Uvh novell-groupwise-admin-<version>.rpm

When you get to "admin" you can just press tab and then entire file name should be completed for you. That's it. GroupWise snapins should be active again. Remember, this is only a "last resort" solution for when there simply isn't a way to complete a task or fix a problem with the Administration Console!

7 Upgrading GroupWise Post Offices

Upgrading your post offices is very similar to upgrading domains. There are just a few things to keep in mind about your upgrade:

- Your post office cannot be upgraded until the domain that owns the post office is at GroupWise 2014.
- You should use the version of GWCheck that is designed for your version of GroupWise. Thus, if you have multiple post offices and will not upgrade them all at the same time, make sure you have not only your GroupWise 2014 GWCheck available, but also that you keep the older standalone versions of GWCheck on hand until you have upgraded those older post offices.
- The GWIA, while an SMTP server, also serves as a client when it is used for IMAP4 and POP3. Once you upgrade your GWIA to GroupWise 2014, you will only be able to use POP3 and IMAP4 to GroupWise 2014 post offices.
- If you upgrade a post office to GroupWise 2014 and that post office owns users who typically proxy to other users on older GroupWise post offices, you will not be able to upgrade those users' clients until all post offices are upgraded.
- If you have multiple post offices, you will need to wait on upgrading WebAccess until all of the post offices have been upgraded, or use two separate WebAccess servers to handle both versions of GroupWise.

So, as you can see, it's a good idea to get your post offices upgraded to GroupWise 2014 on a scheduled roll-out so that you are not surprised by any of the possible issues with mixed post offices. That said, may sites operate in a "mixed" system quite nicely for an extended period of time. You must simply make sure that your plans take the above caveats into account.

How Does the Upgrade Work?

At the post office level, a GroupWise upgrade is really just a database conversion from one version to another. The former GroupWise post office database, is RECOVERED by the Admin Service's administrative thread and CONVERTED to the new version. This requires three simple components:

- The domain that owns the post office in question must already be upgraded to GroupWise 2014.
- The Post Office Agent software must be at GroupWise version 14
- The dc (dictionary files) in the post office directory must be at version 14

We realize that this sounds simplistic, but it really is quite simple. When you upgrade your post office, you are simply recreating your post office database to be a GroupWise 2014 database.

If you are moving from GroupWise 7 or later to GroupWise 2014, there are no structural changes outside of the post office database to be concerned with. However, if you are upgrading from GroupWise 6.5 or earlier, you will notice an interesting new feature. Prior to GroupWise 7, GroupWise had 25 message databases in the ofmsg directory structure. These are shared databases that are randomly divided amongst your users, no matter how many users are on a post office. Upon creation, a user is assigned to a message database, and all mail "sent" from that user goes into this database number. In GroupWise 6.5 and earlier, a post office with 50 users ends up with the same number of message databases as a post office with 5000 users!

This was not a huge issue for many years. However, as the usage of e-mail increased over time, these databases grew larger and larger. While GroupWise seemed to handle the bloat of the databases just fine itself, it started to cause issues for backup software, the time it took to perform a GWCheck, etc., etc. Additionally, FLAIM databases (which all GroupWise user and message databases are) have a limit of 4 GB per database. Thus, it has become more important over time to distribute the data over a larger number of databases to prevent database files from reaching the FLAIM limit.

With GroupWise 7, Novell increased the number of message databases to 255. This allows for better load balancing of the message store. There are some interesting side effects of this change though that are important to know about. If you are upgrading to GroupWise 2014 from GroupWise 6.5 or earlier, users will be reassigned to these new database numbers immediately. For example, Danita's database went from being number 21 under GroupWise 6.5 to number 91 under GroupWise 7. As mentioned, this is an immediate change. As soon as a user logs into the GroupWise 2014 post office (regardless of the client version) and sends a message, that message will be saved into the new database. All previous messages will remain in the former message database. So, in the case of Danita, she now has messages linked in her sent items to both **msg21.db** and **msg91.db**.

While this is mostly a technical discussion, and doesn't really impact your users in any noticeable way, you should know what happens if you have post offices at a version older than GroupWise 7 that you do not upgrade right away. You will start to see these newer, higher numbered databases appearing even in GroupWise 6.5 or earlier post offices. This is due to how the GroupWise system works. If Danita sends a message to a user on a different post office, the message is placed in **msg91.db** on Danita's post office. That message is then sent through the MTAs to the second post office, and when it is saved, it is placed in **msg91.db** on THAT post office. This poses no problems. The older post office agents will look into any database that is referenced in a message header. The important thing to remember is that this is normal and you should not be concerned when you see these "oddly" numbered databases in the older post office directories. Be careful not to assume that these files are not needed and get too tidy and delete them!

Enabling SOAP

Prior to GroupWise 2012, SOAP only needed to be enabled if you were running the GroupWise Mobile Server, the DataSynchronizer Mobility Server, or another third party product that requires SOAP access. With GroupWise 2014, it will be a very rare occurrence to not need SOAP enabled for your post offices. Not only do the aforementioned processes require SOAP access, but WebAccess requires SOAP to be enabled at the POA in order for WebAccess to function. Thus, it will be important for almost all Post Office Agents to support SOAP. Follow these steps to enable SOAP for all post offices that will have users who access GroupWise via WebAccess:

In ConsoleOne, click on the GroupWise System Globe, and perform the following steps:

1. In the dropdown list that shows "Users", change the setting to "Post Office Agents."
2. Find the POA for your post office, right-click and choose Properties.
3. Now click on the triangle in the GroupWise tab and change to Network Address.
4. Make sure that there is a port listed for SOAP for your Post Office Agent. The default SOAP port is 7191.
5. Now, on the GroupWise tab, change to the Agent Settings screen. Verify that SOAP is enabled for the POA.
6. Save your changes.

Preparing the Post Office Database

When you are ready to continue your upgrade, we will first check the post office database to make sure that it is ready to upgrade. If you will be upgrading a Domain at the same time as your Post Office, you can do the verification in ConsoleOne. In ConsoleOne, select the post office object and choose **Tools|GroupWise Utilities|System Maintenance|Validate Database**. If your database shows as valid, you can proceed. If for some reason the database does NOT validate, you should rebuild it. In order to rebuild the database you must first shut down the POA and make sure that no users can attach to the post office directly. At this point, we are going to shut down the post office agent for the upgrade anyway, so if you need to rebuild your database, first follow the instructions immediately below on shutting down your post office agent. Once the post office agent is shut down, return to ConsoleOne and choose **Tools|GroupWise Utilities|System Maintenance**, and this time choose Rebuild Database.

If the domain that owns this post office has already been upgraded on a different server, you must do the validation from the owning domain's GroupWise 2014 server at the command line. Please see the section entitled *"Validating or Rebuilding a Post Office Database"* on page 130 to prepare your post office database.

Upgrading Your Post Office

In the *"Installing the GroupWise Administration Service"* chapter, you installed the software required to take your post office to GroupWise 2014, but your post office has not actually upgraded. This will not happen until you run the Upgrade wizard from the Installation Console. If you are upgrading a Domain and Post Office at the same time, please go to *"Domain With Post Office (GWIA optional)"* on page 52 section to complete your upgrade.

If your Post Office is on a server without a domain, continue with these instructions.

138 | Upgrading GroupWise Post Offices

Back in the *"Installing the GroupWise Administration Service"* on page 25, we loaded up the Installation Console after installing the Administration Service. Now we need to look at the upgrade steps for our system.

Hopefully you set your Installation configuration to use "user" mode as we described in "Changing the Installation Console Access Method". Otherwise you will need to follow the "token" instructions above in that section to access the Installation Console (assuming it's been more than 5 minutes since you completed the installation of the files and received your first token).

1. Go to **https://yourserver:9710/gwadmin-console/install**

    We have set our installation mode to "user", so we can login with our "gwinstall" user we defined above.

Figure 7-1: The Installation Login Screen

2. We now see the Installation options screen

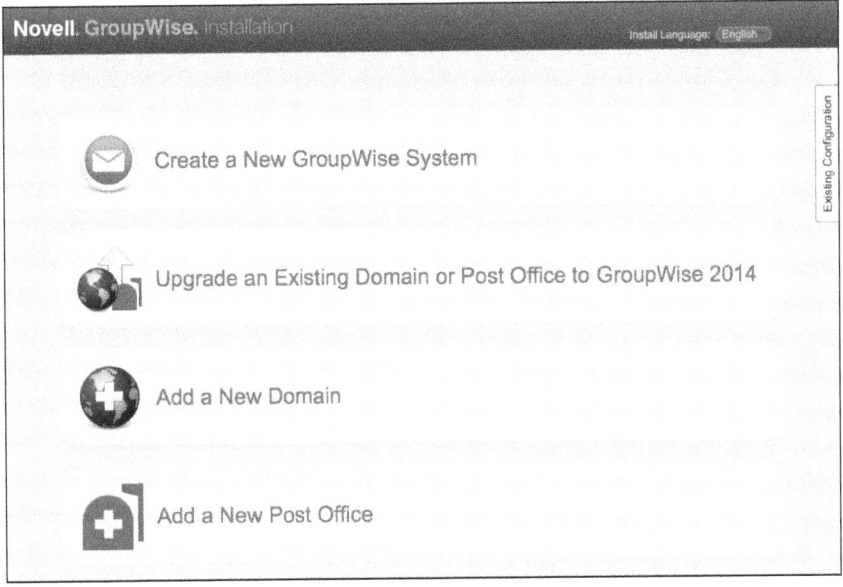

Figure 7-2: Installation Options

3. Click on "Upgrade an Existing Domain or Post Office to GroupWise 2014". In our figure below, when we click on the "Upgrade" option, we see our post office called Caledonia.

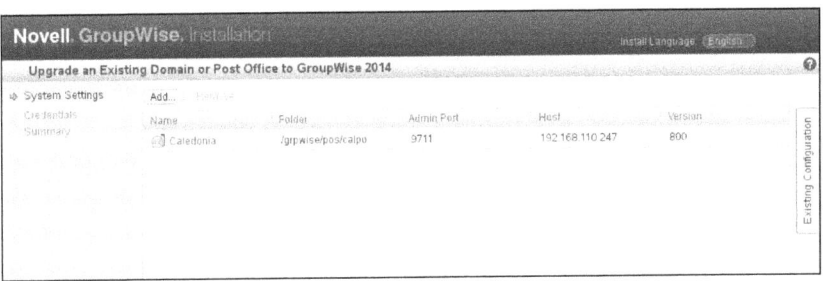

Figure 7-3: Post Office to upgrade

This lists the path of our post office, the Admin Port that has been assigned, the IP address or host name of the server is listed, and the version shows as 800.

1. With your post office properly listed in the upgrade section, click Next.

    You will be prompted for location and credentials of your Primary Domain admin service (unless for some reason it is also in the upgrade list).

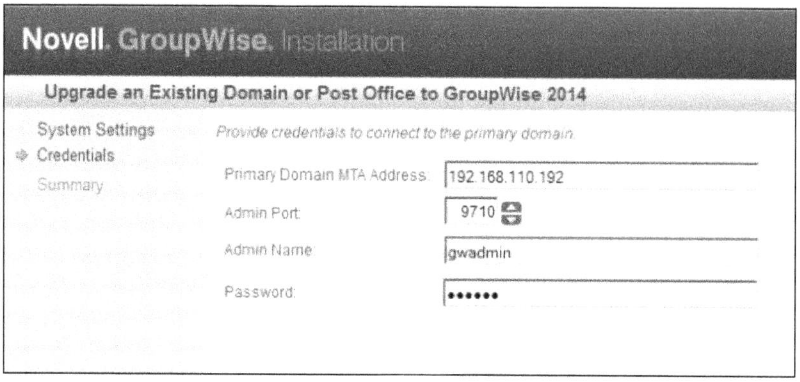

140 | Upgrading GroupWise Post Offices

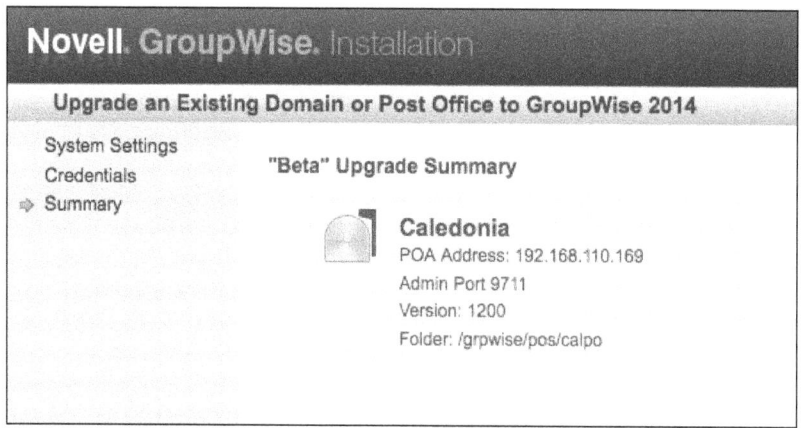

Figure 7-4: Connecting to the Primary Domain to complete an upgrade

2. You will now see a summary screen. In the figure below, our GroupWise system is called "Beta", so you see the name of the system, the post office to upgrade, and the settings for the post office.

Figure 7-5: The Upgrade Summary Screen

Click Finish to complete the upgrade. In the background, the Administrative Service will prepare the post office for upgrading and launch the POA to complete the process.

The Admin Service, MTA and POA all have the ability to upgrade the pertinent databases. The process for upgrading is thus: in the Installation Console, you choose the databases to be upgraded. The installation process then copies the 2014 dictionary (dc) files to the pertinent directories, and instructs the Admin Server to proceed to upgrade. The dc file is essentially a text file that contains the database schema for creating a GroupWise 2014 database. The **gwpo.dc** shows the version number at the very top line as #VERSION=1400. This version number at the top of the file verifies that you have the GroupWise 2014 dc file in your post office directory. The Admin Service looks at the database to see if it is eligible to upgrade (i.e., the owning domain has already been upgraded). The Admin Service will launch a recovery of the database, effectively converting the post office to GroupWise 2014. You will see a notice to restart your MTAs and POAs, and a link to access your Administration Console. However, the URL in the link presented to you is for the local server. Since we are upgrading a Post Office on a server that is remote from its domain, there is no access to the Administration Console on the URL you are given. You will need to access the URL for your domain server instead.

In our experience, a restart is not required.

Geek note: the MTA and POA still have the ability to upgrade the databases as well, but it's a job that's been officially delegated to the Admin Service.

If you are watching during the upgrade procedure, you will see the **creating.dbb** and **recover.dbb** files described above temporarily in the post office directory. Here's an example

```
-rw-r--r--  1 root root  39983 Jan 27 14:15 0127gwbk.001
-rw-r--r--  1 root root 301056 Feb  5 15:37 creating.ddb
-rw-r--r--  1 root root    877 Feb  5 15:37 dzrec.log
    .
    .
    .
    .
-rw-r--r--  1 root root 784384 Feb  5 15:37 recover.ddb
-rw-r--r--  1 root root      4 Sep 27 14:11 uid.run
```

To verify that the post office is version 14, you will launch the Administration Console and check the version in the properties of the domain. We'll do this below in the *"Verifying the Upgrade"* section below.

Verifying the Upgrade

When you completed your upgrades in the sections above, go to the section on *"Verifying the Upgrade"* on page 55 in the *"Upgrading GroupWise Domains"* chapter to check on your upgrade.

Configuring and Verifying a DVA for your Post Office

If you are upgrading from GroupWise 2012, it is likely that you have a GroupWise Document Viewer Agent installed on your server, and the upgrade would have simply upgraded the GWDVA executables, and the GWDVA will continue to work as always. If, however, you upgraded from GroupWise 8, you may or may not have a GroupWise Document Viewer Agent configured. You can check this on your upgraded server.

- On Linux, run **rcgrpwise status.** If a DVA is installed and configured, it will be clearly visible in the list of running agents.
- On Windows, go to the Administration Tools|Services. If a DVA is installed and configured, it will be listed in services as GroupWise DVA.

If there is no DVA running, we will install one.

1. From a Terminal Window/Command Prompt, change to the **<serverfiles>\admin** directory
2. run the following command (if on Linux you may need to proceed the command with **./**)

    gwadminutil services -i -dva

3. Check that the service was installed

    - On Linux, run **rcgrpwise status**. You should see a gwdva listed, but "unused". Run **rcgrpwise start gwdva** to start the DVA.
    - On Windows, click **Start|Administrative Tools|Services** (or choose Action|Refresh if Services is still loaded). Look for the GroupWise DVA. Right-click the service and choose Start.

Now that the DVA is installed and running, we can create a GroupWise object for the DVA so that it can be assigned to your post office. To do this, we go to the Administration Console in our web browser.

1. Log into the Administration Console (see *"Logging Into the Administration Console"* on page 117.
2. Click on System.
3. Choose Document Viewer Agents
4. In some cases during the upgrade your DVA will have been properly created. However, it is our experience that generally there will be no DVA for your current Post Office listed here. Click New.
5. In the creation window, enter a name for your DVA (Perhaps in our case Caledonia DVA), enter the IP address and port for the DVA you just created. The default port is 8301.

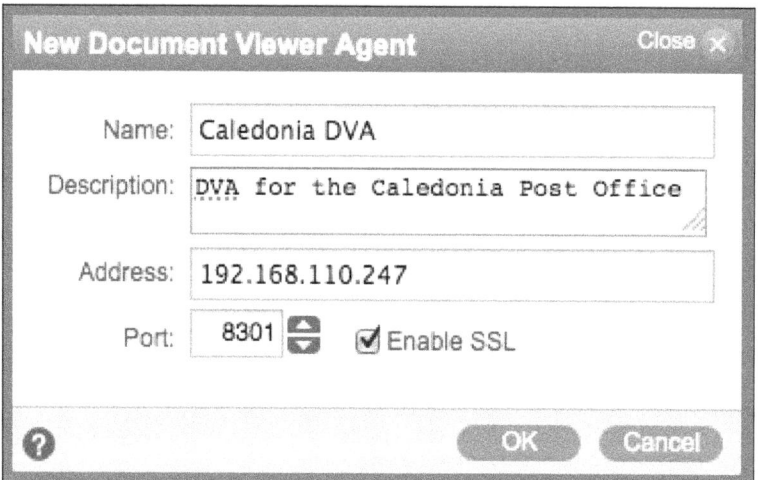

Figure 7-6: Configuring the DVA

6. When you Click OK, the object will be created, and it should appear in the DVA list. Close the DVA list,

7. Now, click on Post Offices in the list on the left hand side of the Administration Console.
8. Choose your Post Office and click on its name to open the link.
9. Scroll to the right and click on the Document Viewer Agent tab,
10. As we mentioned above, there are times when this is properly populated, but the likelihood is that no DVA is listed here. Click on Add Document Viewer Agent.

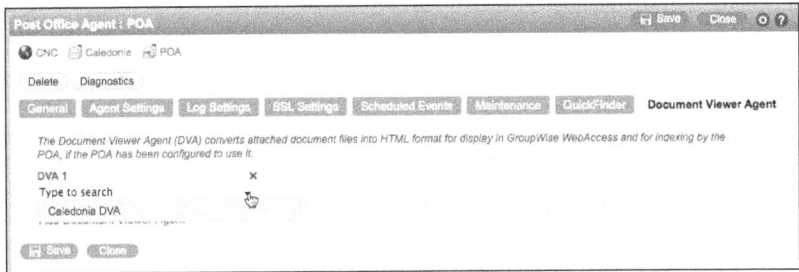

Figure 7-7: Adding the DVA to the Post Office Agent

11. Click the dropdown (or start typing the name you gave the DVA agent earlier) and choose your DVA.
12. Click Save. It may seem that nothing has happened. If you were watching, you would see the Save icon on the top toolbar flicker. If you are unsure, close this window and click on the POA and Document Viewer Agent tab again just to verify.

Log into the Upgraded Post Office

It's now time to log into your new POA and verify that everything is working as desired. You can do this with your current GroupWise client, or upgrade to the GroupWise 2014 client.

Once you have logged into your mailbox, there are a few tasks that you should perform to ensure that everything is working properly

- Send a message to yourself. This should pop into your mailbox almost immediately.
- Send a message to a user on the same post office, and verify that it is received.
- Send a message to a user on another post office if applicable and verify that it was received
- Send a message to an external recipient through your GWIA and verify that it was received.
- Send a message from an external sender to your user through the GWIA and verify that it was received.
- If you use GroupWise Document Management aopen an existing document and verify that you are able to access it properly. If there are problems, check Troubleshooting below.
- Create a new document in GroupWise DMS and verify that it creates and saves properly.

Troubleshooting

There are very few things that can go wrong during a post office upgrade. If you find that your post office refuses to show as a GroupWise 2014 post office in the Administration Console do a couple of things:

- Double-check that the upgrade procedure copied the new dc files into the post office directory. Open the **gwpo.dc** and **ngwguard.dc** files with a text editor to verify that they are in fact the GroupWise 2014 files.
- Double-check that the domain owning this post office is actually a GroupWise 2014 domain (i.e., it shows as version 1400 in the Administration Console).
- Unload and reload the POA to see if this solves the problem.
- It is possible that communications issues have prevented the post office database from receiving the news that its parent domain is a GroupWise 2014 domain and thus is allowed to upgrade. Remember that just loading the GroupWise 2014 agent software is not enough. If all else fails, rebuild the post office database. See *"Validating or Rebuilding a Post Office Database"* on page 130.

Once all of these tasks are performed successfully, you are DONE with the Post Office upgrade.

When you are ready to continue, just turn to the next chapter in your upgrade plan.

8 Upgrading GroupWise WebAccess

With GroupWise 2012, Novell made some major changes to WebAccess, which continue with GroupWise 2014. There is no longer a GWINTER (WebAccess Agent) for GroupWise WebAccess. Rather than having the WebAccess Application (web server) speak to the WebAccess Agent to gather information for the user, the WebAccess Application speaks directly to the POA via SOAP.

Also, the directory objects for the WebAccess Application are no longer used. If you have read our books on manually configuring GroupWise WebAccess on Apache, you will know that these agents were always "optional" and were essentially just a GUI interface for editing the web server and WebAccess configuration files. From here on out, you will need to make configuration changes directly to the **webacc.cfg** file if you wish to modify your WebAccess Application settings. We will go over some of those settings later in this chapter.

Finally, the GroupWise 2014 WebAccess cannot service users on post offices that have not been upgraded to GroupWise 2014. In other words, if you will not upgrade all of your post offices rapidly (perhaps over a weekend or other "off" time such as a long holiday), you will either need to leave your WebAccess at your current GroupWise version, or have two separate WebAccess installations to provide for both your older post offices and your new GroupWise 2014 post offices.

GroupWise 7 and later WebAccess installations can access a GroupWise 2014 post office with no major downsides (we have not checked. Of course, your users will not be able to utilize any of the new features of the GroupWise 2014 WebAccess, but the users will be able to log into the upgraded PO through a GroupWise 7 or later WebAccess installation.

If you are running GroupWise WebAccess along with the GroupWise Monitor Application and/or the GroupWise Calendar Publishing Host on the same server, all of these must be upgraded in the same upgrade cycle or the other applications will not work until they are upgraded.

Preparing For The Upgrade To GroupWise 2014 WebAccess

For the Web Server running the WebAccess Application you will need one of the following:

SLES 11/OES 11

Apache 2.2 plus:

- Tomcat 6.0 or later (installed via YaST for SLES, or during GroupWise installation for OES11)
- JRE 5 or later
- ModProxy Module

Windows Server 2008/2008 R2/2010

Microsoft Internet Information Server (IIS) 7 or later plus:

- Tomcat 6 or later
- JRE 5 or later
- Jakarta Connector 1.2 or later
- ISAPI Support

Firewall Considerations

The GroupWise 2014 WebAccess Application requires access to the SOAP port on each Post Office Agent in the system. This is typically port 7191. The GroupWise 2014 WebAccess Application also requires access to at least one GroupWise Document Viewer Agent (GWDVA) in the system. This is generally port 8301. Ensure that your firewall does not block this access by the WebAccess Application.

While we do not wish to get into a huge server placement discussion here, web server placement IS important, especially if you are upgrading from a system prior to GroupWise 2012. With GroupWise 8 and earlier, the web server only needed to talk to one WebAccess Agent on port 7205 (although it was possible to configure fault-tolerance and have multiple WebAccess Agents accessible by the Web Server). With GroupWise 2012 and later, ALL post office agents need to be accessible on the SOAP port, and at least one GWDVA needs to be accessible. Thus, if you place your web server in the DMZ, you potentially need to open many more "holes" into the inside. If you place the web server inside of your network, you only need to open port 433 (and 80 if you insist, but you should use SSL, so in reality you could get by with only port 443 being open to the internal web server).

To make your WebAccess installation fault tolerant, you could use an L4 switch and round-robin between multiple WebAccess server installations.

Shutting Down the WebAccess Agent

If you are upgrading from GroupWise 8 or prior, the WebAccess Agent will not be available in GroupWise 2014. When you upgrade your WebAccess to GroupWise 2014, you will need to shut down the WebAccess Agent and remove references to the agent in your startup.

Linux

We assume you are running the WebAccess Agent on your Linux server as a daemon. If, however, you are running the WebAccess Agent with its GUI consoles, unload the agents through the GUI console. Finally, to shut down your WebAccess agent, type the following commands at a terminal prompt:

> **/etc/init.d/grpwise status**

or simply

> **rcgrpwise status**

Look to find the name of your WebAccess Agent. For example, when we type the above command, we see:

> **Checking status [webac80a.cnc]**   **running**

This indicates that our WebAccess Agent is named webac80a.cnc. So, to shut down this agent we will type

> **/etc/init.d/grpwise stop webac80a.cnc**

or simply

> **rcgrpwise stop webac80a.cnc**

We also need to remove the WebAccess Agent from the **gwha.conf** file on windows to prevent it from attempting to start when GroupWise starts up. Edit the /etc/opt/novell/groupwise/**gwha.conf** file and remove the section for the WebAccess Agent. It will look like the following:

> **[webac80b.cnc]**
>
> **server = /opt/novell/groupwise/agents/bin/gwinter**
>
> **command = /etc/init.d/grpwise**
>
> **startup = webac80b.waa**
>
> **delay   = 2**
>
> **wait   = 10**

This entire section should be removed in order to avoid having the GWINTER load. (Although loading it wouldn't really hurt anything. It just would not be useful!)

Windows

For Windows, you should also shut down the WebAccess Agent and disable the service. If you are running the agents as services, go into the services console from the Control Panel, right click on the GroupWise WebAccess Agent and choose stop (see Figure 8-1). Right-click the agent service again, go to properties, and disable the service.

If you are not running the WebAccess Agents as a service, go to the agent console and exit via F7 or from the agent menu. You should then go into the startup folder and delete the shortcut for the WebAccess Agent.

148 | Upgrading GroupWise WebAccess

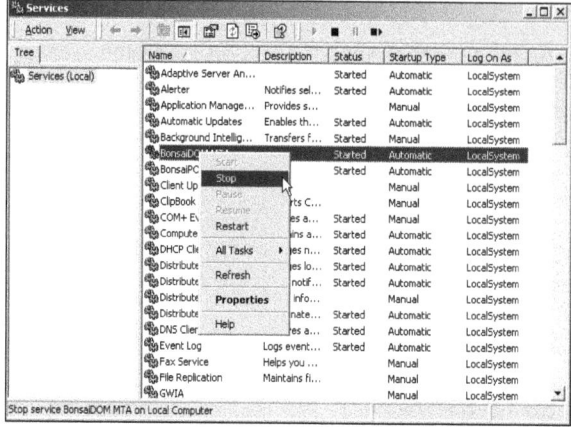

Figure 8-1: Stopping a Windows service

Upgrading WebAccess

Linux WebAccess Installation

1. If you are in a GUI file browser like Nautilus or Konqueror, just click on **install.sh** in your extracted software directory, and choose Run in Terminal (this is a text based installation, and will only run from the terminal). If you are at a terminal window, type **./install.sh** in the directory where the script resides. Here's the installation screen!

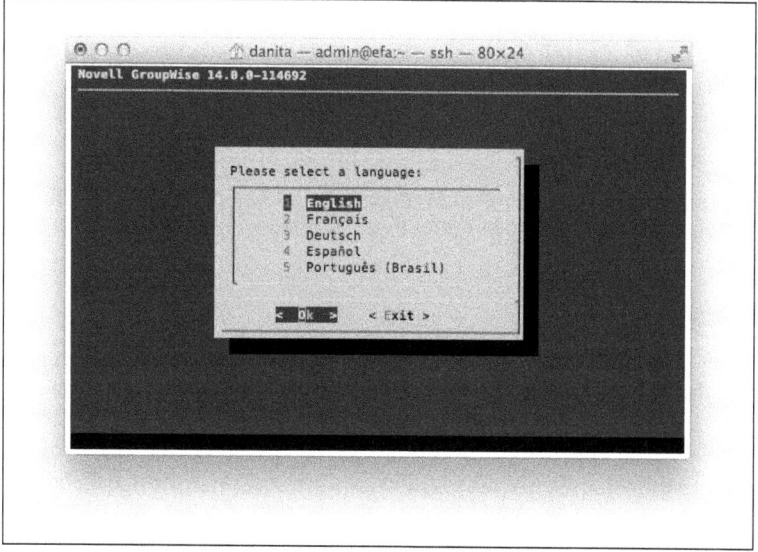

Figure 8-2: The Installation Window

Notice that this is no longer a GUI installation. Everything is text based. In many builds of this installation routine, we have noticed that the arrow keys do not work, and you must use the tab key. If you have issues with arrowing around, use the tab and shift-tab.

2. You have 5 languages to choose from here. Choose your language, and we'll move on.
3. At the next screen you will have two choices: Documentation and Installation. Documentation will attempt to open a web browser and take you to the Novell docs. Remember that the installation can be done in a totally text based environment, thus if you have no GUI/browser available to you, you will only be able to view the **Readme** if you choose to look at the documentation.
4. The next screen will present you with the EULA. When you agree to the EULA you are moved to the following screen:

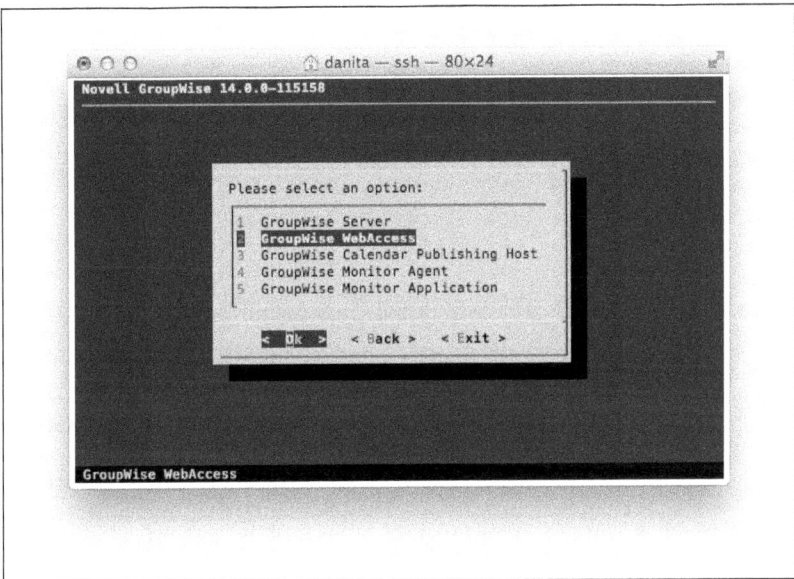

Figure 8-3: The Main Installation Screen

5. Here we will choose to install GroupWise Webaccess. Choose OK.
6. Next you have the option of Install or Configure

150 | Upgrading GroupWise WebAccess

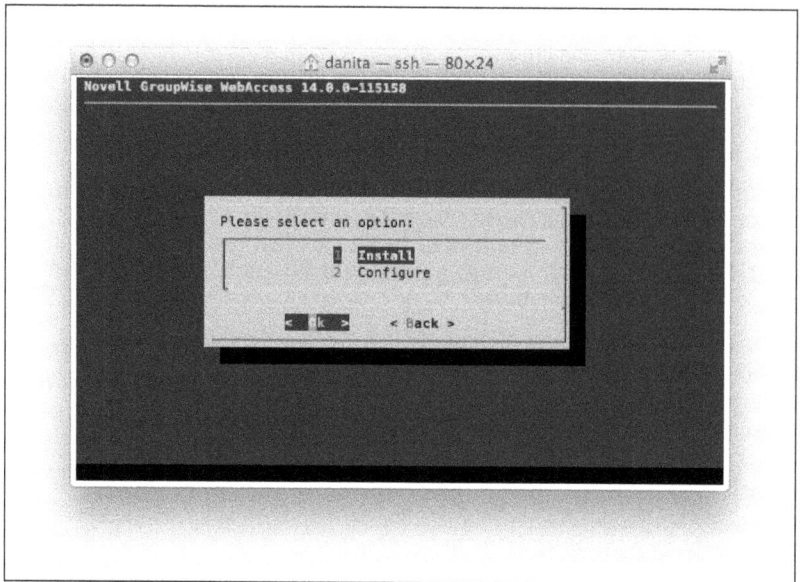

Figure 8-4: Installation Screen

We'll of course choose Install. This will install the actual files. We will later go to configure.

7. The installation routine will copy the necessary files to the server (and check the server repositories for needed updates to server software. Apache and Tomcat will also be restarted.

   Once the files are installed, you will receive a prompt to "press any key to return . . .". This will take you back to the Install/Configure menu.

8. Next we will choose Configure. At the next screen choose 1 to Continue.

9. In the following figure you see the text that says "Specify the network address and port of the Post Office Agent. Please note that this is two different fields, but you will not see the "port" field until after you enter the network address. Do not get confused and think you need to put the port on the same line as the network address. You need only enter one POA location for WebAccess to work. WebAccess will connect to that POA and if the user requesting access belongs to a different post office, standard post office redirection will send the user to the proper POA.

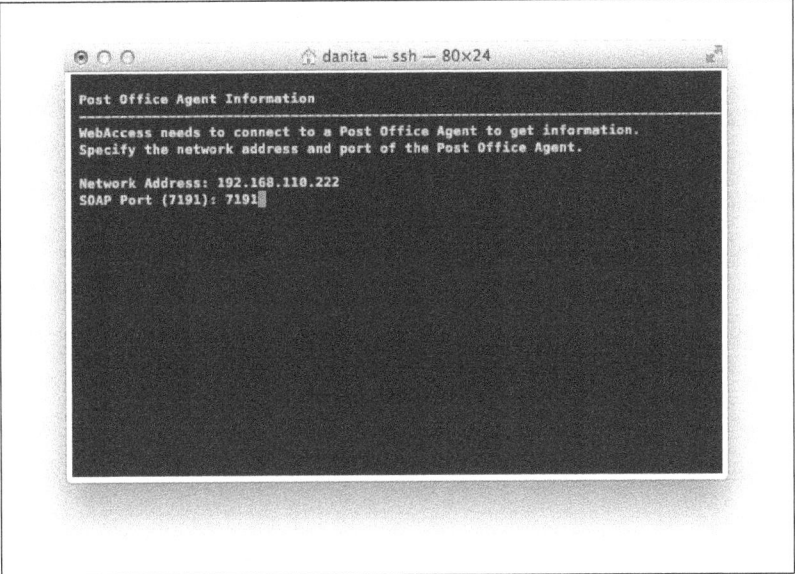

Figure 8-5: Post Office Agent SOAP setup

10. The next screen will be the same, except it is for the GWDVA information. We will discuss more about the DVA below. The DVA port is 8301 by default.

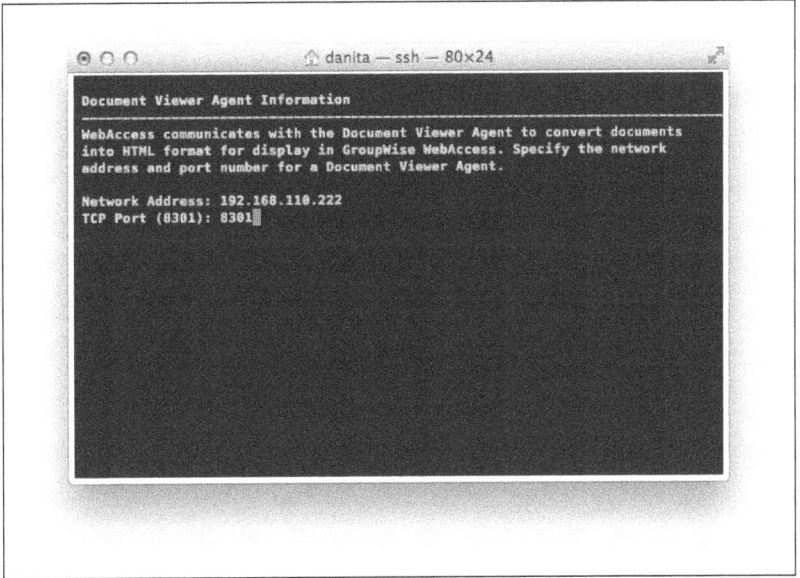

Figure 8-6: DVA Port Setup

11. The next screen indicates the location of Apache and Tomcat. Unless you have manually configured a different instance of Apache, these paths should be correct.

152 | Upgrading GroupWise WebAccess

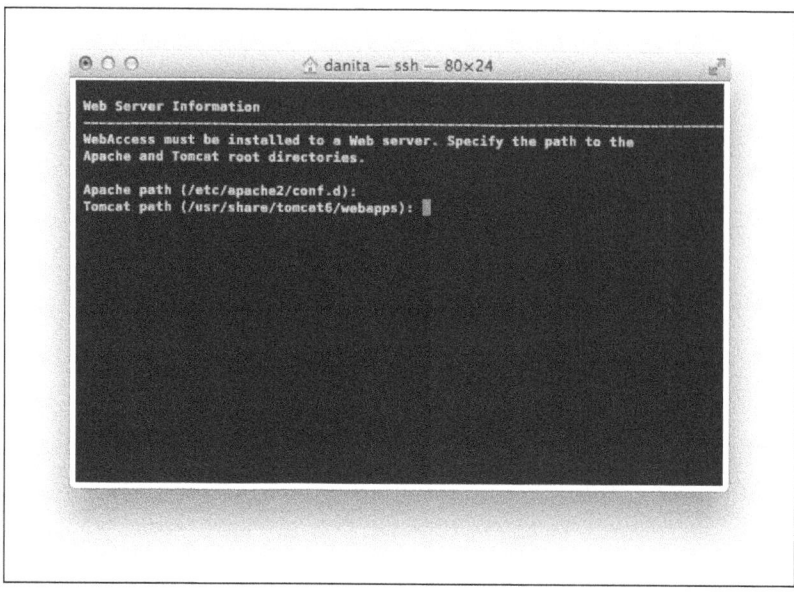

12. The configuration will finish, and you will be returned to the Install/Configure screen. Choose Back and then Exit.

13. While the installation should restart Apache and Tomcat, to be thorough, you should do the following steps:

    /etc/init.d/apache2 restart

    and

    /etc/init.d/tomcat6 restart (SLES 11)

    or

    /etc/init.d/novell-tomcat6 restart (OES)

    Even though deep down we know that OES uses novell-tomcat6, sometimes we also restart tomcat6 for good measure.

Windows WebAccess Installation

1. From Windows Explorer, double-click on **setup.exe** in your installation directory. Here's the installation screen!

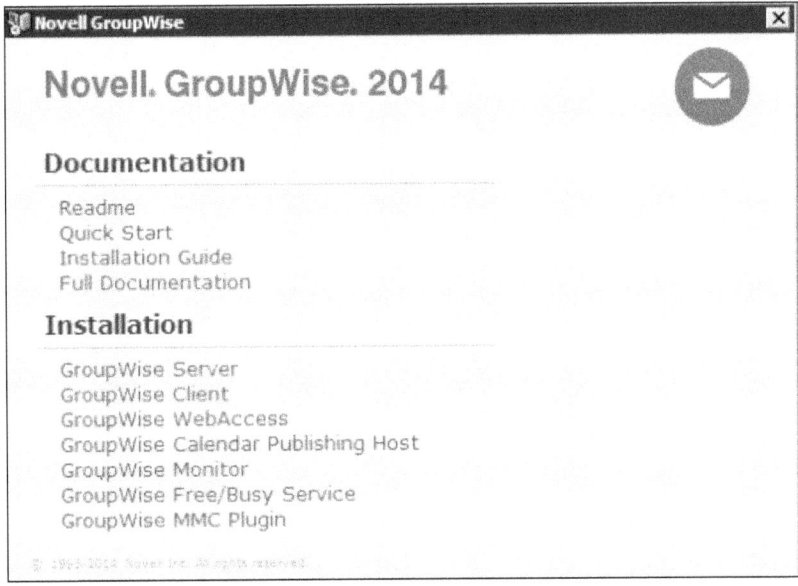

Figure 8-7: The Installation Window

2. Here we will choose to install WebAccess.
3. Choose your language.
4. The WebAccess installation routine will be launched. When you see the Installation Welcome screen, press Next.
5. Here you will choose the Web Server Information. Unless you have more than one web server location running on this server, the default location is where you should place GroupWise WebAccess. Click on Default Web Site and click next.
6. In the following figure you will enter the information for the network address and port of the Post Office Agent. You need only enter one POA location for WebAccess to work. WebAccess will connect to that POA and if the user requesting access belongs to a different post office, standard post office redirection will send the user to the proper POA.

154 | Upgrading GroupWise WebAccess

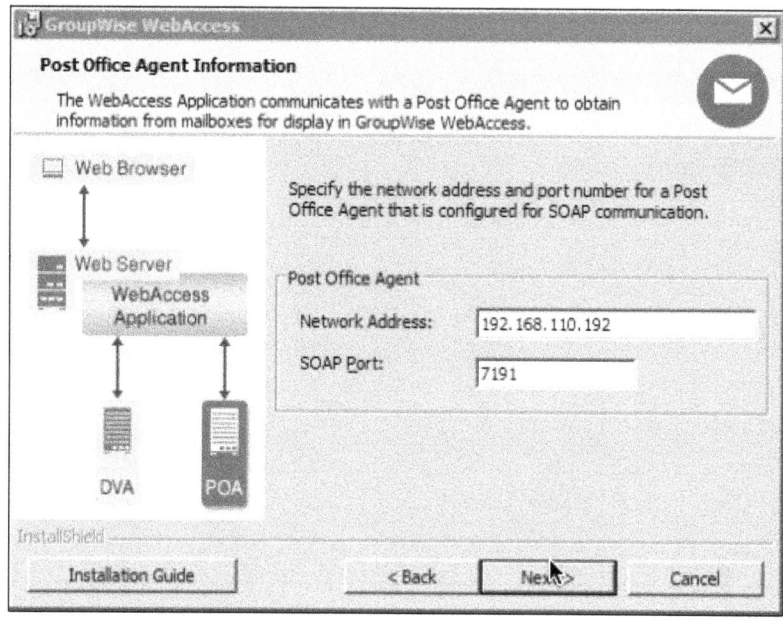

Figure 8-8: Post Office Agent SOAP setup

7. The next screen will be the same, except it is for the GWDVA information. We will discuss more about the DVA below. The DVA port is 8301 by default.

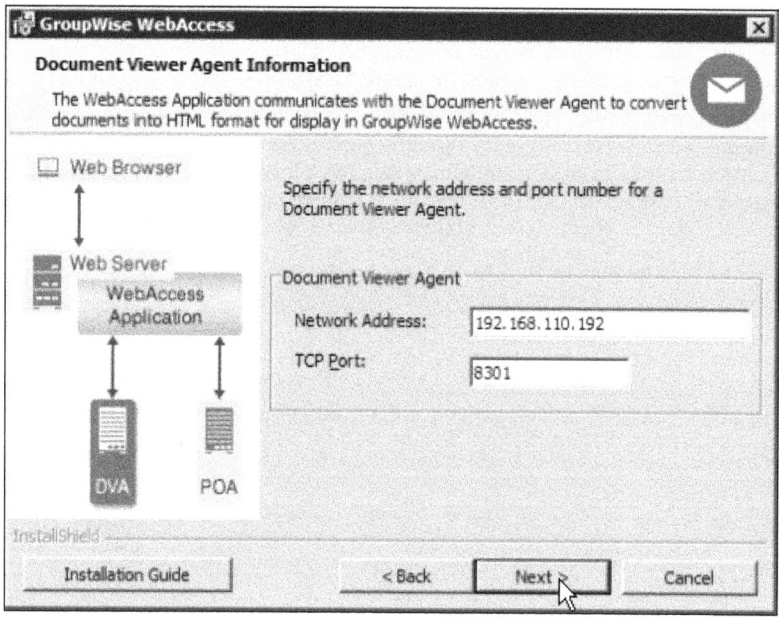

Figure 8-9: DVA Port Seetup

8. At the summary screen, check your settings, and click Install.

9. You will be prompted to either shut down IIS manually, or allow the installation to shut it down for you. Click Yes when you are ready.
10. The installation will proceed, and you will see the final screen, and your WebAccess installation is complete.

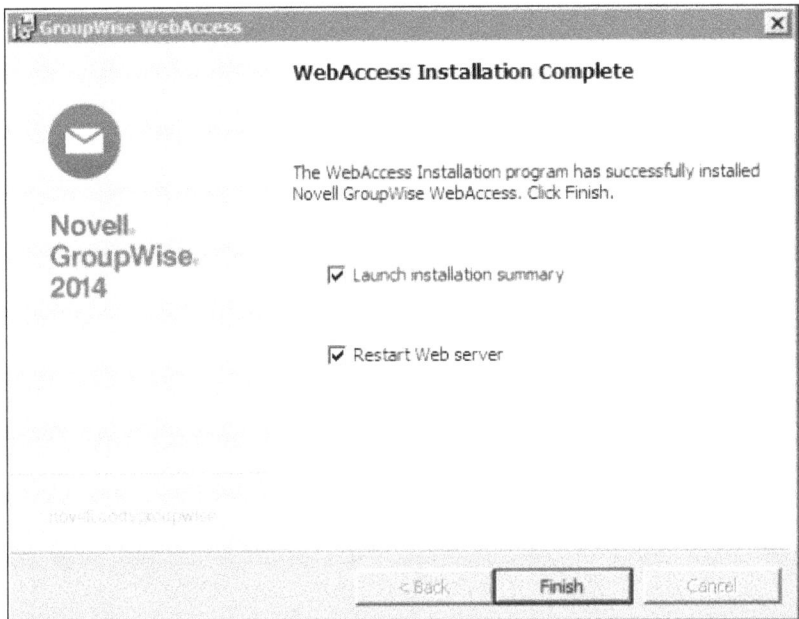

Figure 8-10: The Completed WebAccess launch

11. Click Finish to return to the Main GroupWise Installation screen.

Loading the GroupWise WebAccess Application

Linux

The commands for loading the Apache web server and Tomcat on Linux are as follows:

/etc/init.d/apache2 start

and

/etc/init.d/novell-tomcat6 start (OES)

or

/etc/init.d/tomcat6 start (SLES)

You can also check status, stop and restart using these scripts. For example:

/etc/init.d/apache2 restart

Most SLES/OES commands are also available from any location through a search path by appending "rc" to the command. For example,

rcapache2 restart

OES will auto-start both Apache and Tomcat on a reboot. To ensure that your WebAccess is functional after a reboot of SLES, do the following:

chkconfig apache2 on

chkconfig tomcat6 on

Microsoft Windows Server

The GroupWise WebAccess Application is designed to start when the Microsoft IIS Service and Web Server is started. The Microsoft IIS Web server is designed to start with the Microsoft Internet Information Server service is started. To restart the service, open the Internet Information Services (IIS) Manager from the Administrative Tools menu. Click on your Web Server (top left). On the right side you will see options to Restart, Start and Stop the server.

Configuration Options

The majority of WebAccess optimizations are done through the **webacc.cfg** file. This file is found in the following locations:

Linux:	/var/opt/novell/groupwise/webaccess
Windows:	c:\Novell\GroupWise\WebAccess on the Web server

The original webacc.cfg file on a particular server will be very orderly, and broken into distinct sections. As you patch and update your server over time, new settings will be saved to the bottom of the file in a section called "Values added by install to update config file". If you change information in the file, make sure to look at the end to ensure that you do not have conflicting values, as the final value will win!

There are many interesting options in the webacc.cfg. We encourage you to look through the file to see what might interest you.

Following are some important configurations options pertaining to the upgrade that you should know more about. After any changes, restart Apache and Tomcat (see the section above for *"Loading the GroupWise WebAccess Application"* for instructions on restarting these processes.

Configuring Additional Post Office Agents

The GroupWise WebAccess Application talks directly to post office agents in your GroupWise system to gather the information necessary to show in WebAccess. During installation, you can only supply one post office agent address. However, you can supply as many POA designations as you like, and the WebAccess Application will attempt them in order until it finds a POA that responds. This is only for initial connection to the GroupWise system. Adding additional post offices here adds fault tolerance. For example, if POA1 is down, and it is the only Post Office Agent defined in webacc.cfg, then all users in your system are locked out of WebAccess. Adding additional "entry points" for the WebAccess Application allows you to continue to provide WebAccess services to users of those Post Offices that are active.

If the user logging in does not belong to the POA that is contacted by the WebAccess Application, the redirection table will send the WebAccess Application to the proper location.

In the webacc.cfg, search for Provider.SOAP.1.ip - for example:

> **Provider.SOAP.1.ip=192.168.110.237**
>
> **Provider.SOAP.1.port=7191**

Copy these two lines and change the "1" to a "2" in each line, and modify the IP address and port.

> **Provider.SOAP.2.ip=192.168.110.238**
>
> **Provider.SOAP.2.port=7191**

Do this as many times as necessary, making sure to have two lines for each SOAP provider number you add.

Configuring Additional Document Viewer Agents

As with the Post Office Agent, you can only configure one instance during installation. Modify the following information to add additional DVAs to your webacc.cfg:

In the webacc.cfg, search for Provider.DVA.1.ip - for example:

> **Provider.DVA.1.ip=192.168.110.237**
>
> **Provider.DVA.1.port=8301**

Copy these two lines and change the "1" to a "2" in each line, and modify the IP address and port.

> **Provider.DVA.2.ip=192.168.110.238**
>
> **Provider.DVA.2.port=8301**

Do this as many times as necessary, making sure to have two lines for each SOAP provider number you add.

Configuring HTTP Monitor for WebAccess

Like the other GroupWise Agents, you can configure a web based monitor for WebAccess administration activity. The **webacc.cfg** file contains the following lines:

> ###
>
> # Application Administration Tool
>
> # Invoked on the URL
>
> # (e.g. http://<server>/gw/webacc?action=Admin.Open)
>
> ###
>
> Admin.WebConsole.enable=true

Admin.RestService.host=127.0.0.1

Admin.RestService.port=9710

You can turn this on or off. By going to your server at the URL specified, you can log in and view logged in users, configuration and log files.

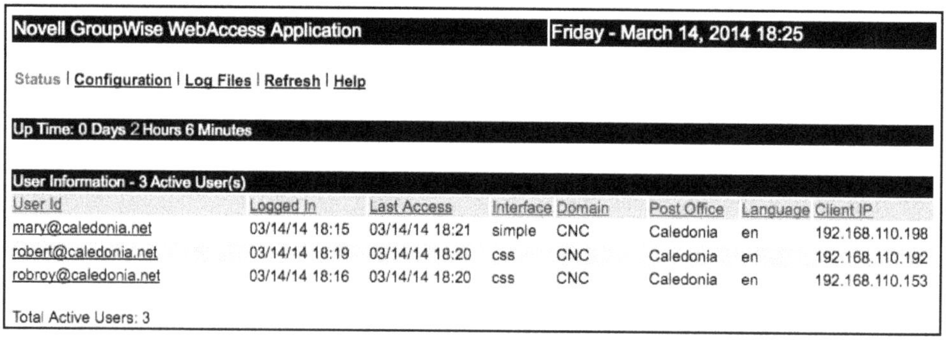

Figure 8-11: The WebAccess Administration Console

Setting the GroupWise 2012 WebAccess as Your Default

If your system will have more than one version of WebAccess in order to accommodate older GroupWise post offices, you can choose to have a single entry point for all of your users. For example, you may already have **https://mail.yourdomain.com/gw/webacc** pointing to your GroupWise 2012 or older WebAccess. Rather than having to direct users to multiple locations, you can continue to have **https://mail.yourdomain.com/gw/webacc** as the entry point for all users, and redirect users on older post offices to **https://gw12.yourdomain.com/gw/webacc**. In order to do this, you must make a change in the **webacc.cfg file**, and of course create an A Record in DNS for your secondary WebAccess server (in our example, **gw12.yourdomain.com**).

This setting is found in the **webacc.cfg** file as:

#Redirect.url=http://gw8.novell.com/gw/webacc

simply remove the pound sign and change the URL to match your desired URL. Once the system is restarted, if a user logs into your http://mail.yourdomain.com/gw/webacc location, their POA will indicate it is not a GroupWise 2013 post office and the WebAccess Application will redirect the user to the older GroupWise WebAccess Application. The user will be required to enter their WebAccess credentials again. These credentials are not passed through to the redirected server.

Figure 8-12: Redirecting to an older WebAccess server

Security Timeouts

GroupWise 2012 brought a new set of security timeouts to WebAccess, and they are still effective for GroupWise 2014. When a user logs into WebAccess, the user has the option on the main login screen to choose whether the computer is public or private. This allows for users who access GroupWise solely via WebAccess, from a private computer at home or at the office to have a longer timeout value set. These values are listed in the **webacc.cfg** as:

    Security.timeout=20

    Security.Private.timeout=480

Setting the "Private" timeout to a higher value "in minutes" prevents users in a more secure setting from timing out multiple times a day, no doubt reducing their frustration!

Deleting Unneeded eDirectory Objects

In prior versions of GroupWise, when you installed WebAccess, an object representing the WebAccess Agent (Gateway) was created in eDirectory and the GroupWise view. Also, objects for the WebAccess Application were created (most commonly under the GroupWise domain object itself, but realistically they could be anywhere!). These objects are no longer used, and can be removed from eDirectory to avoid confusion. We recommend that you give your system a few days to settle down before you delete them, but once everything is working as you expect you can delete the following items:

- GroupWise WebAccess Agents no longer in use. Make certain you export any access control settings you might need as outlined above before you delete the objects!
- GroupWiseProvider Objects
- LDAPProvider Objects
- GroupWiseWebAccess Object
- NovellSpeller Objects

Troubleshooting

There are settings in the webacc.cfg that pertain to how the new admin console connects to the GroupWise Administration Service.

```
###########################################################################
# Application Administration Tool
###########################################################################
Admin.WebConsole.enable=true
Admin.RestService.host=127.0.0.1
Admin.RestService.port=9710
```

There are a couple of reasons why these default settings might not work for you:

- If you are running WebAccess on a server that does not have a GroupWise Administration Service running, the setting of 127.0.0.1 will be invalid. You will need to change it to the proper ID address.
- If you have an MTA running on this server, but it is set to bind to a specific IP address, the Admin Service will also not be listening on localhost (127.0.0.1) and you should change this to the specific location. Surprisingly, if your MTA is set to a host name rather than an IP address, the Admin Service could complain if you enter an IP address here. Test to see which works properly for you.
- If you have modified the default port for your Admin Service, you will also need to change the information here.

Once you are ready to continue, just turn to the next chapter in your upgrade plan.

9 Upgrading GroupWise Monitor

Upgrading the GroupWise Monitor is essentially installing the new GroupWise software for the monitor agent and optionally the Monitor application. If you have a GroupWise 5.5EP Monitor (where have you been???), you will need to totally reinstall your Monitor from scratch. As you know, GroupWise Monitor is similar to the GroupWise WebAccess as it existed prior to GroupWise 2012, in that it has two components, the GroupWise Monitor "Agent" and a web application that can be installed on your web server. (Of course, as we discussed earlier, beginning with GroupWise 2012, GroupWise WebAccess no longer has an "Agent" and is driven entirely by the WebAccess Application and SOAP at the POA.)

While the Monitor setup seems similar to our prior versions of WebAccess, it is quite a bit different. The Monitor Web Application is dependent upon a Monitor Agent being installed somewhere in your system. However, the Monitor Agent is not at all dependent on the Monitor Web Application, and can be used entirely "stand-alone" without the Monitor Web Application being installed at all. It is very rare that the Monitor Agent is run on a server that does not contain a domain (although it is possible by attaching to an MTA via the MTP port). We provide these steps only for reference. If your Monitor Agent is on the same server as a domain, it has already been upgraded during the GroupWise Server installation!

If you are running GroupWise Monitor Application along with GroupWise WebAccess and/or the GroupWise Calendar Publishing Host on the same server, all of these must be upgraded in the same upgrade cycle or the other applications will not work until they are upgraded.

Preparing for the Upgrade

There is very little preparation that must be made for the GroupWise Monitor upgrade. It can reside anywhere, and no database adjustments are made when it is installed. You must shut down the existing Monitor agent, or course (on Linux or Windows), and it's best to also shut down Apache and Tomcat if you are installing the Monitor Web Application. In fact, if your Monitor Agent was on the same server as any of the domains you have previously upgraded, the new Monitor Agent Software has already been installed, and you can continue on with *"Installing your Agent Software" on page 162*.

GroupWise High Availability Agent Considerations

As we mentioned in *"GroupWise High Availability Agent Considerations" on page 12*, if you are using the High Availability Agent, the settings will not come over after the upgrade. Thus, before you install the Monitor Agent you must copy your High Availability settings so that you can re enable the GWHA afterwards.

Edit the **/etc/init.d/grpwise-ma** script and find your MA_OPTIONS settings. For example, ours are:

MA_OPTIONS="--hauser gwha --hapassword gwhapassword --hapoll 120 --httpagentuser gwweb --httpagentpassword gwweb --httpmonuser gwmon --httpmonpassword gwmon"

Save this information in a text file for use in *"Re-enabling the GroupWise High Availability Agent"* below in this chapter.

Installing your Agent Software

This section will talk about installing just the Monitor Agent on Windows and Linux. The monitor agent is required to monitor your GroupWise system. The Monitor Application is not required, but does add some nice enhancements and functionality.

The installation for the GroupWise Monitor is pretty much the same whether you are upgrading or if you are installing from scratch. The important thing to remember is that you should make a copy of your **monitor.xml** file before you begin. The upgrade procedure should use the current **monitor.xml** file that it finds in the directory you specify in the installation (providing it is the same directory where your existing GroupWise monitor resides). However, having a backup is always nice, particularly if you have made customizations on your GroupWise Monitor.

Windows

1. Make a copy of your **monitor.xml** file. This will typically be c:\gwmon.
2. From the Windows machine where Monitor will run, go to your **<installationfiles>** and run **setup.exe**.

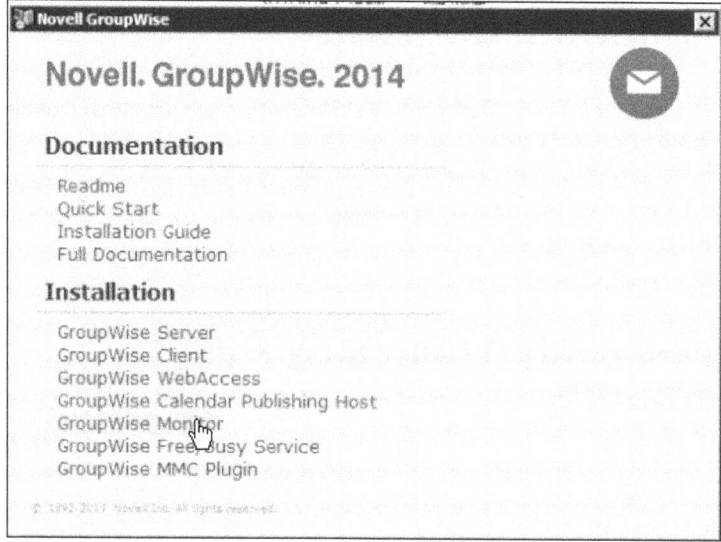

Figure 9-1: Installing GroupWise Monitor

3. Proceed to the GroupWise Monitor: Components Screen. Uncheck "GroupWise Monitor Application", click Next. Note however: If you do intend to have both the Monitor Agent and the Monitor Application on this same server, you must do them at the same time. Otherwise the installation attempts to uninstall the option you deselect. If you are installing both, refer to the steps in *"Installing the Monitor Application Software"* if you need assistance with the installation prompts.

4. Select the local path where you wish to install the GroupWise Agent. Note that the default has changed from **c:\gwmon** to **C:\Program Files\Novell\GroupWise Server\ Monitor**. This is one time when you can easily change this location without having trouble with the setup. If you choose to move your Monitor to this new location, just copy the **monitor.xml** from your former installation into the new directory if necessary.

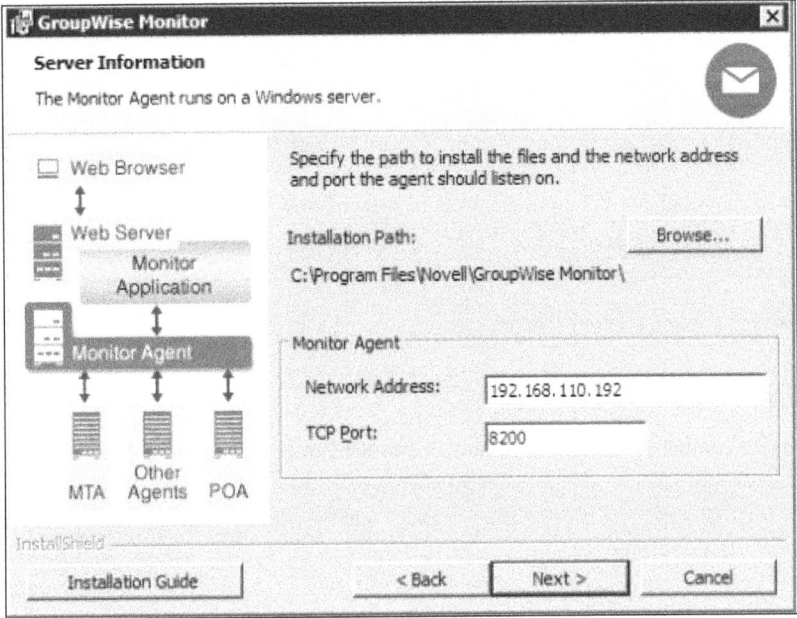

Figure 9-2: Monitor Server Information

5. Also verify that the IP address and Port are correct. Click Next

6. Define the path to any of your GroupWise domain databases. You can use any domain you wish. Choose the domain that the Monitor Agent machine has the easiest access to. Since all of your domains have access to information about all agents in your system, any domain can be used for the Monitor connection. The Monitor Agent will simply query the domain to find IP address, Port and HTTP user and password information for all agents in the system. Click Next.

164 | Upgrading GroupWise Monitor

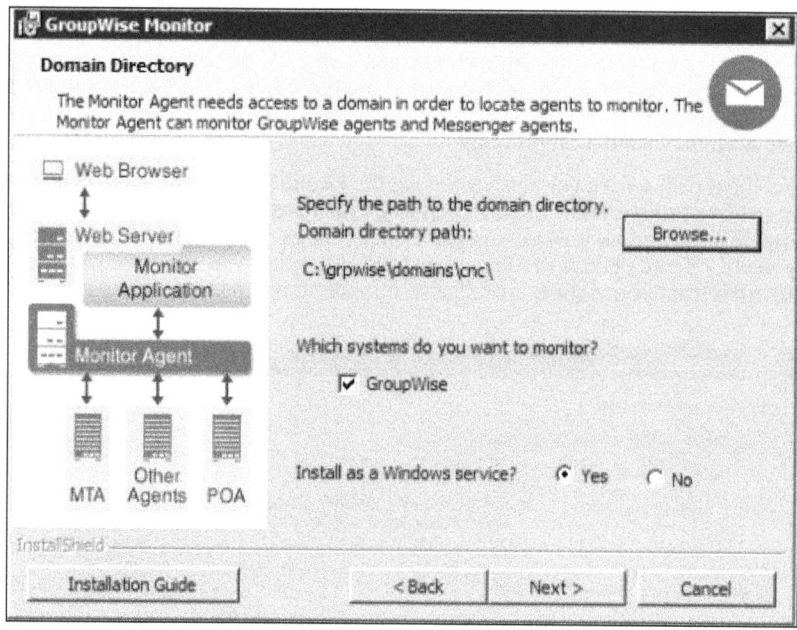

Figure 9-3: Choose Your Domain Directory

7. You will then be given a summary of the Agent install. Verify that this information is correct and Click Next.

8. When the installation is complete, you may launch the GroupWise Monitor Agent.

9. A shortcut was created for you under the GroupWise Monitor menu. Monitor will run as a service on port 8200. This shortcut is provide a GUI access to the Monitor screen. You can also access it at http://yourserver.com:8200.

After the installation, if you changed the location of your GroupWise Monitor Agent files, you must copy your **monitor.xml** from the old location into this new location in order to preserve your settings. Restart the GroupWise Monitor service and load your Monitor agent with the GroupWise Monitor shortcut to verify that your Monitor Agent loads properly, and that your previous settings are being honored.

Linux

If your GroupWise Monitor Agent was installed on the same Linux server as any other GroupWise Agent, the Monitor Agent software will already have been upgraded by the time you read this chapter. As a matter of fact, if your Monitor Agent was already on this Linux box, you do not even need to do any configuration. However, if you are installing to a new server, here are the quick steps needed to install the Monitor.

1. As root, run the **install.sh** script in your **<installationfile>** folder.
2. Choose your Language.
3. Choose Installation.

The Caledonia Upgrade Guide for GroupWise 2014 In-Place Upgrade | **165**

4. Accept the License Agreement.
5. Choose GroupWise Monitor Agent

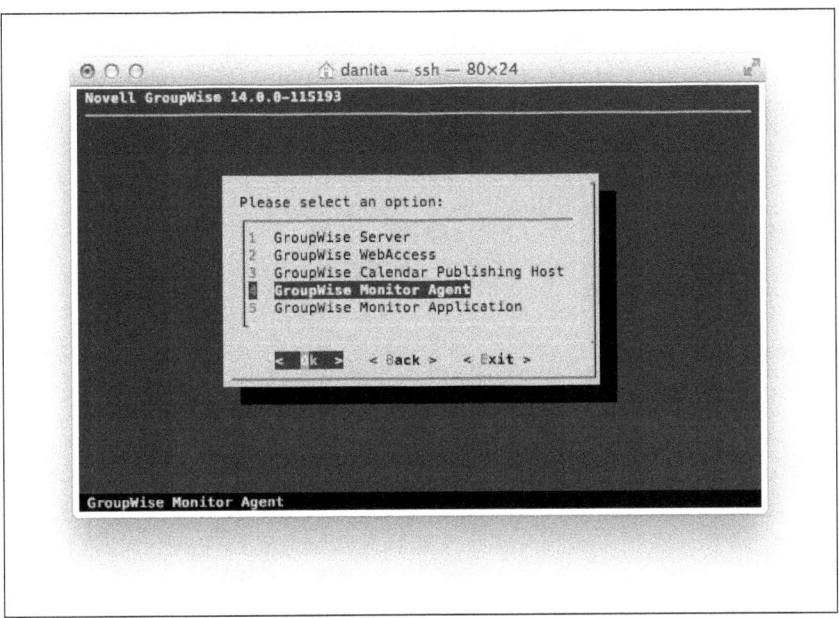

Figure 9-4: Installing the GroupWise Monitor Agent

6. Choose Install. The installation will launch and shut down any agents running if necessary. Press any key to continue after the installation completes.

At this point, the new monitor software has been installed, and you can reload the Monitor Agent. However, if for some reason you need to reconfigure the Monitor agent, follow these steps.

1. Choose Configure.
2. Type 1 to Continue.
3. Type 1 to choose GroupWise (this is a left-over screen from when you could also monitor Messenger).
4. Enter the location of a GroupWise Domain that is easily accessible from the Monitor machine. This can be any GroupWise Domain (primary or secondary) in your system.

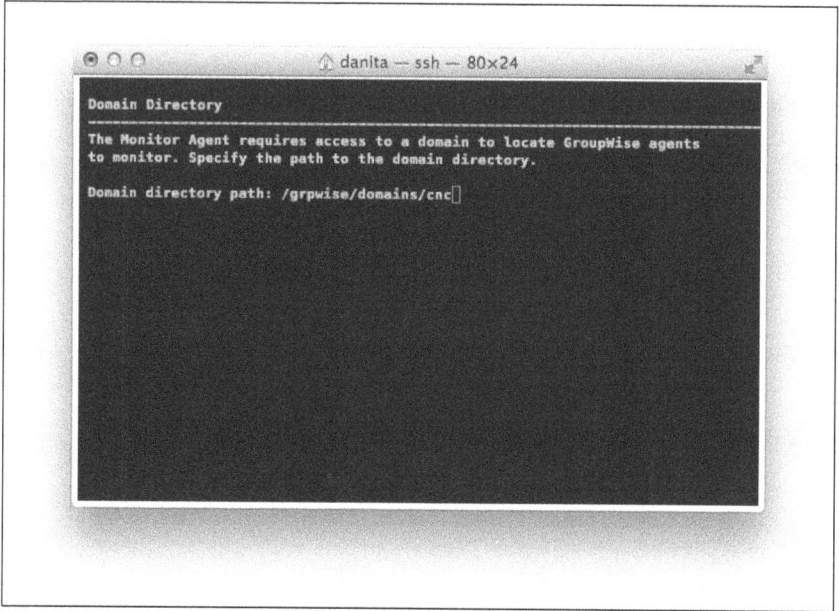

Figure 9-5: Domain Directory for Monitor Agent Installation

5. You will be notified that the Monitor Agent has been configured, and you can choose to start the Monitor Agent on startup. Press any key when prompted and exit setup.

To start the Monitor Agent now, run **/etc/init.d/grpwise-ma start** or simply **rcgrpwise-ma start**

Once the Monitor Agent is loaded, you can check the upgrade by going to the IP address and port where the Monitor Agent is running. For example http://192.168.100.237:8200.

Verify that your settings are correct.

Re-enabling the GroupWise High Availability Agent

If you are using the GroupWise High Availability Agent, the original GWHA settings are not preserved during your upgrade of GroupWise Monitor. Thus you will be required to do a bit of reconfiguring. During our preparations in *"GroupWise High Availability Agent Considerations"* above, we had you copy your MA_OPTIONS line and place it in a text file for user in our reconfiguration.

After the Monitor Agent has been installed, check your GroupWise Monitor agent to verify it loaded (i.e. go to http://yourserver:8200). If the agent is loaded, and operational, go back to your Linux server and type:

rcgrpwise-ma stop

Now, go edit **/etc/sysconfig/grpwise-ma.** Look for the line that starts GROUPWISE_MA_OPTIONS. Replace the switches there with those that were in your MA_OPTIONS you saved earlier. Our line would look like this:

GROUPWISE_MA_OPTIONS="--hauser gwha --hapassword gwhapassword --hapoll 120 --httpagentuser gwweb --httpagentpassword gwweb --httpmonuser gwmon --httpmonpassword gwmon"

Note that the option has changed from **MA_OPTIONS** to **GROUPWISE_MA_OPTIONS**.

Now start the Monitor Agent again:

rcgrpwise-ma stop

Test the High Availability Agent by shutting down one of your agents. For example, we might shut down the MTA on our system:

rcgrpwise stop CNC

What the status of the agent (either through the monitor or by running **rcgrpwise status**) to verify that the agent restarts.

Troubleshooting GWHA

The gwha service should still be configured. You can verify this by going to /etc/sysconfig and looking at the gwha file. Unless this file has a line that reads

disabled = yes

then the service is still enabled. If the above line has appeared, remove it.

If the Monitor Agent will not load, double check the hauser and hapassword switches. If you type them by hand, remember that it is hapassword, not hapass and Danita tends to type (over and over!).

Troubleshooting the GroupWise Monitor Agent

There are very few things that can go wrong during a Monitor upgrade. The only problems we typically see have to do with the following:

- You neglect to keep a copy of your **monitor.xml** in case of difficulties.
- You change the location of the Monitor installation files on Windows during the installation (either accidentally, or on purpose) and then do not reconfigure the agent to update the startup files for the server.

Installing the Monitor Application Software

Windows Monitor Application Installation

To install the Monitor Application perform the following:

1. From the Windows server where IIS is installed, go to your **<installationfiles>** and run **setup.exe**.

2. Proceed to the GroupWise Monitor: Components Screen. Uncheck "GroupWise Monitor Agent", click Next. Please note: If you do in fact plan on having both the Monitor Agent and the Monitor Application on the same server, you must check both here. If you uncheck the Monitor Agent, and it is already installed on your server, the installation will attempt to remove it! Thus, if you need to install both, keep both checked here. Refer back to the section above on *"Installing your Agent Software"* if you need assistance with the prompts in this installation

3. Indicate the IP address or DNS Name of the server where the Monitor Agent is running (i.e., the server where you installed the Monitor Agent above). Also define the HTTP Port that the Monitor Agent is listening on (the default for the HTTP Port for the Monitor Agent is 8200.) Click Next

> NOTE: If you are not sure what HTTP Port the GroupWise Monitor Agent is listening on, do the following. For the Windows agent, go to the GroupWise Monitor Agent screen and select Configuration|HTTP. For the Linux agent, check the monitor.xml file in /opt/novell/groupwise/agents/bin.

4. Choose the web server instance you wish to use on this web server (typically the default)

5. At the Summary screen, confirm that everything is configured as you would like it to be. Then click Finish to start the installation.

6. During the installation, you may be prompted about shutting down the web server and Java and overwriting newer files. You should choose the affirmative answer for all of these questions.

7. When the installation is complete you will be prompted to launch the Installation Summary and restart the web server.

Linux Monitor Application Installation

Here are the quick steps needed to install the Monitor Application on Linux.

1. As root, run the **install.sh** script in your **<installationfile>** folder.

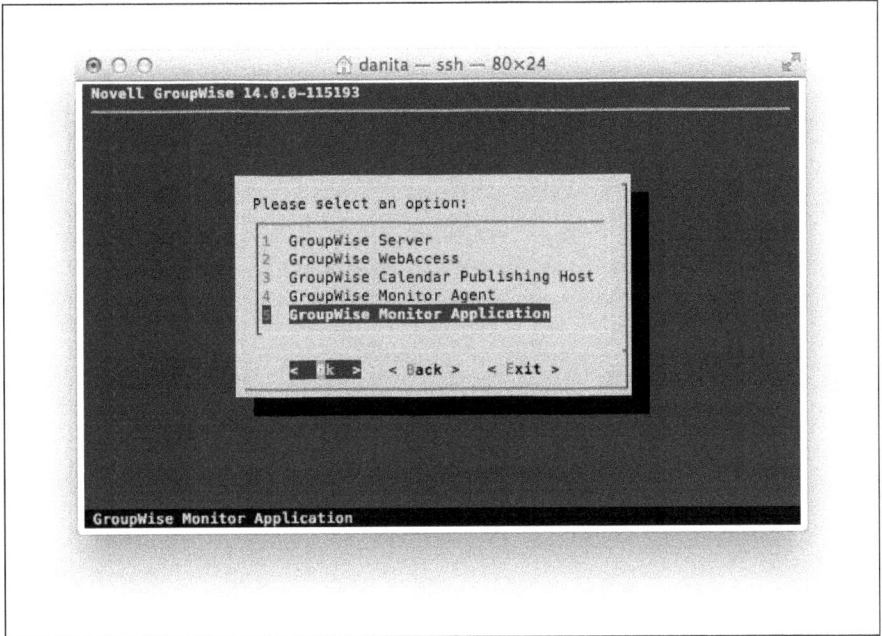

Figure 9-6: GroupWise Monitor Application Installation

2. Choose your Language.
3. Choose Installation.
4. Accept the License Agreement.
5. Choose GroupWise Monitor Application
6. Choose Install
7. The installation will begin.
8. After the files are installed, choose Configure
9. Press 1 to continue
10. Enter the IP address of the Monitor Agent.
11. Enter the Port. The default is 8200

170 | Upgrading GroupWise Monitor

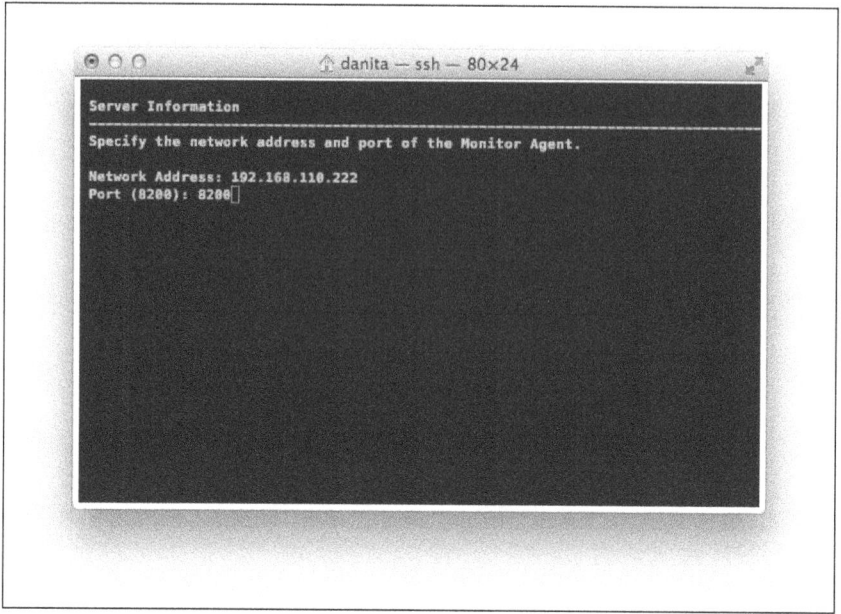

Figure 9-7: Monitor Application Server Settings

12. At the next screen, unless you have configured custom locations for Apache and/or Tomcat, the defaults should be correct.

13. After the installation, you will be instructed to restart Apache2 and Tomcat6

Loading The GroupWise Monitor Application

Now we will load the web server and the Tomcat. The instructions for loading the web server or Tomcat are different based upon the platform you are using.

Linux

Assuming you are using the default Apache2 and Tomcat6 installations on your Linux server, load the components thusly:

/etc/init.d/apache2 start

and

/etc/init.d/novell-tomcat6 start (OES)

or

/etc/init.d/tomcat6 start (SLES)

You can also check status, stop and restart using these scripts.

Microsoft IIS – Web Server

The GroupWise Monitor Application is designed to start when the Microsoft IIS Service and Web Server is started. The Microsoft IIS Web Server is designed to start with the Microsoft Internet Information Server Service is started under Control Panel|Administrative Tools|Services.

Logging Into GroupWise Monitor Application

Just point your browser to

https://yourserver.com/gwmon/gwmonitor.

For example:

https://groupwise.caledonia.net/gwmon/gwmonitor.

Once you are ready to continue, just turn to the next chapter in your upgrade plan.

10 Upgrading the GroupWise Calendar Publishing Host

Upgrading the GroupWise Calendar Publish Host is relatively painless, and can be done as soon as the Post Offices it services are upgraded.

If you are running GroupWise Calendar Publishing Host along with GroupWise WebAccess and/or the GroupWise Monitor Application Host on the same server, all of these must be upgraded in the same upgrade cycle or the other applications will not work until they are upgraded.

There are new administration options for the Calendar Publishing Host though, and you will need to read the section below on

Preparing for the Upgrade

There is very little preparation that must be made for the GroupWise Calendar Publishing Host upgrade. It can reside anywhere, and no database adjustments are made when it is installed. You must know the name of your Calendar Publishing Host. To find this information do the following:

1. In the Administration Console, click on System|Calendar Publishing.
2. You will see a list of your Calendar Publishing Hosts.

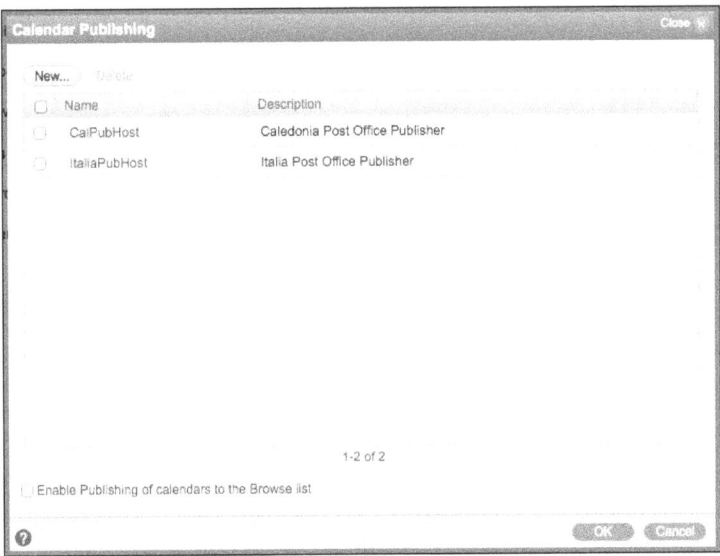

Figure 10-1: List of Calendar Publishing Hosts

3. Note the name of the Calendar Publishing Host that you are upgrading. In our case it is CalPubHost.
4. Now click on Post Office Agents, and choose the Post Office Agent in question. Ours is for our Caledonia Post Office.
5. Click on the Agent Settings Tab.
6. Scroll to the bottom of the page to view the Calendar Publishing Host settings. Note the Port Number. The default is 7171

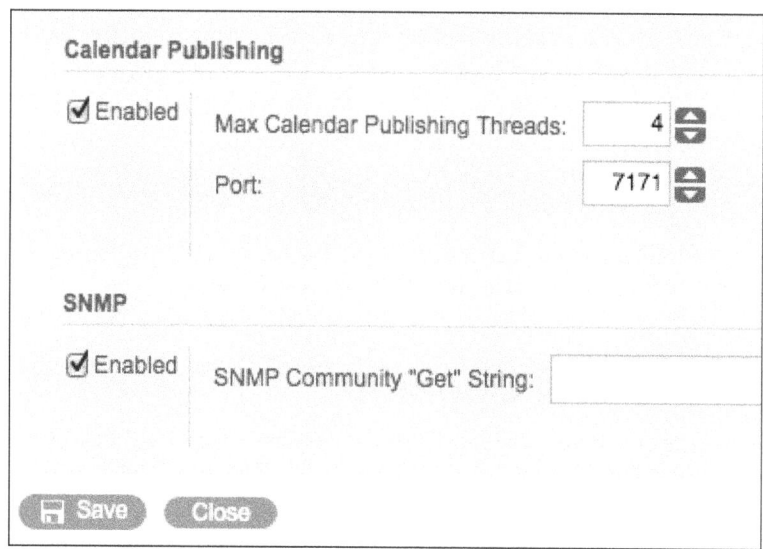

Figure 10-2: The Calendar Publishing settings

Close this Window if you choose.

Installing the Calendar Publishing Host Software

Windows

To install the Calendar Publishing Host software perform the following:
1. From the Windows server where IIS is installed, go to your **<installationfiles>** and run **setup.exe**.
2. Choose GroupWise Calendar Publishing Host.

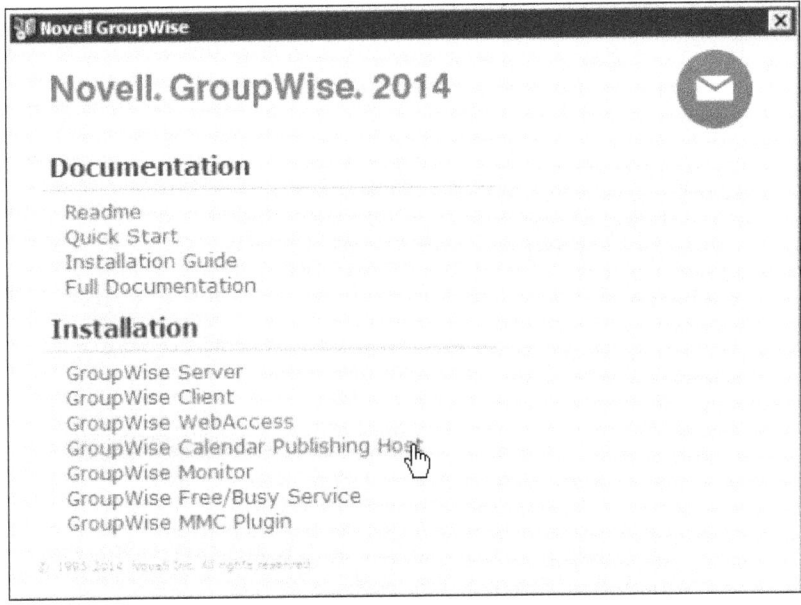

Figure 10-3: Installing the Calendar Publishing Host

3. Choose your language.
4. At the prompt, click next
5. Accept the license agreement.
6. Enter the Calendar Publishing Host Name. In our case this is CalPubHost
7. Choose the IIS web server instances for your Calendar Publishing Host
8. Enter the IP address of the POA for your Calendar Publishing Host. Ours is 192.168.110.192
9. Enter the Calendar Publishing Port Number that we looked up above. The default is 7171.
10. At the Summary screen, confirm that everything is configured as you would like it to be. Then click Install.
11. During the installation, you may be prompted about shutting down the web server and Java and overwriting newer files. You should choose the affirmative answer for all of these questions.
12. When the installation is complete you will be presented with steps to configure your Calendar Publishing Host. Since this is an upgrade, that should already be completed. Click Next.
13. You will be prompted to launch the Installation Summary and restart the web server.

Linux

Here are the quick steps needed to install the Calendar Publishing Host on Linux.

1. As root, run the **install.sh** script in your **<installationfile>** folder.
2. Choose your Language.
3. Choose Installation.

176 | Upgrading the GroupWise Calendar Publishing Host

4. Accept the License Agreement.
5. Choose GroupWise Calendar Publishing Host.

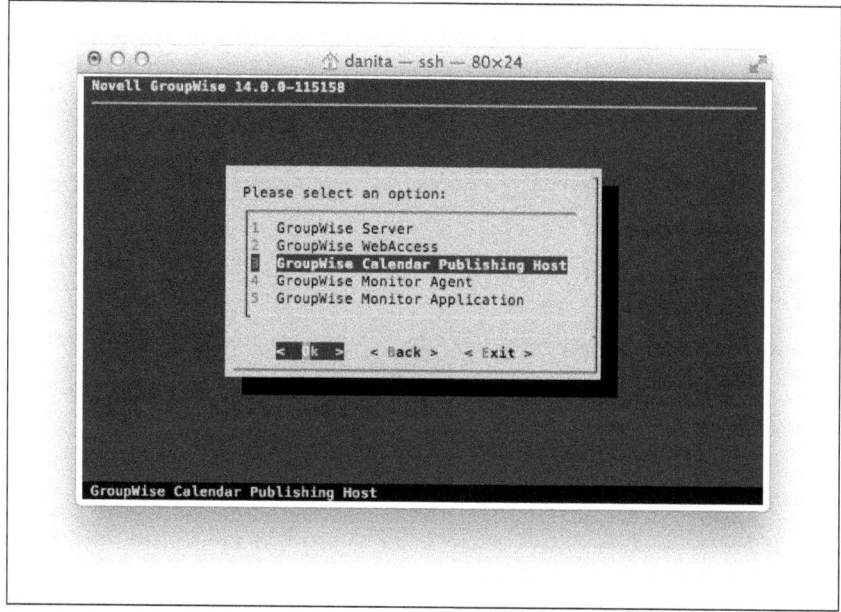

Figure 10-4: The Calendar Publishing Host Installation

6. Choose Install
7. The installation will begin. Tomcat and Apache will be unloaded during the installation. Press Any Key to Continue.
8. After the files are installed, choose Configure
9. Press 1 to continue
10. Enter the Calendar Publishing Host Name. In our case this is CalPubHost
11. Enter the IP address of the POA for your Calendar Publishing Host. Ours is 192.168.110.192
12. Enter the Calendar Publishing Port Number that we looked up above. The default is 7171.
13. At the next screen, unless you have configured custom locations for Apache and/or Tomcat, the defaults should be correct.
14. After the installation, you will be instructed to restart Apache2 and Tomcat6

Loading The GroupWise Calendar Publishing Host

Now we will load the web server and the Tomcat. The instructions for loading the web server or Tomcat are different based upon the platform you are using.

Linux

Assuming you are using the default Apache2 and Tomcat6 installations on your Linux server, load the components thusly:

/etc/init.d/apache2 start

and

/etc/init.d/novell-tomcat6 start (OES)

or

/etc/init.d/tomcat6 start (SLES)

You can also check status, stop and restart using these scripts.

Microsoft IIS – Web Server

The GroupWise Calendar Publishing Host is designed to start when the Microsoft IIS Service and Web Server is started. The Microsoft IIS Web Server is designed to start with the Microsoft Internet Information Server Service is started under Control Panel|Administrative Tools|Services.

Checking the GroupWise Calendar Publishing Host

Just point your browser to

http://yourserver.com/gwcal

For example:
http://groupwise.caledonia.net/gwcal

You will see any published calendars that are available for the System.

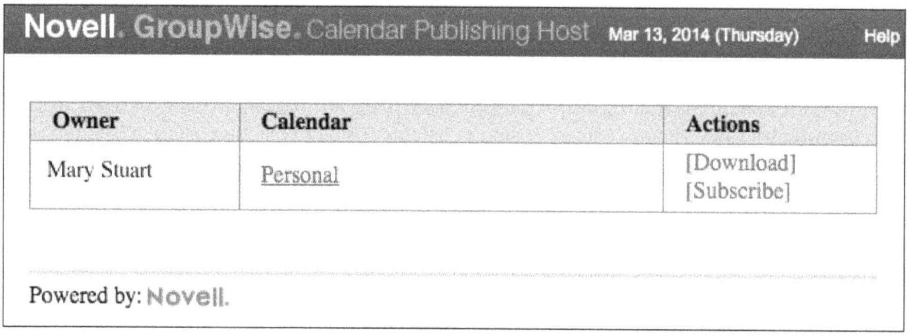

Figure 10-5: Published Calendars

Configuring Calendar Publishing Host Administration

After you have upgraded your Calendar Publishing Host and have verified that it is working, it's time to look at the new administration options. Similarly to WebAccess, Calendar Publishing Host now has its own configuration file on the web server.

Let's go to look at this file.

Linux: /var/opt/novell/groupwise/calhost/calhost.cfg

Windows: c:\novell\groupwise\calhost\calhost.cfg

This file will look very similar to the webacc.cfg that you are probably familiar with.

Enable the CalHost Administration Console

1. In your favorite text editor, search for the line that reads

    Admin.WebConsole.enable=false

2. If this is preceded by a # sign, remove the # to activate this line
3. change false to true.

Now you must restart Tomcat on your server

For Linux, run

/etc/init.d/novell-tomcat6 start (OES)

or

/etc/init.d/tomcat6 start (SLES)

On Windows, click Start > Administrative Tools > Services. Then right-click Tomcat 6, and click Restart.

Load the CalHost Administration Console

To load the CalHost Administration Console, navigate to your server in a web browser like this:

http://yourserver.com/gwcal/admin

You will be prompted to login. Use your gwadmin user credentials you created when we set up the system. Any user who has rights as a Post Office Administrator or higher can log into this console with their own GroupWise credentials.

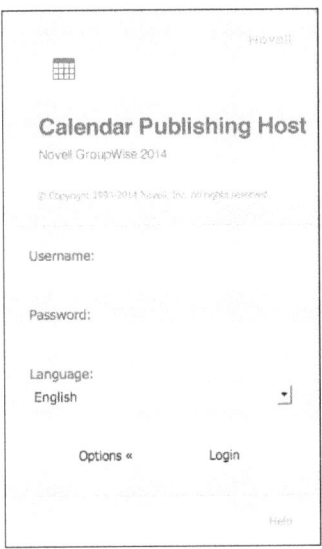

Figure 10-6: Logging into the Calendar Publishing Host Administration Console

Post Office Settings

You will be presented with the following screen:

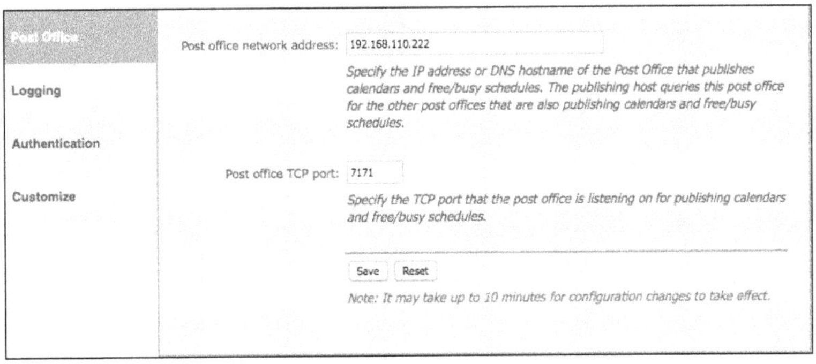

Figure 10-7: The Calendar Publishing Host Administration Console

This screen will show you the settings that were migrated to the new Calendar Publishing Host configuration during upgrade. If the IP address of your POA were to change, you would edit that here.

We'll quickly run through the other screens of this administration console.

Logging Settings

On the Logging Screen you can set your logging settings.

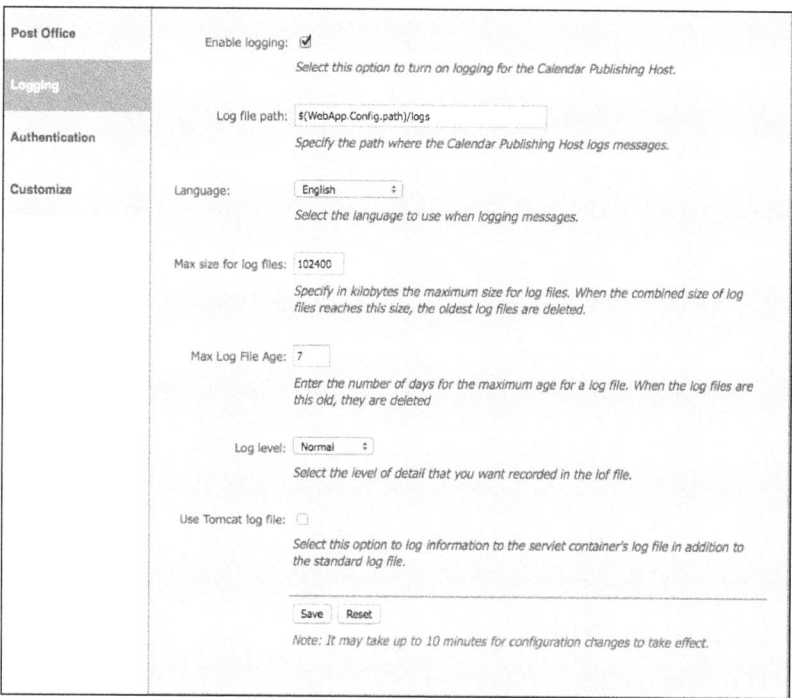

Figure 10-8: The CalHost Log Settings

These settings are very similar to the logging settings for all of your GroupWise agents. The one addition here is that you can choose to log both to the GroupWise agent logs and the Tomcat logs if you desire.

Authentication Settings

If you need to change which Administration Service the Calendar Publishing Host Admin authenticates to, you can do so here.

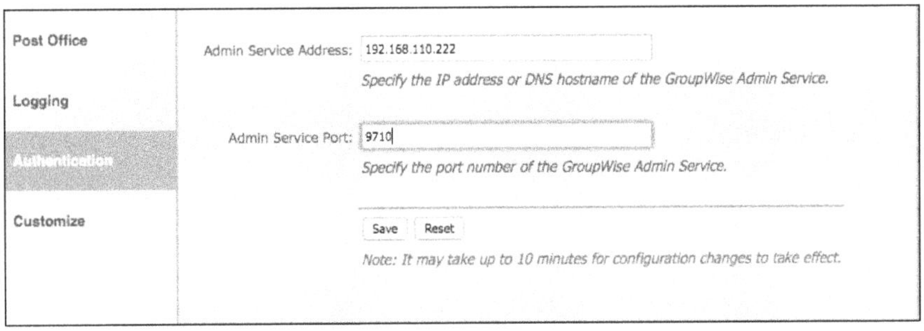

Figure 10-9: Calendar Publishing Host Admin Authentication Settings

Please be aware that this can be affected by the settings we described in *"Verifying MTA Network Settings"* on page 12.

Customize

If you click on the Customize tab, you can change the way the published calendars page looks. For example, we've added a Caledonia logo, changed the text and placed the changed text at the bottom edge of the logo.

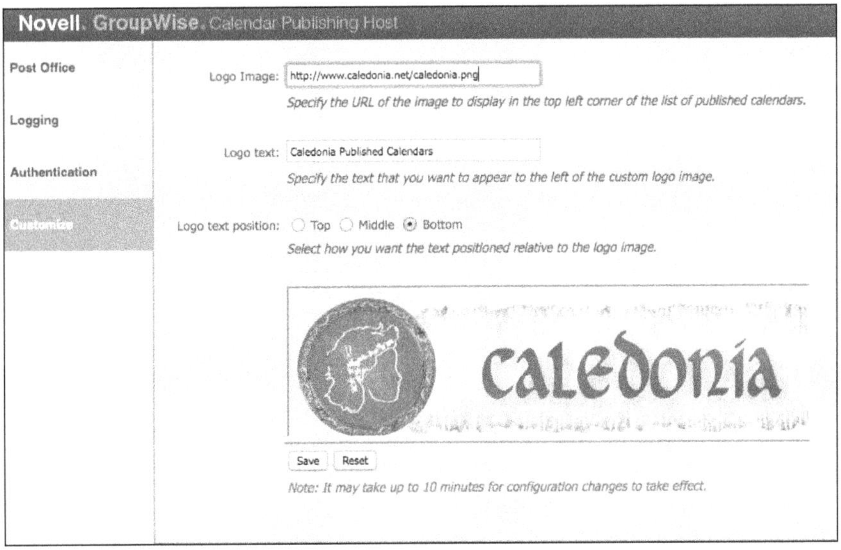

Figure 10-10: Client Customization Settings

Figure 10-11: CalPub Customizations

Updating your Changes

You will notice that on all of the setup screens above there is a notice that you may need to wait up to 10 minutes for changes to occur.

There is a setting in the **calhost.cfg** that defines this time

Config.Update.check=10

While it would be possible to set this for a shorter timeframe, you can also simply restart Tomcat to effect a change immediately.

For Linux, run

/etc/init.d/novell-tomcat6 start (OES)

or

/etc/init.d/tomcat6 start (SLES)

On Windows, click Start > Administrative Tools > Services. Then right-click Tomcat 6, and click Restart.

Troubleshooting

There is little that might go wrong with the actual Calendar Publishing Host upgrade. That said, the addition of the Calendar Publishing Host Administration Console can have its moments!

There are settings in the **calhost.cfg** that pertain to how the new admin console connects to the GroupWise Administration Service.

```
##########################################################################
# Application Administration Tool
##########################################################################
Admin.WebConsole.enable=true
Admin.RestService.host=127.0.0.1
Admin.RestService.port=9710
```

There are a couple of reasons why these default settings might not work for you:

- If you are running the Calendar Publishing Host on a server that does not have a GroupWise Administration Service running, the setting of 127.0.0.1 will be invalid. You will need to change it to the proper ID address.
- If you have an MTA running on this server, but it is set to bind to a specific IP address, the Admin Service will also not be listening on localhost (127.0.0.1) and you should change this to the specific location. Indeed, if your MTA is set to a host name rather than an IP address, the Admin Service could complain if you enter an IP address here. Test to see which works properly for you.
- If you have modified the default port for your Admin Service, you will also need to change the information here.

Once you are ready to continue, just turn to the next chapter in your upgrade plan.

11 Upgrading GroupWise Clients

Most sites find that upgrading the GroupWise client is the last thing they do, simply because it seems to be time consuming and requires a lot of pre-planning. There are many ways to upgrade the GroupWise client, depending on the size and needs of your organization. Smaller sites will have desktop administrators move from desktop to desktop, installing the new GroupWise client (and many sites use this as an opportunity to do other desktop cleanup that has been pending for awhile). Other sites will want more automated solutions. We will look at a number of ways to get your GroupWise system upgraded quickly and smoothly.

Choosing Your Windows Client Installation Method

There are several methods that can be used to upgrade your users to the new GroupWise 2014 Windows client. We'll look at the various methods that Novell provides with GroupWise to upgrade your clients.

- **Manual installation**: Download the combined client executable, and launch it manually at the desktop. You would then walk through the dialogs for the installation.
- **Auto-Update Direct POA Access**: This method relies on the client being notified through the Bump/Build number combination that there is new GroupWise software, and launches the installation when the client logs into the post office.
- **Auto-Update with POA Access Through a Web Server**: Rather than having the POA deliver the files, the auto-update redirects the user to a web server for download.
- **Update through SETUPIP**: This method allow you to distribute the client to remote (or local) users without going through the auto-update process. It is also very handy for rolling out a client upgrade to groups of users, rather than one at a time or at the post office level.
- **Pushing the Client Upgrade through ZCM:** If you use ZCM to manage applications for your users, you can push down the client through ZCM with no intervention by the user.

We'll see how each of these can work for your environment.

The Auto-Update Algorithm

Before we actually get to configuring the post office for the upgrade, we will discuss how the Auto-Update Algorithm affects the upgrade process. GroupWise has a built-in mechanism for notifying the clients that it is time to upgrade. It is called the Auto-Update Algorithm, and it is an integral part of the functionality of the upgrade. While the Auto-Update is very similar to prior versions, there are some differences to take into account, primarily due to the removal of the Software Distribution Directory for GroupWise 2014.

The Auto-Update Algorithm is used in conjunction with the client options, and can be controlled at the Domain, Post Office or even User level for distributing your clients.

In simple terms, here's how the Auto-Update Algorithm works.

- When you install the GroupWise server, the GroupWise Client installation files are copied to the server directories. This is automatic on Linux, and you are given the option to disable this on Windows (but it is the default to include the Client Auto-Update Repository. On Linux this is in **/opt/novell/groupwise/agents/data/** and on Windows at **c:\Program Files\Novell\GroupWise Server\data**.

- When a post office is created, it gets a "bump" or software version number associated with it (0 at creation). The Bump Number is controlled by the Administration Console, and written to the **wpdomain.db** and **wphost.db** for the post office in question. This number is also written to the workstation's registry. This has come to be known as the "Bump" number because it is called that in the Windows Registry. Internally to the GroupWise databases though, this is known as the "Software Version" number.

- GroupWise 2014 has a **version.ini** file that has a "Build" Number in the file. This was formerly the **software.inf** file.

  sample **version.ini**

  [General]

  BuildNumber=4863

- The Client Options settings in the Administration Console define which users/posts offices/domains should be auto-updated.

All of these components work together to ensure that clients are notified of the update. We will use auto-update in some of our methods below, and show you other ways to deliver your software without using the auto-update mechanism.

Auto-Update through Direct POA Access

Follow these steps to set up your post office for Auto-Update through the direct POA access method:

1. The installation routine (see *"Installing the GroupWise Administration Service"* on page 25) copies the client files into the server directories.

2. The client software is copied to **/opt/novell/groupwise/agents/data/client/setup/win32/** directory.

3. In order to better control the client software installation, we need a new directory under here, also called **win32**. So you will need to create a directory so that you have **/opt/novell/groupwise/agents/data/client/setup/win32/win32**, and yes that is **/client/setup/win32/win32**. You are not seeing double.

4. There are a couple of files in the installation directory that do not get copied to the GroupWise server directories, and we will need them in this **win32** directory.

   - **<installationfiles>/client/setup.cfg**
   - **<installationfiles>/client/win32/setup.ini**

   Copy both of these files into **<documentroot>/gwclient/win32/win32**.

You should then change them to reflect your wishes upon installation. We have samples of these files later in this chapter.

In prior versions of GroupWise, the **setup.cfg** file contained settings for enabling auto-update and controlling its use. This has been removed from the **setup.cfg**, and is now control in the Client Options in the GroupWise Administrative Console. Like all client options, these can be set by user, post office or domain. Let's do an example of this for a specific post office.

1. Log into the GroupWise Administration Console.
2. Click on Post Offices.
3. Choose your Post Office from the list of available Post Offices.
4. Click on the Client Options tab.
5. At the bottom left of the Client Options is Client Auto-Update. Click on that setting.
6. In the Client Auto-Update settings you have some options here, which we will discuss:

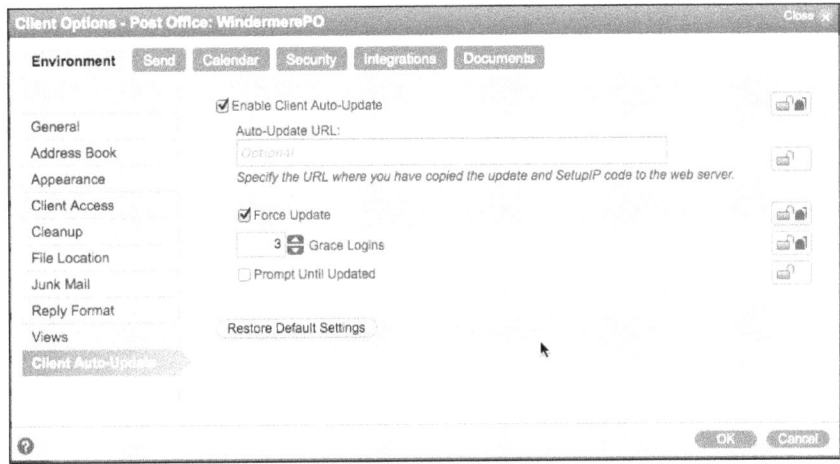

Figure 11-1: Auto-Update Options

- Enable: check this box to enable the auto-update.
- Auto-Update URL: We will discuss this in the next section. For this particular purpose, we will leave this blank.
- Force Update: This setting was formerly in the **setup.cfg** file. If you wish to require your users to update check this. This works in conjunction with:
  - Grace Logins: How many times should a user be able to cancel out of the update before being forced to allow the auto-update to occur.
- Prompt Until Updated: If the user chooses to cancel the update, will s/he be nagged about it until the update is completed.

Finally, before anything will really happen, the administrator must increment Bump Number. The administrator cannot choose the Bump Number, only increment it. To better understand this, let's look at the Bump Number (also known as the "Software Number").

1. In the GroupWise Administration Console, click on Post Offices, and then select the Post Office you wish to modify.

188 | Upgrading GroupWise Clients

2. In the Post Office settings, click on the "Diagnostics" dropdown along the top of the settings and select Display Object.
3. Scroll through the listing until you find "Software Version" In our figure, this is version "1"

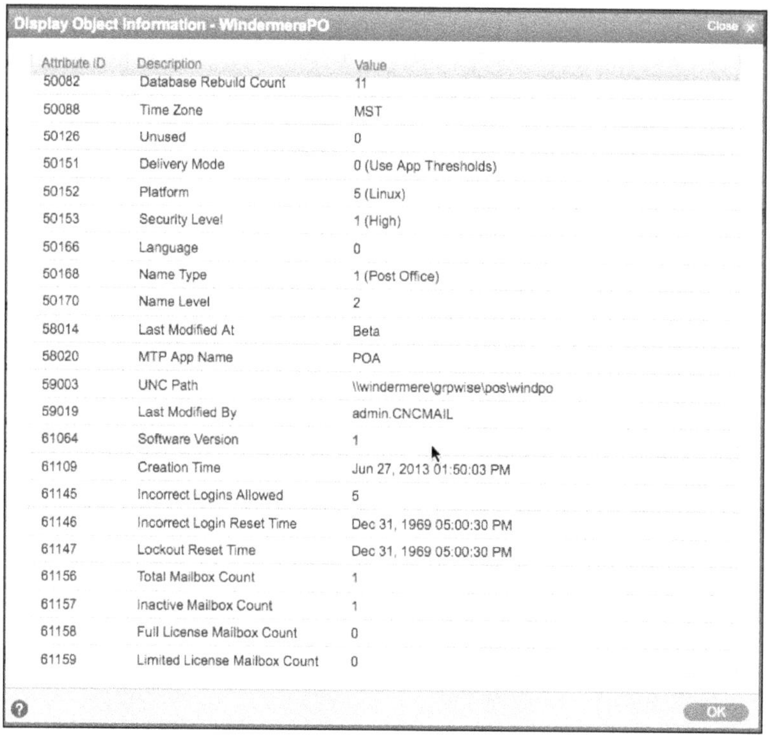

Attribute ID	Description	Value
50082	Database Rebuild Count	11
50088	Time Zone	MST
50126	Unused	0
50151	Delivery Mode	0 (Use App Thresholds)
50152	Platform	5 (Linux)
50153	Security Level	1 (High)
50166	Language	0
50168	Name Type	1 (Post Office)
50170	Name Level	2
58014	Last Modified At	Beta
58020	MTP App Name	POA
59003	UNC Path	\\windermere\grpwise\pos\windpo
59019	Last Modified By	admin.CNCMAIL
61064	Software Version	1
61109	Creation Time	Jun 27, 2013 01:50:03 PM
61145	Incorrect Logins Allowed	5
61146	Incorrect Login Reset Time	Dec 31, 1969 05:00:30 PM
61147	Lockout Reset Time	Dec 31, 1969 05:00:30 PM
61156	Total Mailbox Count	1
61157	Inactive Mailbox Count	1
61158	Full License Mailbox Count	0
61159	Limited License Mailbox Count	0

Figure 11-2: The Internal Software Version Number

To increment the bump number for a post office, follow these instructions:

1. In the GroupWise Administration Console, click on Post Offices, and then select the Post Office you wish to modify.
2. In the Post Office settings, click on the "More" dropdown along the top of the settings.
3. Choose Client Auto-Update

Figure 11-3: Choosing Client Auto-Update

4. When you click the Trigger Update, the Bump Number will change.

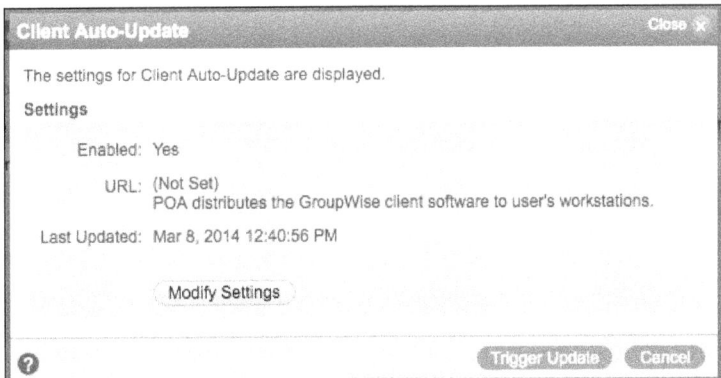

5. This increments the Bump Number for the post office by one. If you follow the above instructions again for Display Object, you will see that the Software Version is one higher than before,

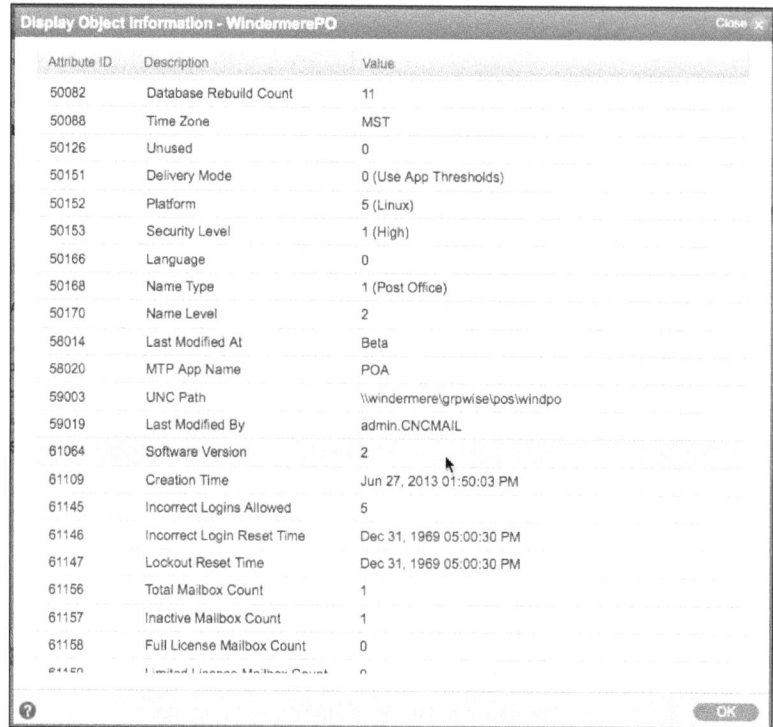

Figure 11-4: Incremented Software Version

6. As we will explain in a few minutes, if you want your users to upgrade, clicking this button multiple times will not cause problems. However, clicking it just once when you do NOT want to upgrade will cause you some headaches!

The stage is now set to initiate your auto-update. The next time a user logs into the post office, the following exchange will occur.

1. The client on the user's PC will query the POA and ask what the Bump Number is.

2. The client on the user's PC then compares this Bump Number to the registry value in **HKEY_LOCAL_MACHINE\SOFTWARE\Novell\GroupWise\Client\5.0\NewSoftwareBump**. For 64 bit machines, this is now in **HKLM\software\Wow6432node\novell\groupwise\client\5.0\NewSoftwareBump**. If this number is different (higher or lower), then the client continues on to ask for the Build Number.

3. The Build Number is found in both the **version.ini** file in the Client Software Update Repository, and in the workstation registry. **HKEY_LOCAL_MACHINE\SOFTWARE\Novell\GroupWise\BuildNumber** or **HKEY_LOCAL_MACHINE\SOFTWAREWow6432Node\Novell\GroupWise\BuildNumber.** The client looks at this value, and if the new value in the **version.ini** file is higher, the client then continues the update query process.

4. The client then compares the settings in Client Options that affect this user (so user/post office/domain), and if Update has been enabled, the upgrade begins.

It is important to note that the workstation must have access to write to the registry in order for the auto-update process to work. If the workstation cannot write the new Bump and Build numbers to the registry, it will not upgrade, and it will not give the user any indication that there is new software.

Once you know these key steps, it's easy to see where odd messages users receive about software updates come from. Here are a couple that we see frequently:

- "There is new GroupWise software available; however you can not access it at this time": This error can occur if the bump number on the post office in question is different than the one in the workstation's registry, and the Build Number is higher, but the user cannot receive the files. For a standard auto-upgrade through the POA, this should not happen, but if you are using a web server for the auto-update, and the web server is unavailable, you might see this message.
- "There may be new GroupWise software available. However, the auto-update process was unable to access the GroupWise Software directory. Please contact your administrator": This one is interesting, because it means that the bump number is different on the post office than on the workstation, but the **version.ini** cannot be accessed to verify that the software is actually newer.

If you have an easy method to change the registry at your workstations, you can also simply change the value in the **HKEY_LOCAL_MACHINE\SOFTWARE\Novell\GroupWise\Client\5.0\NewSoftwareBump** or **HKLM\Software\Wow6432Node\Novell\GroupWise\Client\5.0** to "0". This will ensure that the Bump Number in the registry is different than what is in the **wphost.db** file, and will restart the upgrade query for all (or a subset if you choose to only change the registry for a group of users) of your workstations.

Auto-Update with POA Access Through a Web Server

In the prior section, we saw the following figure:

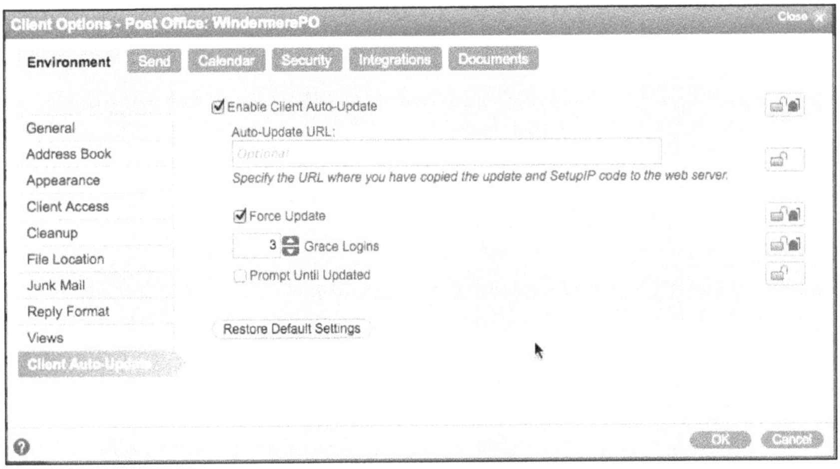

Figure 11-5: Auto-Update Options

We promised to explain the Auto-Login URL, and so here we are! In prior versions of GroupWise, the Software Distribution Directory (SDD) was used to distribute software for Auto-Update. While the POA was responsible to "hand off" the update of the software to the client, it was required that the user logged into the Windows workstations have read rights to the Software Distribution Directory in order to run the installation routine.

GroupWise 2014 has abandoned the SDD, and has instead compressed the installation files at the Post Office server. In order to continue to provide auto-update for even the smallest of sites with very limited server resources and administrative staff, auto-update at the POA was developed, so that out-of-the-box, without too much additional configuration, auto-update could be delivered to users. Thus, if you use the direct access as described above, the POA will actually deliver the installation files to the users for decompressing and installation.

On an already very busy post office, this can cause some slowdowns first thing Monday morning when all of your users arrive and are presented the auto-update option! To alleviate this, Novell has added a new "web server delivery" method for auto-update. This is very similar to SETUPIP, but requires less configuration, and is still reliant on the auto-update algorithm we described above.

Preparing the Web Server

The steps will be very similar to the above. The first thing you must do is configure your web server. We will not go through installing and setting up a web server for you. Refer to the documentation of the server on which you wish to install web services. There is no reason why you cannot use your GroupWise WebAccess server for this purpose if you choose, or you could fire up a small server for the dedicated purpose of providing GroupWise client installation functionality.

The steps are the same for Apache2 on Linux or IIS on Windows. You must simply start at your document root. On SLES/OES, this is **/srv/www/htdocs**. On IIS this would be **c:\inetpub\wwwroot**. We will refer to this from here on out as simply **<documentroot>** for both Windows and Linux.

1. Create a new folder under the document root. You can name it anything you like, but **gwclient** seems reasonable!

2. The installation routine (see *"Installing the GroupWise Administration Service"* on page 25) copies the client files into the server directories.

3. The client software is copied to **<serverfiles>/agents/data/client/setup/win32/** directory. Copy the entire **<serverfiles>\agents\data\client\setup\win32** into your web server **<documentroot>\gwclient** folder that you created above so that you have **<documentroot>/gwclient/win32** on the server.

4. In order to better control the client software installation, we need a new directory under here, also called **win32**. So you will need to create a directory so that you have **<documentroot>/gwclient/win32/win32** (yes, that's two **win32** folders).

5. There are a couple of files in the installation directory that do not get copied to the GroupWise server directories, and we will need them in this **win32** directory.

    - **<installationfiles>/client/setup.cfg**
    - **<installationfiles>/client/win32/setup.ini**

    Copy both of these files into **<documentroot>/gwclient/win32/win32**.

    You should then change them to reflect your wishes upon installation. We have samples of these files later in this chapter.

Apache Specific Settings

On Apache on Linux, depending on the settings of your server, you may need to give specific access rights to this folder structure before the web server will actually deliver files for you. So perform the following steps for this.

1. Go to the **/etc/apache2/conf.d** folder on your Linux server.

2. Create a new text file here and call it something like **gwclient.conf**. The name is not really important as long as it has a **.conf** extension. Just name it something that will make sense to you later.

3. Place the following contents in this file:

   <Directory /srv/www/htdocs/gwclient>

      Options Indexes

      AllowOverrides None

      Order allow,deny

      Allow from all

   </Directory>

4. Restart Apache2. i.e., type **rcapache2 restart**

IIS Specific Settings

On Windows Server, you will need to give specific access rights to your GroupWise client files before the web server will actually deliver the files to your users. Here are the steps required to accomplish this:

1. Click Start > Administrative Tools > Internet Information Services (IIS) Manager.

2. Expand the Local Computer object, expand the Sites folder, expand your website, then select the client software directory that you created above under *"Preparing the Web Server"*. Here we will enable directory browsing so that the **gwclient** directory can be accessed:
   - In the Features View, double-click Directory Browsing.
   - In the Actions pane, click Enable.
   - Click the client software directory to return to the Features View.

3. Next, to configure IIS to allow the download of the client software files:
   - In the Features View, double-click MIME Types.
   - In the Actions pane, click Add.
   - In the File name extension field, type .* (a period followed by an asterisk).
   - In the MIME type field, type application/octet-stream.
   - Click OK.

4. Click the client software directory to return to the Features View.

Is is possible that you have configured file filtering at a higher level in this website. Is so, you must also configure IIS to not filter out files in the client software directory:

1. In the Features View, double-click Request Filtering.

2. Click Allow File Name Extension.
3. In the File name extension field, type .* (a period followed by an asterisk).
4. Click OK.

Finally, we will restart IIS. You can do this one of two ways:
1. In IIS Manager, click on the IIS Server Name
2. In the left-hand column choose "Restart Server"

Alternately, you can restart the IIS service as follows:
1. Click Start > Administrative Tools > Services.
2. Right-click World Wide Web Publishing Service, and click Restart.

Web Server Cleanup

Both Linux and Windows leave some files around that will cause trouble with the download of the GroupWise files.

On Windows, specifically, there is a file called **web.config** in your document root (typically **c:\inetpub\wwwroot**). This file, while important, will trip up the download of your GroupWise files. To avoid issues, right-click on the file, go to Properties and change the file to "hidden".

For both servers, look in the **win32\win32** directory for any temporary files that might have been created when you were editing the **setup.cfg** and **setup.ini** files. On Linux, these typically end with a ~ - for example, **setup.cfg~**. These extraneous files can also cause download issues. Delete them.

Test the Software Availability

Regardless of your web server platform, you should test to verify that the client software is available from a browser. Follow these instructions to do so:
1. From your browser, navigate to http://web_server_address/gwclient (assuming this is the directory you chose for your installation).
2. Verify that you can see files and or directories related to your installation.

Enabling Auto-Update in GroupWise

In prior versions of GroupWise, the **setup.cfg** file contained settings for enabling auto-update and controlling its use. This has been removed from the **setup.cfg**, and is now control in the Client Options in the GroupWise Administrative Console. Like all client options, these can be set by user, post office or domain. Let's do an example of this for a specific post office.
1. Log into the GroupWise Administration Console.
2. Click on Post Offices.

3. Choose your Post Office from the list of available Post Offices.
4. Click on the Client Options tab.
5. At the bottom left of the Client Options is Client Auto-Update. Click on that setting.
6. In the Client Auto-Update settings you have some options here, which we will discuss:

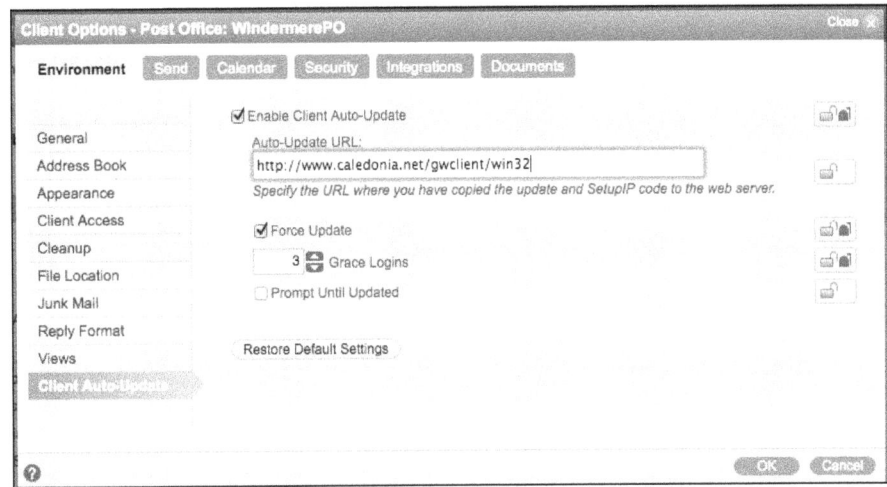

Figure 11-6: Auto-Update Options

- Enable: check this box to enable the auto-update.
- Auto-Update URL: Put in the path to your web server, including the **gwclient** directory we created.
- Force Update: This setting was formerly in the **setup.cfg** file. If you wish to require your users to update check this. This works in conjunction with:
    - Grace Logins: How many times should a user be able to cancel out of the update before being forced to allow the auto-update to occur.
- Prompt Until Updated: If the user chooses to cancel the update, will s/he be nagged about it until the update is completed.

Finally, before anything will really happen, the administrator must increment Bump Number. The administrator cannot choose the Bump Number, only increment it. To better understand this, let's look at the Bump Number (also known as the "Software Number").

1. In the GroupWise Administration Console, click on Post Offices, and then select the Post Office you wish to modify.
2. In the Post Office settings, click on the "Diagnostics" dropdown along the top of the settings and select Display Object.
3. Scroll through the listing until you find "Software Version" In our figure, this is version "1"

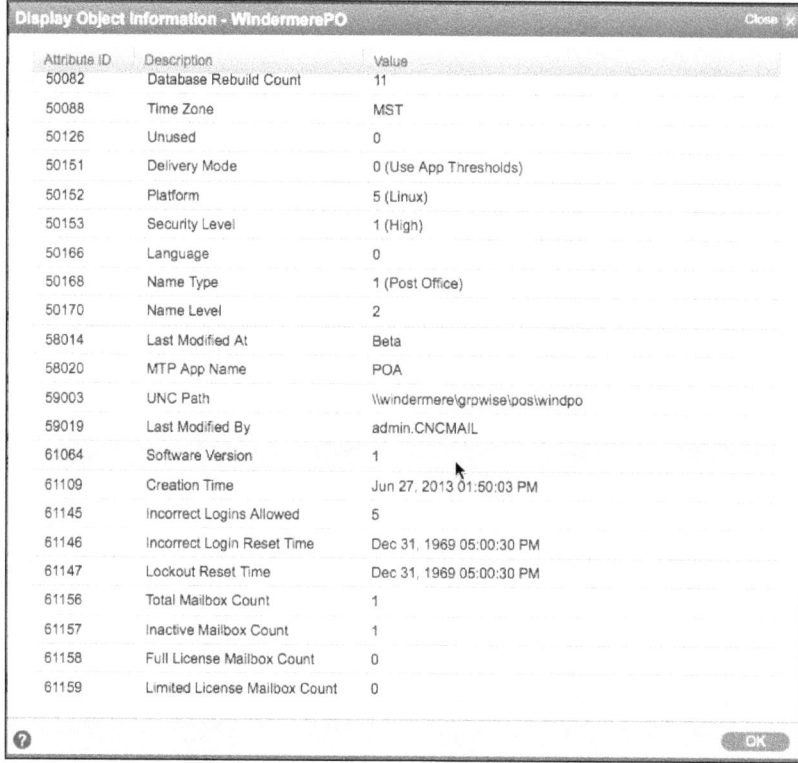

Figure 11-7: The Internal Software Version Number

To increment the bump number for a post office, follow these instructions:

1. In the GroupWise Administration Console, click on Post Offices, and then select the Post Office you wish to modify.
2. In the Post Office settings, click on the "More" dropdown along the top of the settings.
3. Choose Client Auto-Update

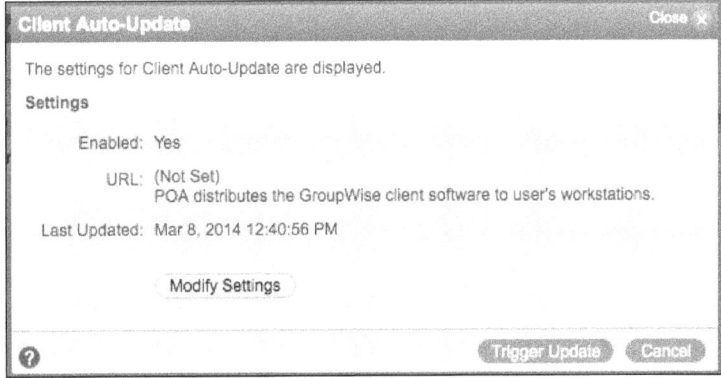

Figure 11-8: Choosing Client Auto-Update

4. When you click the Trigger Update, the Bump Number will change.

5. This increments the Bump Number for the post office by one. If you follow the above instructions again for Display Object, you will see that the Software Version is one higher than before,

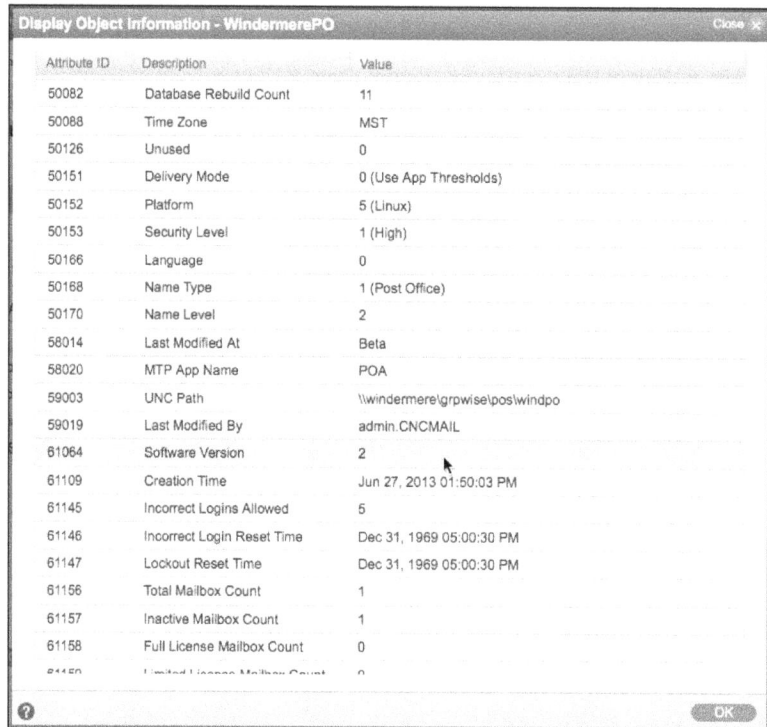

Figure 11-9: Incremented Software Version

6. As we will explain in a few minutes, if you want your users to upgrade, clicking this button multiple times will not cause problems. However, clicking it just once when you do NOT want to upgrade will cause you some headaches!

The stage is now set to initiate your auto-update. The next time a user logs into the post office, the following exchange will occur.

1. The client on the user's PC will query the POA and ask what the Bump Number is.

2. The client on the user's PC then compares this Bump Number to the registry value in **HKEY_LOCAL_MACHINE\SOFTWARE\Novell\GroupWise\Client\5.0\ NewSoftwareBump**. On 64 bit OS this is **HKLM\software\Wow6432node\novell\ groupwise\client\5.0\NewSoftwareBump** If this number is different (higher or lower), then the client continues on to ask for the Build Number.

3. The Build Number is found in both the **version.ini** file in the Client Software Update Repository, and in the workstation registry. The client looks at this value, and if the new value in the **version.ini** file is higher, the client then continues the update query process.

4. The client then compares the settings in Client Options that affect this user (so user/post office/domain), and if Update has been enabled, the upgrade begins.

It is important to note that the workstation must have access to write to the registry in order for the auto-update process to work. If the workstation cannot write the new Bump and Build numbers to the registry, it will not upgrade, and it will not give the user any indication that there is new software.

Once you know these key steps, it's easy to see where odd messages users receive about software updates come from. Here are a couple that we see frequently:

- "There is new GroupWise software available; however you can not access it at this time": This error can occur if the bump number on the post office in question is different than the one in the workstation's registry, and the Build Number is higher, but the user cannot receive the files. For a standard auto-upgrade through the POA, this should not happen, but if you are using a web server for the auto-update, and the web server is unavailable, you might see this message.
- "There may be new GroupWise software available. However, the auto-update process was unable to access the GroupWise Software directory. Please contact your administrator": This one is interesting, because it means that the bump number is different on the post office than on the workstation, but the **version.ini** cannot be accessed to verify that the software is actually newer.

If you have an easy method to change the registry at your workstations, you can also simply change the value in the **HKEY_LOCAL_MACHINE\SOFTWARE\Novell\GroupWise\Client\5.0\NewSoftwareBump** or **HKLM\software\Wow6432node\novell\groupwise\client\5.0\NewSoftwareBump** to "0". This will ensure that the Bump Number in the registry is different than what is in the **wphost.db** file, and will restart the upgrade query for all (or a subset if you choose to only change the registry for a group of users) of your workstations.

Upgrading the GroupWise Client with SETUPIP

Earlier in this chapter we discussed how you can now trigger auto-update by domain, post office or even user. However, there is no way to multi-select subsets of users and edit their client options, or change the client options of a group.

This is where SETUPIP really shines, because you can configure a distribution of the GroupWise client, and then you can simply distribute a small executable to multiple users (via email, or placing it on a web server for download) and manage a more controlled rollout of the client.

SETUPIP requires a web server to serve up the client files. When you deliver the GroupWise client using SETUPIP, it downloads a compressed version of the GroupWise client from a file called **setupip.fil**. Any additional languages you wish to include will only add 3-5 MB per language to the download. After everything is downloaded, SETUPIP launches the GroupWise client **setup.exe** installation program from the users local hard drive and the installation begins.

Additionally, SETUPIP can be used to install GroupWise fresh on a PC that has never had GroupWise before. This allows you to get the client to remote workers who have never had their laptops in the office!

Configuring Your Web Server

You can use any web server available that allows connections on port 80. Here are the steps to configure your web server. The procedure is almost identical to our previous settings under *"Auto-Update with POA Access Through a Web Server"*.

The steps are the same for Apache2 on Linux or IIS on Windows. You must simply start at your document root. On SLES/OES, this is **/srv/www/htdocs**. On IIS this would be **c:\inetpub\wwwroot**. We will refer to this from here on out as simply **<documentroot>** for both Windows and Linux.

1. Create a new folder under the document root. You can name it anything you like, but **gwclient** seems reasonable!

2. The installation routine (see *"Installing the GroupWise Administration Service"* on page 25) copies the client files into the server directories.

3. The client software is copied to **<serverfiles>/agents/data/client/setup/win32/** directory. Copy the entire contents of **<serverfiles>\agents\data\client\setup\win32** into your web server **<documentroot>\gwclient** folder that you created above.

4. In order to better control the client software installation, we need a new directory under here, also called **win32**. So you will need to create a directory so that you have **<documentroot>/gwclient/win32/win32**.

5. There are a couple of files in the installation directory that do not get copied to the GroupWise server directories, and we will need them in this **win32** directory.

    - **<installationfiles>/client/setup.cfg**
    - **<installationfiles>/client/win32/setup.ini**

    Copy both of these files into **<documentroot>/gwclient/win32/win32**.

    You should then change them to reflect your wishes upon installation. We have samples of these files later in this chapter.

6. In the **win32** folder you will have all of the available language files (e.g. **setupip.xx**, where **xx** is an appropriate language designation such as en for English or **fr** for French-France. If you have more than one language file the client will be presented with a list of languages that can be downloaded and extracted. If the user selects more than one language, the GroupWise Client will be installed in all of the selected languages. You should remove all language files from this folder for languages that are not needed for your organization. If only one language file exists, users will not be prompted to select languages for the installation. If you require more than one language file for your system, configuring your **setup.cfg** file will allow you to set the default language. Also, you must indicate "Yes" for any languages you wish to have installed. Otherwise only the default language will be installed.

Apache Specific Settings

On Apache on Linux, depending on the settings of your server, you may need to give specific access rights to this folder structure before the web server will actually deliver files for you. So perform the following steps for this.

1. Go to the **/etc/apache2/conf.d** folder on your Linux server.

2. Create a new text file here and call it something like **gwclient.conf**. The name is not really important as long as it has a **.conf** extension. . Just name it something that will make sense to you later.

3. Place the following contents in this file:

    <Directory /srv/www/htdocs/gwclient>

       Options Indexes

       AllowOverrides None

       Order allow,deny

       Allow from all

    </Directory>

4. Restart Apache2. i.e., type **rcapache2 restart**

IIS Specific Settings

On Windows Server, you will need to give specific access rights to your GroupWise client files before the web server will actually deliver the files to your users. Here are the steps required to accomplish this:

1. Click Start > Administrative Tools > Internet Information Services (IIS) Manager.

2. Expand the Local Computer object, expand the Sites folder, expand your website, then select the client software directory that you created above under *"Preparing the Web Server"*. Here we will enable directory browsing so that the **gwclient** directory can be accessed:

    - In the Features View, double-click Directory Browsing.
    - In the Actions pane, click Enable.
    - Click the client software directory to return to the Features View.

3. Next, to configure IIS to allow the download of the client software files:

    - In the Features View, double-click MIME Types.
    - In the Actions pane, click Add.
    - In the File name extension field, type .* (a period followed by an asterisk).
    - In the MIME type field, type application/octet-stream.
    - Click OK.

4. Click the client software directory to return to the Features View.

Is is possible that you have configured file filtering at a higher level in this website. Is so, you must also configure IIS to not filter out files in the client software directory:

1. In the Features View, double-click Request Filtering.
2. Click Allow File Name Extension.
3. In the File name extension field, type .* (a period followed by an asterisk).
4. Click OK.

Finally, we will restart IIS. You can do this one of two ways:

1. In IIS Manager, click on the IIS Server Name
2. In the left-hand column choose "Restart Server"

Alternately, you can restart the IIS service as follows:

1. Click Start > Administrative Tools > Services.
2. Right-click World Wide Web Publishing Service, and click Restart.

Web Server Cleanup

Both Linux and Windows leave some files around that will cause trouble with the download of the GroupWise files.

On Windows, specifically, there is a file called **web.config** in your document root (typically **c:\inetpub\wwwroot**). This file, while important, will trip up the download of your GroupWise files. To avoid issues, right-click on the file, go to Properties and change the file to "hidden".

For both servers, look in the **win32\win32** directory for any temporary files that might have been created when you were editing the **setup.cfg** and **setup.ini** files. On Linux, these typically end with a **~** - for example, **setup.cfg~**. These extraneous files can also cause download issues. Delete them.

Test the Software Availability

Regardless of your web server platform, you should test to verify that the client software is available from a browser. Follow these instructions to do so:

1. From your browser, navigate to http://web_server_address/gwclient (assuming this is the directory you chose for your installation).
2. Verify that you can see files and or directories related to your installation.

Now that you've configured your web server, we can create the **setupip.exe** that will control the installation of the GroupWise client through the web server. The next section entitled *"Configure and Generate the setupip.exe Executable"* will explain this process.

Configure and Generate the setupip.exe Executable

The **setupip.exe** file is used to download and launch the GroupWise client installation over an IP connection to a web server. When executed, the **setupip.exe** file downloads the compressed GroupWise client and then launches the **setup.exe** file. The **setupip.exe** file contains the location (URL) to your web server(s) where you have hosted the GroupWise client as explained previously. The procedure to create the **setupip.exe** file is a Windows application (**writeip.exe**). If your GroupWise server is on Linux, this presents a bit of a complication, because you have not "installed" server files on Windows in order to extract these files. There are a couple of ways to get access to these files for our purposes. A few ideas are:

- If this is an OES server, place the **<serverfiles>/agents/client** directory and your **<installationfiles>** on a NCP accessible drive.
- Configure SAMBA for shares to the **<serverfiles>** and **<installationfiles>** and map drives from Windows to these SAMBA shares.
- Download the Windows GroupWise full distribution and extract the files by doing the following:
  - After downloading the full Windows distribution zip file, right-click on the file and choose "Extract All" and place it in a directory of your choice. For example **c:\temp\gwinstall**. This would then serve as your **<installationfiles>** directory for the rest of this SETUPIP section.
  - change to this new **<installationfiles>\server\win64** directory

- run **setup.exe /extract c:\temp\gwserver** (or any location you choose). Use this location as your **<serverfiles>** location for accessing the required client files.

Our preference is actually the latter. In any event, you must have access from Windows for this process!

To generate your **setupip.exe** follow these steps.

1. From your **<serverfiles>/data/client/setup/win32** folder, run the utility called **writeip.exe.**

2. In the WRITEIP utility fill in the DNS name or IP address of the web server with the appropriate location to the GroupWise client directory on the web server. Based on the previous section this would be **http://<your server IP or DNS name>/gwclient**

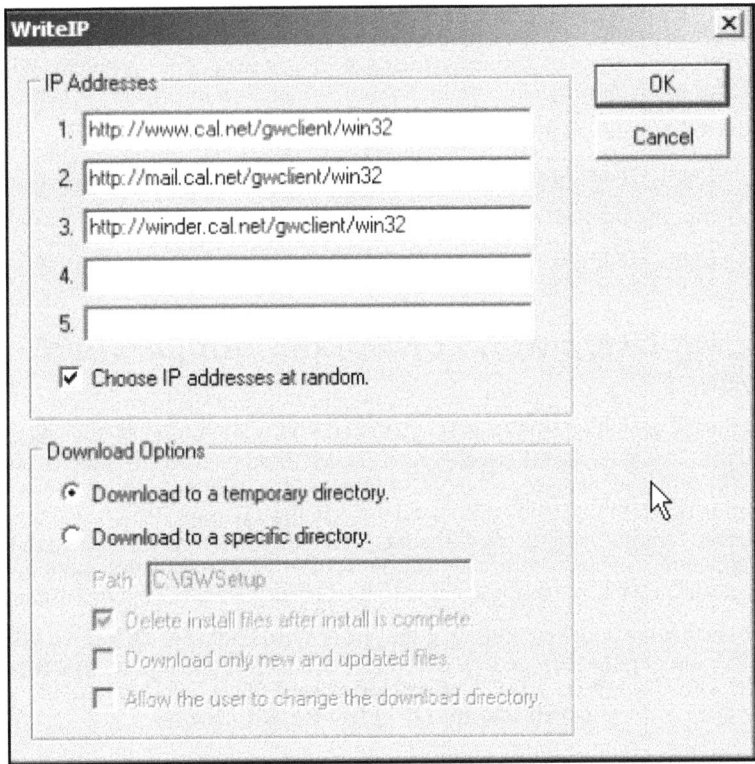

Figure 11-10: The Write IP interface

NOTE: You can define multiple web servers for the GroupWise client download. This allows the client to be downloaded randomly from the sites you define if you check this option. Otherwise, if the first web server is down, the client will be downloaded from the next web server on the list. If you are providing SETUPIP functionality for users both on your network and across the Internet, you might want to provide URLs with both private and public IP addresses to the same web server location.

204 | Upgrading GroupWise Clients

3. After filling in the information in the WRITEIP utility select the OK button, which will generate a new executable in the **<serverfiles>/agents/data/client/setup/win32** directory called **setupip.exe**.

4. Copy the **setupip.exe** file to the into the **<documentroot>/gwclient** directory of the web server.

5. You can instruct users to set up their GroupWise client by going directly to http://yourserver.com/gwclient/setupip.exe - then when they download this file, the installation of the client will begin.

6. Alternatively, you can email the **setupip.exe** to your users. Instruct them to save the attachment locally, close groupwise and run **setupip.exe** to upgrade.

Troubleshooting SETUPIP

The SETUPIP utility makes a file called **setupip.err** in the Windows program directory. The Windows program directory is usually **c:\windows**. If you experience problems with SETUPIP, look at this file for some clues.

Some of the more common problems with SETUPIP are

- not putting in the entire path to the files in the http: links
- not configuring the web server to be able to access the files
- having errors in the gwclient.conf on Apache

Upgrading Users with ZENworks Configuration Management

The following information is applicable to ZENworks Configuration Management (ZCM) 10.3 through 11.3. If you have earlier versions of ZCM, these instructions may not work in your environment. We will not cover any other ZCM versions for this guide. Also, we will not cover every permutation of ZCM that you might need for installing GroupWise. If you are using ZCM, we assume you are familiar with the ZCC dialogs, and that you know how to assign your own relationships and requirements to your application bundles. The steps below are only intended to show the part of the ZCM setup that is specific to the GroupWise 2014 client installation.

The first thing that we do when preparing the GroupWise client for ZCM is to generate the GroupWise MST file required for the installation. This is done by using the **gwtuner.exe** file that is supplied with GroupWise 2014. The **gwtuner.exe** file is found in both the Linux and Windows distributions in **<installationfiles>\admin\utility\tools.**

As you can probably see, **gwtuner.exe** is a Windows application, and it needs access to files from the **<installationfiles>\client** folders. The Zenworks Control Center needs access to both the **<installation files>** and the **<serverfiles>** folders. If your GroupWise server is on Linux, this presents a bit of a complication, because you have not "installed" server files on Windows in order to extract these files. There are a couple of ways to get access to these files for our purposes. A few ideas are:

- If this is an OES server, place the **<serverfiles>/agents/client** directory and your **<installationfiles>** on a NCP accessible drive.
- Configure SAMBA for shares to the **<serverfiles>** and **<installationfiles>** and map drives from Windows to these SAMBA shares.
- Download the Windows GroupWise full distribution and extract the files by doing the following:

- After downloading the full Windows distribution zip file, right-click on the file and choose "Extract All" and place it in a directory of your choice. For example **c:\temp\gwinstall**. This would then serve as your **<installationfiles>** directory for the rest of this ZCM section.
- change to this new **<installationfiles>\server\win64** directory
- run **setup.exe /extract c:\temp\gwserver** (or any location you choose). Use this location as your **<serverfiles>** location for accessing the required client files.

Our preference is actually the latter. In any event, you must have access from Windows for this process!

1. Run the **gwtuner.exe** file. You will see the information in Figure 11-11.

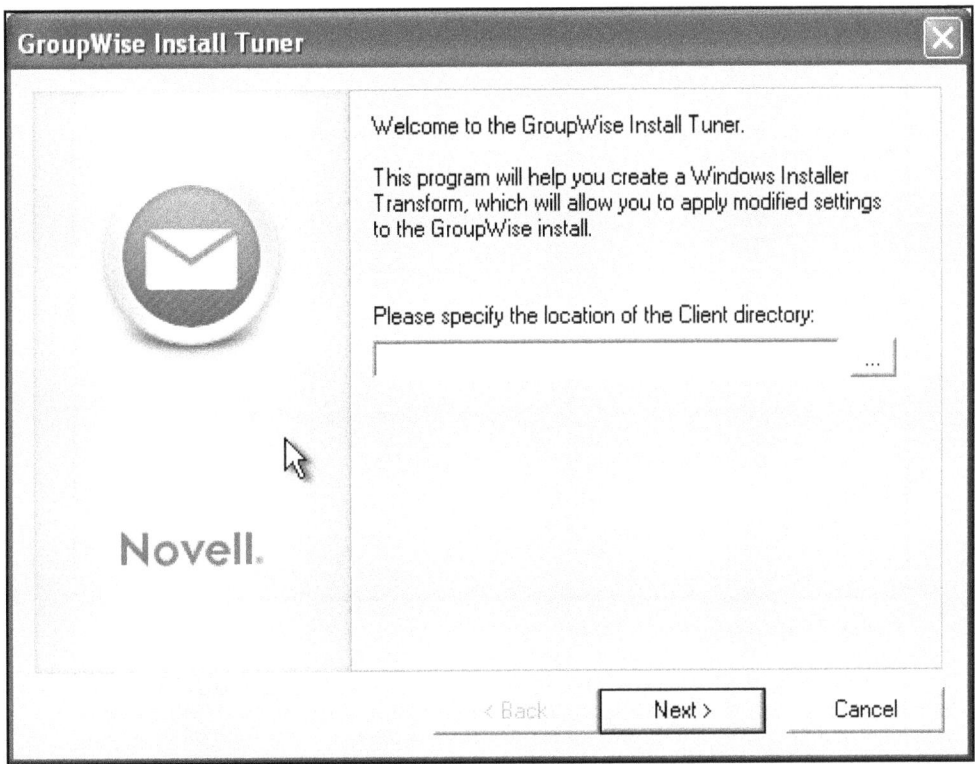

Figure 11-11: The GWTuner Client Directory Window

2. At this screen, enter the location of your client directory in **<installationfiles>** folder.
3. The next screen shows the options for the installation. For our purposes, we wish to have ZCM control the client entirely, so we will go over the options here. In order to allow ZCM to control these options, we are unchecking most of the boxes in the dialog:
    - **Install path**: Enter your installation path. The default is shown in the figure below.
    - **Program folder:** This is the name of the Program folder, should you choose to create one (as you will see later, we will not be creating a program folder during our setup).

- **Add GroupWise to the Desktop:** If you choose, you can add a GroupWise icon to the desktop during installation. For our purposes this is unchecked, as we will allow ZCM to control this
- **Add GroupWise to the Quick Launch:** We can also add an icon to the Quick Launch. We are leaving this unchecked.
- **Add Notify to the Startup folder:** We wish to control this with ZCM, so we are leaving this unchecked.
- **Install Internet Browser Mail Integration:** This adds "mail to" functionality to your browsers to launch GroupWise when a "mail to" link is clicked.
- **Add icons to the Start Menu:** If we leave this checked, the Program folder listed above will be created for the Start Menu.

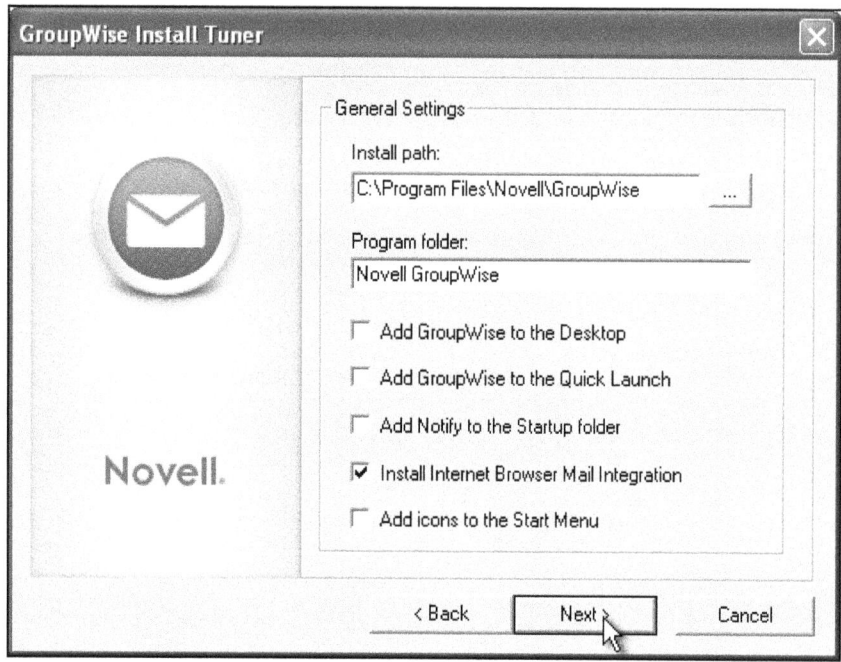

Figure 11-12: The GWTuner General Settings

4. The next screen will allow you to choose the languages you wish to install. You can, of course, choose as many languages here as you require. If you choose more than one language, the next screen will prompt you for the default language for the installation.

5. When you click Finish, your **groupwise.mst** file will be created in the **win32** directory under the **<installationfiles>\client\win32** folder.

Now that our **groupwise.mst** file has been created, we can configure the ZCM routine to deliver this client to the workstation. Novell has made some modifications to the GroupWise and ZCM settings that allow this to happen with much less work that in past versions. As we saw in the *"Upgrading the GroupWise Client with SETUPIP"* section above, the GroupWise client for SETUPIP is packaged in a file called setupip.fil that contains the complete GroupWise client for distribution. This is found in your **<serverfiles>/agents/data/client/setup/win32** folder. ZCM will be able to use this file, and a few other files to manage the GroupWise installation, rather than thousands of individual files as in the past. The only files we will need for our ZCM repository are **setupip.fil**, **extract_setupip_packs.cmd** and the language files we chose in the GroupWise Install Tuner. So, if we had chosen English and German as our languages to install above, we would need to also have **setupip.en** and **setupip.de** for our bundle. We will walk through those steps now.

1. Launch your Zenworks Control Center in your browser, and choose Bundles.
2. Create a new bundle by clicking on "New" and then choosing "Bundle" and then indicating it is a Windows Bundle and click Next.

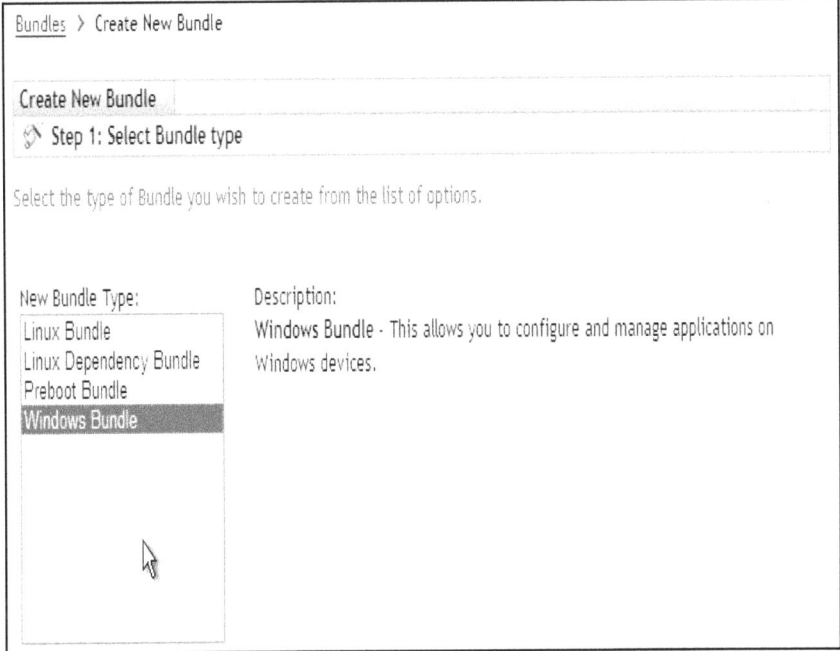

Figure 11-13: Creating a new ZCM Windows Bundle

3. Create this as an empty bundle so that we can configure the actions as necessary.
4. On the next screen we will need to fill in a number of values:
   - **Bundle Name**: Give your bundle a name such as "**GW2014**"
   - **Folder**: The default is **/Bundles**.
   - **Icon**: GroupWise 2014 has specified an icon for this use. Browse to your **<installationfiles>/client/win32** directory and choose **grpwise2014.ico** as your icon file.
   - **Description**: Enter your description for GroupWise 2014 Client here.

208 | Upgrading GroupWise Clients

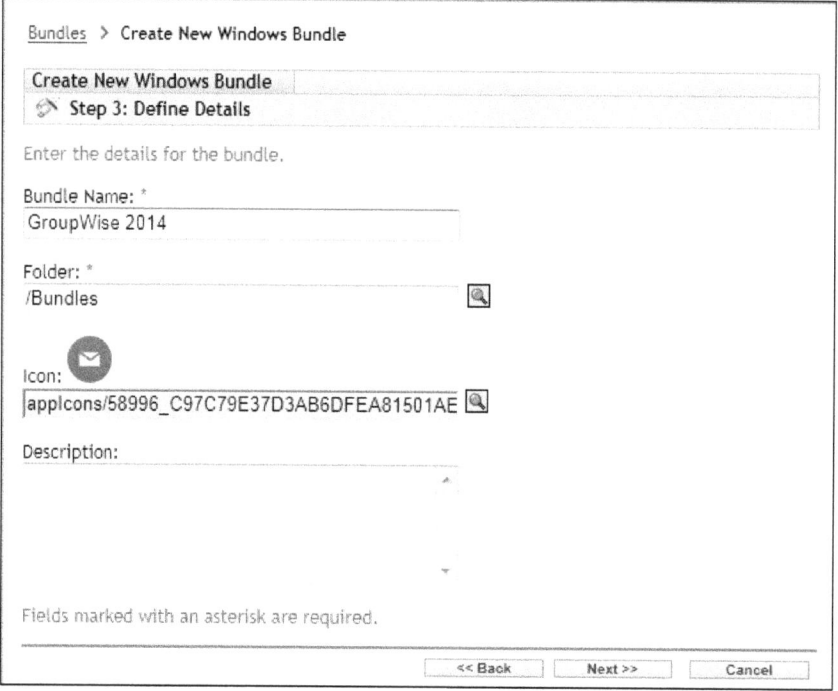

Figure 11-14: Creating the new GroupWise Bundle

5. On the next screen ZCM 11 will allow you to create your bundle as a "Sandbox" version if you choose to do so until you are ready to publish the bundle for installation. Leave "Define Additional Properties" checked here so that we can further customize the application.

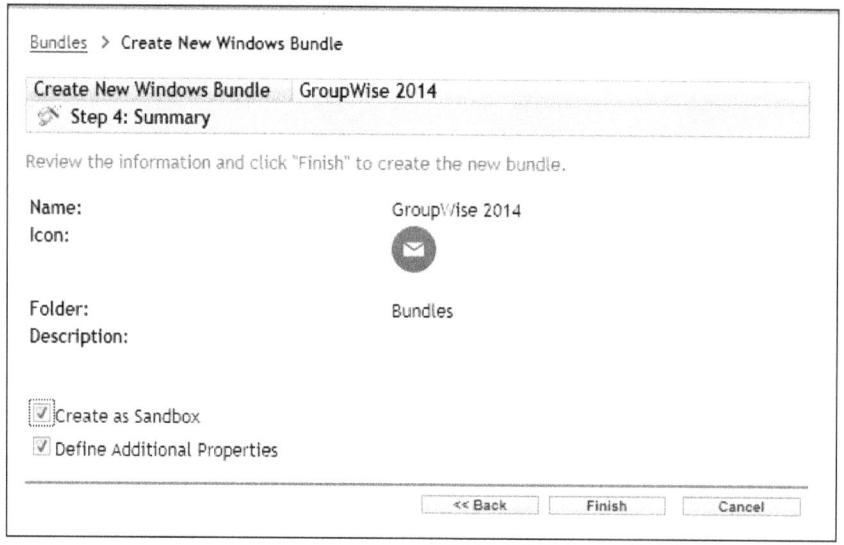

Figure 11-15: The GroupWise Bundle Page

Next we will create some installation actions for our bundle.

1. Click on the Actions Tab, and then the Install tab to create some new actions.
2. For the first Action, choose a Prompt User action. For this action we will use the following values:
    - Name the action something such as "Prompt User that the Client will be installed"
    - User Cancels Allowed: If you wish to force the installation immediately, leave this at 0
    - Seconds to be Displayed: Choose how long the prompt should stay on the screen - perhaps 30 seconds.
    - Click "Add" in the Define Prompts box to type in the text to be displayed. For example "The GroupWise Client will now be installed. Please be patient".
    - Scroll down and select OK to save the action

We'll now create a second action

1. Now, choose "Install File(s)" as a second action. In this action we are essentially having ZCM put the installation files in a temporary location on the workstation so that the **extract_setupip_packs.cmd** can perform the extraction. Name this action something that will make sense to you. For example "Install files to temporary installation folder".
    - Click on Add to get to the Select Files dialog, and click Add again to find the files. This time we need to go to the **<serverfiles>\agents\data\client\setup\win32** folder and select the **extract_setupip_packs.cmd**, **setupip.fil**, and our language files (for example, **setupip.en** and **setupip.de**). Click "Open" to include these files in the Select Files dialog.
    - The **setupip.fil** file is already a compressed file, so it not necessary to compress these files further. Thus, check the box that says "do not compress or encrypt uploaded content".

    When you click Okay, you will see a confirmation screen to show you the files that will be uploaded to your repository.

2. Once the files are uploaded, you will be returned to the Select Files dialog. Now you will need to specify where these files should be placed on the local machine. Remember this is a temporary installation directory, so you can choose any location you like. An example would be **c:\gwclient**. Select Okay.

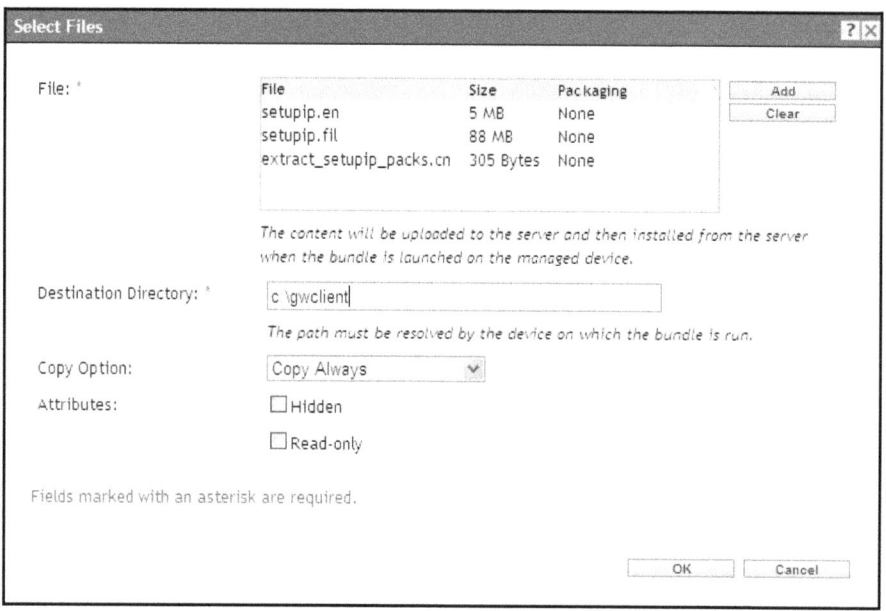

Figure 11-16: The completed Select Files dialog

3. At the next screen, you can select to run this installation as a dynamic administrator user to avoid any rights problems during the copy. Select okay to save this action.

The next action we need to create is one to extract the files from the **setupip.fil** file for GroupWise.

1. Back on the Install Tab, click Add to create a new action, and choose Run Script as the action.
2. In our first action, we copied **extract_setupip_files.cmd** to **c:\gwclient**, so we can enter **c:\gwclient\extract_setupip_packs.cmd** as the Script File Name. The **extract_setupip_packs.cmd** file will then extract all of the files under this directory into **c:\gwclient\win32**. This is important for our final installation step.
3. Click the radio button next to "When Action is Complete" for the wait parameter for this script.

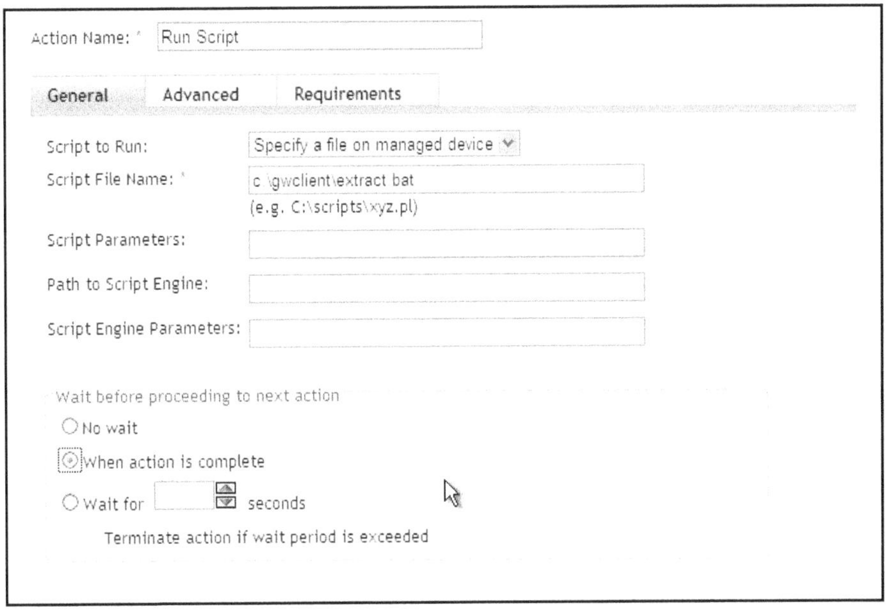

Figure 11-17: Creating the Run Script Command

4. Before you leave this screen, you should give the Action Name a more specific name, such as "Run Script to extract GW2014 files".
5. Choose to run the script as dynamic administrator to avoid problems during the extraction.
6. Click OK and you will now see two actions in your Install tab.

The next step is to copy the MST file that we created with the GroupWise Install Tuner to the local temporary installation directory. The following steps will do this:

1. Click Add again to create a new action. Choose "Install File(s)", and give the action a name that designates that you wish to "Copy **groupwise.mst** to local directory".
2. Click Add to show the Select Files screen, and click Add again to show the add dialog.
3. Browse to your **<installationfiles>/client/win32** directory and choose the **groupwise.mst** file that we created above. Click OK. The file will be uploaded to the ZCM repository.
4. Next you will be asked where this file should be copied. The **extract_setupip_packs.cmd** process created **c:\gwclient\win32** (if you used **c:\gwclient** as your temp directory). This is where the **groupwise.mst** file must reside.
5. Leave the copy option as Copy Always.
6. Change to the Requirements tab and run the process as Dynamic Administrator.

Our final action will be to actually install GroupWise using the **groupwise.mst** file.

1. Again, at the Install Tab, add a new action of "Launch Executable". Name this Action "Launch install.bat for GroupWise 2014".
2. The command name in our case will be **c:\gwclient\win32\install.bat**.

3. For command line parameters you can choose:
   - /unattended - this will show the typical GroupWise progress statuses for the installation
   - /silent - the user will not see anything while GroupWise installs
4. Click on Add under Environment Variables and add the following:
   - **Name**: GW_INST_TRANSFORM_FILE
   - **Value**: **groupwise.mst** - note that this assumes the same folder as the **install.bat** file, which in our case is correct.

   Click Ok.
5. Click on Add under Environment Variables for a second variable to update existing GroupWise installations to match our current installation msi:
   - **Name**: GW_INST_REMOVE_MSI
   - **Value**: True

   Click OK

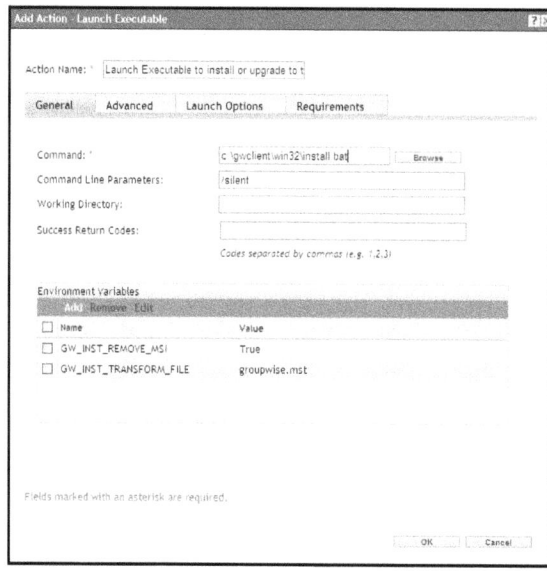

Figure 11-18: Our action for running install.bat

6. Next click on the Advanced tab and select "When action is complete" for the wait time. Also choose to run as dynamic administrator. Click OK.

Next we will create a launch action for the GroupWise 2014 bundle.

1. Click on the Launch Tab, then click on the Add button and choose "Launch Executable" as the type.
2. For the command, you will have "**${ProgramFiles32}\Novell\Groupwise\grpwise.exe**".
3. For command line parameters you can choose any parameters you typically use.

4. Click on the Advance Tab. Since this is for the launch of the client, you should choose "no wait" and "Run as logged in user". Click OK.

5. Apply your changes.

Back at the script parameters for the installation, we had the choice of running the installation in "unattended" or "silent" mode. If you chose silent, you might wish to allow ZCM to control the dialog that users see. To do so, go back to the Summary page of your new bundle, and scroll down until you see "Show Bundle Activity". If you change this to "Yes", ZCM will provide the status information to the user as the application installs.

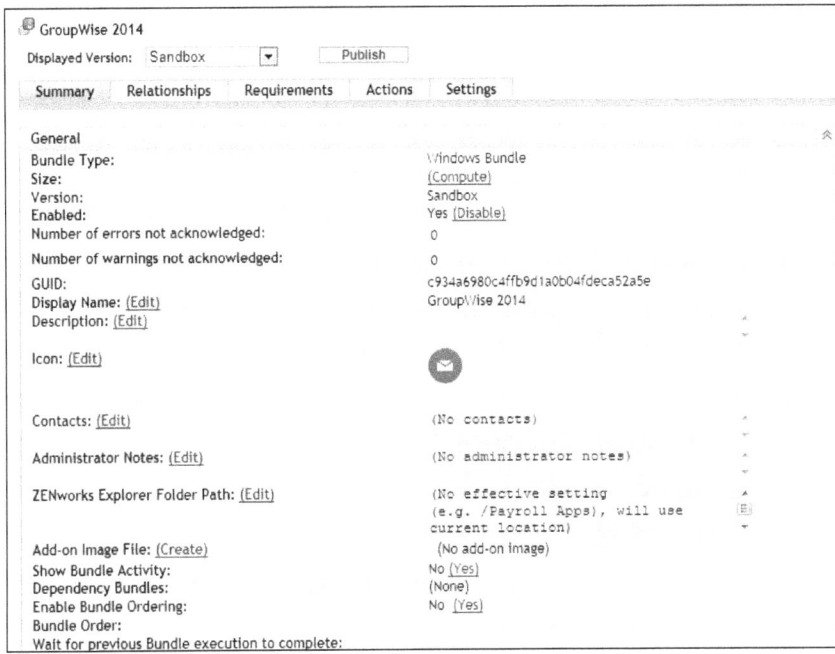

Figure 11-19: Change Show Bundle Activity to Yes

Next, change the "Displayed Version" at the top of the Summary from Sandbox to Published. To do so, click on the "Publish" button, publish as a new version.

To complete your installation, add your relationships, requirements, icon choices and schedule.

SETUP.INI

The **setup.ini** file in the **<installationfiles>\client\win32** directory is full of interesting settings for the Microsoft Installer. It also has one very important setting that you will want to set if you wish to totally automate your installation. You can disable the language dialog in the installation by verifying that the EnableLangDlg setting is set to No (N).

VERSION.INI

The **version.ini** file simply designates the "development version" of the GroupWise software. For the version of GroupWise 2014 we used most recently in this book, the contents of this file are:

[General]
BuildNumber=4863

Whenever the GroupWise client is installed, the Build Number of the GroupWise client is put into the Windows registry. The **BuildNumber** string value is kept in the following registry location:

HKEY_LOCAL_MACHINE\SOFTWARE\Novell\GroupWise

or

HKLM/SOFTWARE\WOW6432NODE\NOVELL\GROUPWISE

SETUP.CFG

As we mentioned above, the **setup.cfg** no longer contains the settings for the auto-update, as those have been moved to the Client Settings in the databases. This is still a very important file in the installation process. There is a **setup.cfg** file that ships with GroupWise 2014 in the **<installationfiles>\client** directory. This is a template file that is used for customizing the GroupWise client installation. This file does not have an effect on the installation of the GroupWise software unless it is copied in to the **<serverfiles>\agents\data\client\setup\win32\win32** directory. If the **setup.cfg** resides in this directory, it will be used to set parameters for the client installation. There are a number of options you can set for the installation through the **setup.cfg** file. Here are some of the more common:

- If you wish to make the installation automatic for the users so that they are asked no questions and only see the progress and ending of the installation:

  ShowDialogs=No

  ShowProgress=Yes

  ShowFinish=Yes

(Remember to also check the **setup.ini** file for EnableLangDlg=N)

- GroupWise Notify will not be put in the Windows startup folder
  Notify=No

- Enable GWCheck at the workstation for Caching clients
  [GWCheck]

InstallGWCheck=Yes
GWCheckEnabled=No

- The Language will be English (or your language of choice).

  [Language]

  Default=English

  English=Yes

Upgrading the Linux Cross-Platform Client

There is no upgraded GroupWise Linux client for GroupWise 2012. The GroupWise 8 client is currently available at http://download.novell.com/Download?buildid=X95cxyoSSiE~ . If you need to install the GroupWise Linux client, follow these instructions.

- Download the GroupWise Linux client from the above location.
- Install the RPM manually from the \client\linux\ directory of the GroupWise Linux installation CD. You can install the RPM as follows:

rpm -Uvh novell-groupwise-gwclient-8.0.0-84910.i586.rpm

SuSEconfig

Of course, the actual version of the RPM will change over time. The name of the RPM above is simply the shipping version.

Upgrading the MAC Cross-Platform Client

There is no upgraded GroupWise Mac client for GroupWise 2012. The GroupWise 8 client is currently available at http://download.novell.com/Download?buildid=X95cxyoSSiE~ . If you need to install the GroupWise Mac client, deploy the groupwise.dmg file to your Mac users.

Auditing the GroupWise Client Upgrade

The GroupWise 2014 POA has a feature that can give you a quick look at who has upgraded to GroupWise 2014. In order to see this feature your GroupWise 2014 POA should support HTTP monitoring and your post office must have enabled the setting for tracking a minimum client version. You can either enable HTTP monitoring in the Administration Console or in the startup file of the POA. The advantage of using the Administration Console to apply these settings is that the POA will pick up the settings dynamically, and you will not need to restart the post office agent.

The minimum client version settings will highlight in red the version number or release date of the GroupWise client for any user who is using a client older than the version or date you indicate.

Upgrading GroupWise Clients

Below is how you can enable these settings through the Administration Console:

1. Click on Post Offices
2. Click on the Post Office you wish to monitor.
3. Click on the Client Settings tab.
4. Enter the version you would like for your Minimum Client Release Version (14.0 would represent the GroupWise 2014 client).
5. Make sure you do not check the box next to the Minimum Client Release or only your GroupWise 2014 users will be able to log in.
6. Click Apply, then OK to exit.

NOTE: If you check the check box to Lock Out Older GroupWise Clients then users will get a message before even entering their GroupWise password that states "The version of GroupWise you are using is older than the minimum version allowed by the system administrator." You need to be careful about enabling the lock out function, as the user will not even be given the opportunity to update their client if you select this option. You may be better off using the grace login option in the Client Options to give the user X number of grace logins before they are able to login without updating.

After enabling these settings you can monitor the client versions from your browser. Go to the POA's http port in this manner from your browser:

http://192.168.100.238:7181

NOTE: If you are not sure what HTTP port your POA is using, you can hit the C/S port (1677) and it will redirect you to the HTTP Port.

You may be prompted for the User Name and Password for the POA HTTP Monitor. Once you have loaded the Web monitor for the POA, click on the C/S Users link. From here you can view the version of GroupWise client that your various users are using. Any user that is using an older GroupWise client than you specified will show up in red. Any user that is using at least the GroupWise client version you have specified will show up in blue.

Hopefully this chapter will get you on your way to finishing up your GroupWise upgrade. Good luck!

Appendix 1: LDAP Attributes Map

Blank cell in eDir or AD column indicates that the standard LDAP mapping is used. Note that AD largely uses the standard LDAP mappings. eDirectory is the "oddball" on several attributes.

GroupWise	LDAP	eDir	AD	
User Name	uid		samAccountName	
GUID	entryUUID	GUID	objectGuid	
Login Disabled		loginDisabled	userAccountControl	
Email Address	mail	eMailAddress		
Extra Email		mail	proxyAddresses	
Description	description			
City	l	physicalDeliveryOfficeName		
Company	o	company	company	
Department	ou		department	
Fax	facsimileTelephoneNumber			
Given Name	givenName			
Home Phone	homePhone			
Middle Name	initials			
Mobile Phone	mobile			
Other Phone	otherTelephone			
Pager	pager			
Location	physicalDeliveryOfficeName			
Postal Code	postalCode			
PO Box	postOfficeBox			
Surname	sn			
State	st			
Street Address	street		streetAddress	
Phone	telephoneNumber			
Title	title			
Name Prefix	personalTitle			
Name Suffix	generationQualifier			

nGWFileID
nGWGroupWiseID
nGWObjectID
nGWPostOffice
nGWVisibility
nGWAccountID
nGWMailboxExpirationTime   These will be synced into eDir by the Admin Service.

www.ingramcontent.com/pod-product-compliance
Ingram Content Group UK Ltd.
Pitfield, Milton Keynes, MK11 3LW, UK
UKHW050411240426
12048UKWH00020B/1451